CAMBRIDGE STUDIES IN CRIMINOLOGY XLVII
General Editor: Sir Leon Radzinowicz

Dangerousness and Criminal Justice

BARNES & NOBLE BOOKS

———

THE HEINEMANN LIBRARY OF CRIMINOLOGY
AND PENAL REFORM

CAMBRIDGE STUDIES IN CRIMINOLOGY

HOWARD LEAGUE FOR PENAL REFORM

DANGEROUSNESS AND CRIMINAL JUSTICE

Jean Floud
and
Warren Young

BARNES & NOBLE BOOKS
TOTOWA, NEW JERSEY

First Published in Britain in 1981 by
Heinemann Educational Books

Published in the U.S.A. 1982 by
Bames & Noble Books, Totowa, New Jersey

Library of Congress Cataloging in Publication Data

Floud, J. E. (Jean E.)
  Dangerousness and criminal justice.

  Bibliography: p.
  Includes index.
  1. Preventive detention—Great Britain.
  2. Indeterminate sentence—Great Britain.
  3. Insane, Criminal and dangerous—Great Britain.
  I. Young, Warren. II. Title.
  KD8340.F56   364.3′0941   82-1762

  ISBN 0-389-20286-X   AACR2

Typeset by The Castlefield Press of Northampton, and
printed by Biddles Ltd, Guildford, Surrey

Contents

PART II – THE DANGEROUS OFFENDER IN ENGLAND TODAY

PART III – PROTECTIVE SENTENCING

The Working Party

Preface

We were convened in May 1976 by the Howard League for Penal Reform to review and report on the law and practice in relation to 'dangerous' offenders. The Academy for Contemporary Problems, Columbus, Ohio had embarked on *The Dangerous Offender Project** and it was hoped that we would be able to make recommendations which would be useful not only in the British context but also more generally. The Howard League has met the cost of our meetings and the preparation of this report.† We are happy to record our appreciation of their generous support for an undertaking which has taught us all a great deal more than we could have learned without the stimulus of organised discussion.

Our attention was drawn to an extensive body of American writing on the difficult issues raised by the practice of preventive confinement (the civil commitment of the mentally ill and, in the administration of criminal justice, the detention of persons awaiting trial, the use of the

The Dangerous Offender Project at the Academy for Contemporary Problems, Columbus, Ohio, directed jointly by John P. Conrad and Simon Dinitz and sponsored by the Lilley Foundation, has produced the following publications since its inception in 1975:
In Fear of Each Other J. P. Conrad and S. Dinitz
The Law and the Dangerous Criminal L. Sleffel
The Search for Criminal Man Y. Rennie
The Dangerous Offender and the Police P. Conrad, S. Dinitz and S. A. Miller
The Dangerous Offender in Custody R. Freeman, J. P. Conrad, S. Dinitz and I. Barak
The Incapacitation of the Dangerous Offender W. Van Dine, J. P. Conrad and S. Dinitz
The Dangerous Juvenile Offender D. M. Hamparian, J. P. Conrad, S. Dinitz and R. Schuster
The Prosecution of the Dangerous Offender W. Lyday, J. P. Conrad and S. Dinitz
The Dangerous and the Endangered J. P. Conrad
The Dangerous Offender Project: Summary of Findings J. Conrad
The Violent Few D. M. Hamparian, R. Schuster, S. Dinitz and J. P. Conrad
†We most gratefully acknowledge the considerable secretarial and other help with the organisation of meetings and the preparation of the Report given by Mrs M. A. Fearnley and Mrs R. Kerruish; and the efficient help with the task of typing the Report given by Miss M. Guy, Mrs P. Paige and Mrs E. Pilmer.

indeterminate sentence of imprisonment and the indefinite commitment of mentally abnormal offenders to special hospitals). The concept of dangerousness itself was the focus of an impassioned and wide-ranging controversy to which there existed no British counterpart: in this country, the validity and necessity of the concept had not been questioned in this way. We were to concern ourselves with only part of the controversial practice in a single jurisdiction, namely the protective sentencing of dangerous offenders in England and Wales. (We had abandoned the original intention to include Scottish law and practice in our survey, following discussion in Edinburgh which brought home to us the full extent of the differences between the two social and legal systems; and the Butler Committee had recently reported on the position of the mentally abnormal offender.) Nevertheless, we felt it necessary to confront the fundamental issues raised in the American controversy and, since they transcended the boundaries of particular jurisdictions, it seemed that we could perform a useful service by reporting on them at some length for the benefit of British and other non-American readers. We, therefore, enlarged the scope of our report to include discussion of the ethical and sociological as well as the more narrowly penological issues implied by our terms of reference.

We were not tempted to broaden the range of our discussion to include the medical and psychological aspects of dangerousness. 'Dangerousness' is not itself a medical or psychological concept and to have inquired into the psychology of the kinds of offenders classed as 'dangerous' would have been an impossible task, beyond our resources of time and competence. Nor did we examine the many practical penological problems raised by the detention of dangerous offenders: to decide the requirements of a regime for such offenders that would be humane and constructive as well as secure is an urgent and important task, but one for another working party of different composition and character. Nevertheless, we did attempt to gain some impression at first hand of the kinds of person referred to as dangerous offenders, and the conditions of their confinement, by visiting a number of prisons and special hospitals to discuss our task with groups of prisoners and members of the prison and hospital administrations. These discussions were most enlightening and we take this opportunity to record our grateful thanks to all those in the institutions listed in Appendix B who received us and gave us their time and the benefit of their experience.

We met 20 times, on most occasions for a full day's discussion. At an early stage in our work we decided not to issue a general invitation for evidence or to invite witnesses to meet us. Instead, we issued the consultative paper which is reproduced in Appendix A and invited written comments from some 50 persons, for the most part professionally concerned with our subject-matter but including a number of arbitrarily selected members of the general public. We were very much helped by the comments of the 40 respondents whose names are recorded in Appendix A: we are most grateful to them for the trouble they took to formulate their views for our benefit.

Throughout the period of our work we kept in close touch informally with the Home Secretary's Advisory Council on the Penal System whose review of maximum penalities overlapped our own work at certain points (Mr Blom-Cooper and Professor Walker were both members of the Advisory Council as well as of our own working party); and with the Prison Department of the Home Office, through Mr Brian Howden who, until his untimely death in May 1977, was an active participant in our discussions and an invaluable guide to the administration of the penal system. He was greatly missed in the later stages of our work. We were fortunate to have a ready successor in Mr Norman Honey, then Governor of Wormwood Scrubs and now with the Prison Department of the Home Office.

We worked our way from very different points of departure to a broad agreement — not on the need for immediate change in the present arrangements, on which point we agreed to differ — but on the principles which should delimit and govern the practice of protective sentencing and on proposals for legislation which would embody them and represent an improvement on present practice if and when the time came for change. None of us would wish to be called to account for every proposition contained in Parts I and II of the report and none of us would wish to endorse in every particular the proposals advanced in Part III. None of us, however, wishes to make any specific disclaimer and our differences of opinion do not call for notes of dissent, still less for a minority report.

Mr Charles Rhodes was a valued colleague. He took a full part in our deliberations and had read and given approval to a draft of this Report in preparation for our final meeting which, in the event, he was unfortunately too ill to attend.

J.F
L.B-C.
M.D.
F.G-H.
J.G.
F.H.McC.
B.McK.
N.D.W.
I.W.
W.Y.

September 1980

Introduction

When we were convened as a working party, the Butler Committee had only recently reported on *The Mentally Abnormal Offender*; the focus of our concern was, therefore, the mentally normal offender. More precisely, we were to look into the powers available to the courts to protect the public from the exceptional, 'dangerous' offender, other than those provided under the Mental Health Act 1959. We did not, as one correspondent put it, 'predicate a false dichotomy between "normal" and "abnormal" offenders, based on whether the courts deal with them under the Mental Health Act or the Criminal Justice Act'. Nor did we seek 'to solve the problems of the dangerous person by ever more clever and intricate sentencing, before the nature of dangerousness has really been understood', as another warned us against trying to do. Ours was not a psychological or medical, but a penological brief. We did not take the existence of 'dangerous persons' for granted; but we agreed at an early stage in our work that there exists a minority of exceptional, high-risk serious offenders who, whatever may be their mental state, cannot be said to be suffering from a definable mental disorder treatable within the mental health system, and who are, therefore, legally sane and the responsibility of the penal system. It was our task to review the arrangements for protecting the public from harm at the hands of such 'dangerous offenders'.

These arrangements are almost wholly discretionary in character. Parliament has listed the non-homicidal offences for which the life sentence is available and in so far as the life sentence has come to be used for protective purposes this amounts to a statutory limitation on the practice of protective sentencing; but in no other respect has the discretion of the courts to provide protection against the risk of serious harm from legally sane offenders been circumscribed by statute.

Early in the history of attempts in the present century to use special sentences for the protection of the public, the distinction was drawn between the 'social nuisance' of the persistent, usually petty, offender and the 'social menace' of the high-risk serious offender; both were held to represent social dangers in the neutral sense of 'danger' as meaning an unacceptable risk of harm. Parliament made attempts in

1908, 1948 and 1967 to deal with the problem of persistence and incorrigibility by means of preventive detention and the extended sentence; but it has been left to the courts to use ordinary determinate sentences or the life sentence to provide protection against the risk of serious harm, in cases where a hospital order is ruled out for one reason or another; and to the executive to see that in exercising their discretion to vary the conditions of security under which prisoners are detained, or to release them on parole or on licence in the course of their sentences, considerations of public safety are given due weight.

The devices of preventive detention and the extended sentence for persistent offenders have met with much criticism, directed in the main against the idea of combating a social nuisance by means of such drastic measures. The wholly indeterminate life sentence has also come under attack. But the wide scope of judicial and administrative discretion to deal with the risk of serious harm has not been questioned.

The size and composition of the class of dangerous offenders which emerges from the exercise of these discretionary powers cannot be precisely determined; but it is small and heterogeneous and it has not aroused controversy. Members of the judiciary and the Home Office, in responding to our Consultative Document, made it clear that they were unaware of any pressing need for change arising from practical experience, either in the powers of the courts or in the arrangements made for the control and supervision of 'dangerous' offenders, apart from the special case of the mentally abnormal offender which had been remitted to the Butler Committee. The use of the penalty of imprisonment was declining and sentences for less serious offences were becoming shorter; the Advisory Council on the Penal System had already embarked on a review of maximum penalties of imprisonment and should shortly issue an interim report on *The Length of Prison Sentences*, to deal with the pressing question of the reduction of sentence lengths for the ordinary offender; but these developments, and their possible implications for the sentencing of 'dangerous' offenders, were not mentioned by our respondents when they cautioned against any move to circumscribe judicial discretion and rationalise the administration of a protective element in sentencing.

All this is in marked contrast with the position in the United States where a patchwork of 'dangerous persons' legislation, involving the extensive use of indeterminate sentences and the withholding of bail from defendants charged with 'dangerous' offences, has provoked widespread attacks on the practice of protective sentencing. Fierce constitutional controversy has centred on the questions whether preventive detention violates the presumption of innocence — whether it punishes a person on the basis of status alone, for 'being dangerous' without conviction for an illegal act; and whether it satisfies the *equal protection* test of 'reasonable classification' and the *due process* test of 'rational relation' (that is, whether the classification of certain offenders as 'dangerous', which effects a severe deprivation of their fundamental rights, can be defended as rational given its purpose and the classes of persons upon which the burdens and benefits are placed).

No such fundamental questions had been raised in this country before we started work. In 1977, however, Professor A. E. Bottoms drew attention to the developments in penal policy that had not been mentioned by our respondents and to the issues raised by the American debate. He remarked upon an emerging 'bifurcation' in penal policy 'which seems increasingly to be isolating selected groups of the "mad" and the "bad" as those against whom we really wish to take serious action, whilst we are prepared to reduce penalties for the remainder'. He saw the revived interest in 'dangerousness' and proposals for new forms of protective sentence (from the Butler Committee and the Scottish Council on Crime) as manifestations of this development, to which he objected that it was the expression of profoundly irrational penal theory, resting on discredited and dangerously misleading beliefs about man and society: for example, that crime is a 'natural' rather than a socially defined category of human behaviour; and that 'dangerousness' is an inherent defect of character — a quasi-medical condition which can be scientifically diagnosed and treated.

Such beliefs are deeply rooted in tenacious social attitudes to crime and punishment and it is right to point the finger at any tendency which threatens to resuscitate them. They are not our beliefs however. Moreover, we do not see the need to invoke them either to explain or to justify 'bifurcation' in penal policy, if by this is meant the attempt to rationalise and formalise the distinction, already recognised by the courts, between the 'ordinary' and the 'dangerous' offender. It is true that this attempt exposes a number of very difficult ethical and penological problems which have not received the close attention they deserve. We hope that our report will stimulate others to take up these problems, for we do not claim to have settled them, and we believe 'bifurcation' to be the rational response to indications of welcome changes in penal policy, of a tendency to make less use of the penalty of imprisonment and to shorten sentences, at any rate for less serious offences.

It is now widely accepted that few of the 'mad' are 'dangerous'; it is a less widely accepted but equally important truism that few serious offenders are 'dangerous', from which it follows that the question of penalties for serious offences, even for the worst cases of such offences, must not be confused with the question of protecting the public against a minority of high-risk serious offenders. Awkward and difficult questions about the legitimate scope of protection against the risk of serious harm may be neglected while sentences within the normal range are long and the permissible maxima are longer still.

But as these conditions change, it becomes increasingly difficult to evade these questions. Against the risk of what kinds and degrees of harm and what kinds of offenders is the public entitled to be protected, if necessary, by means of a sentence which is longer than would be justifiable on other grounds alone? What should be the form and length of 'protective' sentences? What evidential and procedural requirements should govern the imposition and administration of such sentences? The statutes provide no answers and judicial discussion of these matters is sparse, even in connection with the life sentence.

We do not accept the view that these questions do not lend themselves to rational answers; nor that they are improper or even merely impolitic questions to raise in a free society. We accept the validity and necessity of the concept of dangerousness in criminal justice because we accept that there exists a minority of high-risk serious offenders; we cannot agree that, as it was put to us by the Home Office, the intangible element of 'dangerousness' in these cases is not to an acceptable degree a justiciable issue because the facts cannot be put in issue and ascertained with as much certainty as the issue of guilt. There is the same difficulty in principle when the court has to decide whether or not to impose a hospital restriction order on a mentally disordered offender; this, too, involves making a predictive judgment of his conduct. We do not believe that to attempt to rationalise the protective element in sentencing, by confining its use to certain specified circumstances and in accordance with specified criteria, would be to make a 'dangerous' move towards the institutionalisation of an essentially undesirable practice: that it would encourage Parliament to make unwarranted and undesirable inroads upon judicial discretion in matters essentially apt for judgment *ad hoc* and *ad hominem*; and incline the courts to make a habit of protective sentencing. Indeed, it is arguable that it is only the provision of a special sentence which allows courts to exceed the normal range that will lead to any marked lowering of that range. Nor are we persuaded by the evasive arguments which point to dangerous behaviour about which the public is complacent and to socially powerful 'dangerous offenders' who 'get away with it'. We have more sympathy with those who argue that dangerousness inheres in situations, not in persons; that there are no 'dangerous persons' but only dangerous situations, harmful behaviour and unacceptable (or, at least, unaccepted) risks — though this does not so much dispose of the problem as point to its heart.

We hope that this report will show that we have tried to do justice to these various arguments. Some seem to reflect an undercurrent of complacency in the face of developments in penal policy which, in our view, will call sooner or later for change in arrangements which admittedly have worked well enough and may not in everyone's opinion be in immediate need of review or reform; and some reflect an undercurrent of fear for civil liberties believed to be threatened by the admission of the notion of dangerousness into the administration of criminal justice. We came to the conclusion that, whether or not change in the present arrangements is imminent or immediately desirable, it was time to reconsider the ethical and related problems and to formulate the difficulties and dilemmas in terms which would permit us to propose solutions which would be both just and workable.

We believe that our report deals with important issues and that it is timely. We want to make it clear, however, that our proposals are not directed to the problem of controlling the increase in rates of serious crime any more than to the problem of coping with the new social hazards of a modern industrial society. They should be judged according to their purpose, which is to state the conditions for assessing and effecting a just redistribution of certain risks of grave harm: the grave harm that potentially recidivist serious offenders may do their unknown victims and the grave harm which is suffered by offenders if they are subjected to the hardship of preventive measures which risk being unecessary because they depend on predictive judgments of their conduct which are inherently uncertain. That we are far from underestimating the difficulties of doing justice in this matter will be evident, we hope, from our report.

PART I

Dangerousness and Criminal Justice

CHAPTER 1

'Dangerousness' in Social Perspective

Writers on 'dangerousness' and the law frequently argue that the problem needs to be viewed in broad perspective by taking account of the variety of ways in which, in a modern society, people are at risk of suffering grave harm. We were not convened, nor were we competent, to explore the problem of the 'dangerous' offender in broad terms as a social problem: the hard core of our brief was to consider the case for and against protective penological measures. We did, nevertheless, give careful consideration to the arguments advanced by the proponents of a broader, social perspective on the problem. We readily accepted the general argument that no significant reduction in the prevalence of gravely harmful behaviour can be achieved by measures directed solely against individual offenders; and that what are needed are more broadly conceived social policies, directed against harmful social practices or such other features of the social and material environment as can be shown to encourage gravely harmful behaviour. But we found many of the particular arguments deriving from the demand for a broader social perspective to be unsatisfactory on close consideration. In this chapter we present a summary review and critique of a set of interrelated arguments to which we gave careful attention within the limits of our time and competence. They are all prominent in writings about 'dangerousness' and criminal justice and some were put to us by respondents to our Consultative Document.

The unifying theme of these arguments is that protective sentencing is not only an ethically undesirable but also an unnecessary instrument of social policy. It is said that the need for *special* protection against 'dangerous' offenders is exaggerated. People tolerate comparable or even heavier burdens of risk 'when it suits them'; public opinion is misinformed and misdirected by the mass media and is inconsistent in its judgments of danger and irrational in its demands for protection. Not all gravely harmful conduct is penalised nor are all those responsible for it apprehended. The selection in both cases is arbitrary and therefore inefficient. A rational approach to the problem of protecting the public from the risk of grave harm would lead us to construe 'dangerousness' more broadly than at present, applying it to a wider range of conduct and a more representative group of offenders. But in any case, sentencing people to preventive confinement is not effective as a protective measure. This is largely because it is arbitrary and socially discriminatory in its incidence: white-collar and especially corporate offenders are rarely regarded as 'dangerous' but they are disproportionately responsible for the total burden of risk of serious harm, including physical harm, to which the public is exposed. Even if this bias were removed, however, preventive confinement would not make a significant contribution to public safety, so that it cannot be necessary to make use of the concept of 'dangerousness' in criminal justice at all. What is wanted, instead, are measures of social policy that will inhibit and contain harmful conduct without the necessity of locking people up.

In this chapter we consider these arguments, starting with those concerning public perceptions of risk and the attitudes and values that seem to inform people's judgments of danger.

Public Opinion, Risk and Danger

At the heart of the controversy over dangerousness in criminal justice is the ambiguous, historically shifting and essentially political notion of justifiable public alarm. Just as protection against some ills is held to be the responsibility of individuals, not of public authorities, so of some ills it is held that they or the risk of them must be accepted as the normal conditions of life. If there is really general acceptance of a risk, it is hard to see that people are wronged by the failure to remove it; though of course it would be legitimate to try for good reason, even by legislation, to change people's views on the matter. On the other hand, if there really is general alarm and refusal to accept a risk, it can be held that people are wronged by the failure to remove it; for fear is a harm in itself, not to be underrated.

There is little objectivity in perceptions of danger. It is a question of what people are prepared to put up with and why, and not simply of what is in some degree objectively damaging to them. Dangers are unacceptable risks: we measure or assess the probability and severity of some harm and call it a risk; but we speak of danger when we judge the risk unacceptable and call for preventive measures.

Risk is a matter of fact; danger is a matter of opinion. Judgments of danger are not objective in the sense of being perfectly commensurate with risk; but for purposes of public policy they must be rational in the sense of being principled. Rationality requires that comparable risks must be consistently evaluated; and, moreover, for purposes of public policy they must be evaluated on the presumption of an informed and enlightened public opinion. If a risk is deemed unacceptable as a matter of rationally defensible public policy, but the public is complacent, the presumption must be that if properly informed the public would be appropriately alarmed. It is then the duty of the authorities to enlighten public opinion, though this may be an uphill task. As Lord Ashby (1976) points out, they may have to wait until there is an incident of some kind which 'acts like a sort of adrenaline to the public conscience and enables them to make a decision which they know will win approval'. Likewise, a risk ought not to be deemed unacceptable merely because an alarmed public believes it to be greater than it actually is, even though, were the facts as the public believe them to be, alarm would be justified and the risk unacceptable. In this case, too, public opinion should be educated; but the process is likely to be more difficult and protracted since the effect of 'incidents' will be to reinforce the ill-founded alarm. In a free society policy-makers and officials cannot disregard public attitudes. Public opinion is very uncertain and very sensitive to the influence of the news media; but its weaknesses are often misunderstood as well as exaggerated.

Risks are objectively determinable, at least in principle; but ordinary people are rarely in a position to estimate them accurately. Without expert help the public is likely to be misinformed or ill-informed. Dangers, on the other hand, are subjectively determined; which is not to say that they are necessarily irrationally determined, only that the magnitude of a risk, however accurately determined, does not establish it without further argument as acceptable or unacceptable. Determining the magnitude of a risk is one thing; judging that it represents a danger demanding to be averted by preventive measures is another.

It is true that both activities are subject to distorting influences. Lack of information, failure of imagination, the influence of emotion and the persuasions of interested parties all conspire both to distort perception and unbalance judgment. But there is room for disagreement even when the distorting influences are eliminated; for what people think about risks is as much a matter of value as of fact.

The significance of normative considerations is often overlooked when public attitudes are under criticism; and even when these considerations are acknowledged they are often discounted as irrational. The tacit presumption almost always is that the public ought to agree with the experts, not only in their perception of risk, but in their judgment of danger too. It is thought that equal risks of comparable harm must be equally acceptable or unacceptable as the case may be. If they are not, the public is under suspicion of irrationality. Alarm that is not perfectly correlated with an objective assessment of risk is presumed to be irrational; but it may not be so.

The psychology of judgment is a rapidly developing branch of applied psychology and the discrepancies between subjective and objective or lay and professional assessments and evaluations of risk are the subject of a large and growing literature. Lord Ashby offers a penetrating discussion of these matters. He rather despairs of public opinion: 'there is no rationality in the arithmetic of perception' he declares, as he enumerates instances of differences in public attitudes to risks of the same order of magnitude, according to whether or not they are near at hand ('a flood in East Anglia makes a greater impact than a flood in the Ganges'), removed in time (people commonly discount the future and accept long-term more readily than short-term risks of the same order of magnitude), or occur simultaneously ('five people killed in one road accident makes a much greater impact – and will be included in a radio bulletin – than five people killed in five different accidents'). He finds these notions irrational: they are 'much more significant and puzzling', in his view, than other determinants of public opinion: social norms, for example, or the behaviour of journalists and broadcasters.

That these attitudes make for discrepancies between lay and expert perceptions of risk is obvious; and in this sense they are distorting factors. But as factors influencing people's willingness to accept risk, they do not seem to be necessarily irrational.

Fear converts risk into danger and it tends to be inversely proportional to time and distance. This is understandable, for personal vulnerability diminishes with time and distance: the longer the time-span and the greater the distance separating us from predicted harm, the greater the scope for chance and personal initiative to frustrate the harm or shift its incidence. As for clustering, multiple deaths convert an accident into a disaster and this seems to be a different kind of event. It does not seem altogether irrational to fear death by disaster more than death by simple accident, even if the probability is the same in either case; for the circumstances of a disaster are more fearful in themselves for the sense of helplessness is greater. And being rarer and more dramatic than simple accidents, disasters are understandably more newsworthy.

Much perplexity and impatience with the seeming irrationality of public attitudes to risks takes too little account of the implications of the fact that most environmental hazards are man-made; they represent the risk, not just of harm, but of harmful conduct. Risks of harmful conduct are accepted or rejected on different terms from risks of harmful natural events. The more important of the social norms which seem to distort people's perception of environmental hazards are moral norms governing the attribution of responsibility for the harmful consequences of people's behaviour. Everyone is at risk of harm from everyone else and many dangerous deeds are done; but dangerous deeds do not always make dangerous offenders. The principle of absolute liability is intuitively unacceptable, for we are all differently motivated and placed to inflict harm on others.

Actions are judged by their consequences but on the assumption of a rational agency: that is to say, besides the act itself and its consequences, people take into account the circumstances in which it is done, the motives, position and intentions of the agent and the extent of his awareness of relevant circumstances. A risk originating in the intentionally harmful behaviour of a responsible agent is less acceptable than a risk of the same, or even of a larger order of magnitude, originating in behaviour that is not intended to be harmful; and those who place others at risk of intentional harm, providing they are legally responsible for their actions, are more likely to be judged 'dangerous' and to be the subject of preventive measures than those who place others at risk merely of unintentional harm.

When do dangerous deeds make a dangerous offender? It depends in part on the circumstances and state of mind of the offender: are his purposes legitimate and his intentions innocent? Will he be intent on causing harm? If not intent, how easily and in what situations is he likely to be tempted or provoked into causing it? Is he ruthless or merely reckless? Is he self-serving or merely self-indulgent and careless of the consequences of his actions for others? In part, however, it also depends on whether specific prohibitions are likely to be successfully enforced: being the sort of harmful action against which open prohibitions are ineffectual is an important factor in dangerousness.

Fear depends on the way in which harm arises as well as on its kind and degree. Roughly speaking, the easier it is to interpret a given risk of harm as representing a specific threat rather than a generalised hazard, the more likely it is, other things being equal, that it will be viewed as a danger and the offender as dangerous. The prospect of death or injury suffered directly at the hands of another person arouses greater alarm than death or injury suffered as the indirect result of their dangerous or irresponsible behaviour. This does not seem to be entirely attributable to a failure of imagination. There must always be the hope that if it is a question of dangerous and irresponsible, rather than intentionally harmful behaviour, open prohibitions can be made effective. The man who smokes on an oil rig, or the kitchen-hand in a pork-pie factory who neglects the rules of personal hygiene, places large numbers of people at risk but is less likely to be perceived as a 'dangerous' offender than the persistent rapist or homicidal maniac who goes out of his way to inflict harm, even though his victims may be numbered in single rather than in double figures.

Violence is almost universally regarded as the hall-mark of dangerousness. 'Dangerous' offenders are presumed to be violent and violent offenders are presumed to be dangerous – and not only by the news media and the reading and viewing public in general. Violence-prone offenders present special problems of control and they are a cause of public alarm. But not all the harm inflicted with violence is serious of its kind; nor does all harm against persons, which is by definition a serious kind of harm, involve violence. It is understandable, however, that 'dangerousness' and violence should be so often taken to be synonymous: as Bentham remarked, 'force can effect many things that would be beyond the reach of stratagem'. Violence undermines confidence in the usual precautions against harm and it inspires fear by emphasising the vulnerability and helplessness of victims and the ruthlessness or at least the recklessness of offenders.

Some seven thousand people are killed and some three hundred and fifty thousand are injured each year on the roads of Britain, and it is common to deplore the lack of public outrage at the carnage and the resistance both to safety measures, such as compulsory seat-belts and random breath tests, and to specific measures, such as the indefinite disqualification of alcoholic drivers. Undoubtedly, irrationality is a feature of public opinion on these matters; but at the root of the resistance to measures designed to reduce risks is the sense that careless and even dangerous driving are offences of relatively low culpability. Few people would doubt that there is a significant difference between the harm caused by dangerous driving and, say, harm caused by reckless use of firearms. Cars as well as guns may be used in the furtherance of crime, such as robbery, and it is, of course, possible to be guilty of murder by motorcar; but it is assumed that unlicensed guns will be carried with illegal purposes in view and that they are made for killing, whereas cars are made for other purposes, so that there is more room for negligence attending primarily innocent intentions in the use of a car than in the use of a gun. Moreover, it seems likely in the case of cars that forms of public control other than imprisonment will be effective in prevention. To take away a person's driving licence after he has killed someone with his car does not seem so feeble a measure as taking away his gun licence when he has killed someone with his gun. Popular attitudes being what they are, it may not be unreasonable to hold that a man may have more respect for the law forbidding him to drive than respect for the lives of others if he does drive, though this is not to suggest that severer penalties for driving whilst disqualified are not called for.

If the values and attitudes underlying public judgments of danger are defensible, it does not follow that they are applied consistently. This is in part a matter of the availability and distribution of relevant and accurate information about the nature and magnitude of risks of harm, and in part a matter of the appropriateness of the attitudes and values that are given prominence in the presentation of particular issues. That public opinion on any issue is enormously indebted to the news media is obvious. The question is how far the media are responsible for its weaknesses and it is worth noting that, though the public itself is inclined to hold them responsible, on such evidence as there is the case against them is not proven; at least, not in the simplistic form in which it is usually advanced.

The news media, and especially the press, emerge from investigations of their content and presentation in a more favourable light than from surveys of public opinion about them. For obvious reasons they report, in the main, cases that are brought to court and they concentrate on those that make more interesting reading or viewing. It is understandable, therefore, that people should overestimate the proportion of crimes that are prosecuted and also the amount of crime committed by persons of superior socio-economic status. It is surprising, however, that despite the omnipresence of the media, their virtual monopoly of relevant information and opinion and their professional bias towards news-worthiness, public perceptions of crime and its perpetrators should be closer to the picture presented in the official statistics than to that conveyed by the media (Roshier 1973). It may be that the official picture with all its well-known defects is closer to people's actual experience of crime than the selective presentations of the news media.

The media are accused of inaccurate and sensational reporting and of subjecting public opinion to 'surges of synthetic publicity', as Ashby puts it. It is true that, as he remarks, 'there is a fickleness about the way the media take up a cause, give it saturation treatment and then drop it; not always because the matter has been dealt with but just because the news commentators are tired of it'. But this may be regarded in another light as a defect of the virtue that the media are not the uniform agents of a Ministry of Information. In snapshot they are like the curate's egg; in real life they are a political forum.

The sensational publicity given to particular crimes may from time to time hamper the executive discretion to release on parole by labelling a low-risk offender 'dangerous'. But against this may be set the value of sensational publicity given to aspects of prison life in need of reform. And against the cultivation of romantic attitudes to the daring exploits of professional criminals, like train or bank robbers, must be set the feats of investigative journalism that bring to light and follow up the crimes of big business against consumers, employers and members of the general public.

It is a truism that the selection of certain kinds of conduct as making a man eligible to be treated as 'dangerous', out of the large and changing variety of ways in which people in a modern society may place each other at risk of harm, is essentially a political process. Powerful individuals and groups, who are able directly and indirectly to determine the flow and quality of relevant information and the temper of official and public opinion, no doubt do seek to protect themselves and no doubt the powerless are at greater risk of being deemed dangerous. But it is no more than a half-truth born of this truism that differential attitudes to harmful conduct can be traced to the inequalities and injustices of the power structure and that the powerless are singled out for victimisation as dangerous offenders; and that the media are responsible for perpetuating an essentially distorted view of 'dangerousness' and 'dangerous' offenders.

All in all, public judgments of danger do not seem to be as inherently irrational and inconsistent as is sometimes suggested. Fear is a function of personal vulnerability and, at a given level of risk of serious harm, it varies inversely with the time and distance that separates the prospective victim from the predicted harmful event. The notion of culpability, though complex, is not inherently confused. If it is rational to decide the morality of punishing people for the harmful consequences of their past behaviour with reference to their intentions and motives and state of mind and circumstances, it cannot be irrational to take these considerations into account when deciding on the morality of preventing them from causing harm by their behaviour in the future. Nor does it seem to be irrational to take into account the possibility of successfully enforcing specific prohibitions: for if specific prohibitions can be enforced, it is neither necessary nor permissible to subject the doer of harmful deeds to a general deprivation of liberty. Finally, the role of the news media is more complicated and their influence on public opinion is more uneven than is generally allowed when they are accused of encouraging excessive public alarm at rising rates of 'traditional' crime instead of directing attention to the new and greater hazards of modern social life.

Social Hazards of Modern Societies

We come now to arguments against the role of 'dangerousness' in criminal justice which turn not on the question of justifiable public alarm but on the problem of keeping the public safe in modern societies. The category of 'dangerous' offenders is said to be arbitrarily and unfairly defined: it excludes many persons responsible for deaths, serious and lasting injuries and extensive loss and destruction of property, either because the harmful conduct of such persons is not made punishable or because, though punishable, it is viewed and treated leniently so that even a substantial risk of repetition does not make them eligible to be classed as 'dangerous'. It is unreasonable from the point of view of the public interest and inequitable from the point of view of those already under control as being 'dangerous' that persons such as, for example, habitually drunken drivers and keepers of unsafe factories should be excluded from the class of high-risk, serious offenders liable to preventive confinement in the interests of public safety. If anybody is to be treated as 'dangerous' such persons should be. If the need for preventive confinement of 'dangerous' offenders is conceded, the category should be widened to take account of the full range of possibilities of seriously harmful conduct characteristic of modern societies (Bottoms 1977; Carson 1975).

It is doubtful whether modern societies have more than their share of either domestic violence or so-called psychopathic crime – sporadic outbursts of violence, often sexual and sometimes bizarre in character, committed by individuals who seem to combine 'madness' and 'badness' in varying degrees peculiar to themselves. These kinds of offender and also the fluctuating numbers of small-time street robbers who sometimes terrorise whole neighbourhoods are often termed 'dangerous' and the former, at least, are likely to attract long if not life sentences. However, they are not a distinctive feature of modern societies. The respect in which such societies are different is in the extent to which violent crime is professional and political crime, and white-collar crime is corporate crime which causes serious and widespread physical as well as economic harm.

The professional criminal who derives most of his livelihood over a period of time from robbery with violence as an enterprise in which he occupies a position of leadership, management and supervision is as old as the state; and criminal syndicates created to exploit the appetites and weaknesses of ordinary citizens for gambling, betting, drink, narcotics and sex are not much younger. But robberies and rackets are organised professionally on a new scale and at a new level of sophistication in modern societies (Radzinowicz 1968; McIntosh 1975). Activities are concentrated at a high level and are underpinned by violence or the calculated threat of violence. For the organised professional robber, violence is a working tool to be applied at need whilst criminal syndicates are sustained by violence, in the form of extortion, blackmail, torture, intimidation of witnesses, used to enforce payments, maintain protection rackets, ward off detention and prevent conviction, and deal with treachery and defection from the organisation. Few would hesitate to describe such offenders as 'dangerous', simply on account of the persistence with which they pursue their predatory activities and their cynical use of violence, even in its nastiest form. The epithet is likely to seem even more apt when it is realised how difficult it is to bring them to book. The general detection rate for the crimes such persons commit is very low. The organised professional criminal is much less likely than the unorganised amateur to be detected, even if his crime is large and a great concentration of resources is applied to solving it. The organised professional criminal not only causes more serious harm – he takes and keeps more and is more likely to end up killing or maiming someone – but he is much less likely to be detected and convicted than the more or less unorganised amateur who attacks relatively modest targets haphazardly in the open.

Social protest is an important source of violent crime in modern societies. Of course, political violence is not a modern phenomenon. What is new is the immensely increased sophistication and striking power of violence inspired by political motives. The international political background, the geographical range and political *réclame* of modern terrorist demonstrations (assassinations, kidnappings, hijackings, bombings and vandalisation of sites and buildings) are on a scale undreamed of by earlier generations, and they are the product of modern technology and modern means of communications (Mark 1977).

There is undoubtedly a modern class of professional and political dangerous offenders — high-risk serious offenders whose activities are barely contained by the law. They are the product of the greater incentives, the new opportunities and fresh means to familiar forms of crime offered by modern societies. They represent, as it were, crime *à la mode* and they put law enforcement to a severe test (Mark 1977).

However, modern societies also create a physical and social environment in which people's lives, health, wealth and safety are placed at risk in new ways. Modern technology gives rise to new social hazards — the risk of death or permanent injury from the accidents of modern modes of transport and modern forms of energy; and there also emerge new risks from forms of crime which are modern in the sense that they are peculiar to characteristically modern social structures and institutions, such as public and private corporations and organs of central and local government, created to engage in a wide range of economic and social enterprises and activities. Modern crime in this sense is white-collar crime and white-collar crime is a peculiar problem of modern societies. It arises from the opportunities and incentives provided by modern technology and forms of business organisation.

It may well be true, as the critics who argue that disproportional attention is paid to 'traditional' crime allege, that the harm which results from some modern crimes far exceeds that which can result from almost any traditional crime. Consider, for example, the extensive and serious physical harm that can result from offences against laws passed to prevent accidents on the road (such as persistently driving whilst drunk) or to prevent pollution of the environment (such as illegal tipping of toxic industrial waste) or to protect consumers (such as the sale of harmful medicaments, defective cars or contaminated food products) or to maintain health and safety at work (such as failure to regulate the asbestos content of the factory atmosphere). Consider also the extensive and serious harm which can result from offences such as fraud, bribery and corruption, or commercial malpractices such as deceptive selling. In terms of the numbers of lives lost, the number and seriousness of injuries sustained and the value of property stolen or destroyed, the social and economic cost of white-collar crime in modern society is probably greater than that of traditional crime; and the risks of serious physical and economic harm at the hands of white-collar offenders are far greater than at the hands of old-fashioned murderers, robbers and burglars, even when these are working as organised professionals (Pearce 1976).

The control of white-collar crime presents special problems, however. Offenders may be hard to locate and bring to book, especially in serious cases. The serious white-collar offender is more likely to be a corporation than a private individual and corporate misconduct is notoriously difficult to control. Moreover, public attitudes towards white-collar crime and those who commit it are ambiguous (University of Sydney 1979).

The public at large nowadays is arguably at greater or, at least, at as great a risk of serious harm from the impersonal activities of institutions as from the private designs of individuals. Although corporations in the strict legal sense are not modern phenomena, their immense social significance and that of large-scale organisations of similar nature, both profit-making and non-profit-making, is a distinctive feature of modern social life with which it can be argued the law is ill-equipped to cope, its rules and concepts being related to the motives and designs and misbehaviour of individuals acting privately, for the most part independently of complex institutional frameworks. Of course, the law has responded to the rise of large-scale organisations and corporate misdemeanour by extending and adapting the traditional conceptual and practical apparatus of control. But the difficulties are increasing and increasingly evident.

The author of a comprehensive and careful review of criminal sanctions for corporate illegality in the United States (Yoder 1978) points out that the rate of corporate crime is increasing, despite extensive use of the principle of strict criminal liability and severe penalties for corporate offenders who breach the public trust, and despite the fact that judges have not hesitated to send business men to prison. It can be argued that measures directed towards individual corporate executives, both actual (past) or 'dangerous' (potential) offenders, are losing their force and significance. The rise of large-scale organisations in every sphere of social life means a proliferation of executives whose misconduct cannot always be effectively controlled by traditional means, whether these be backward-looking or forward-looking. It is inherent in the nature of large-scale organisations that personal liability for wilful wrong-doing is often difficult to assign and effective sanctions are hard to devise. Moreover, public and professional opinion is uncertain and, possibly, at odds over the best way to proceed.

White-collar crimes are usually committed by white-collar offenders: that is, by persons who are better educated than most and also likely, therefore, to come from the ranks of the socially respectable and relatively prosperous members of the community. There can be no doubt that 'respectable' opinion in all social classes tends to be biased in favour of the average, unaggressive, socially respectable white-collar offender and that sentences of the court sometimes reflect this bias. Such people may be considered offenders but they are not branded as criminals; still less are they likely to be deemed 'dangerous'. If they are brought to book they are more likely to be fined than imprisoned, and in the frequent cases where the offender is in the service of a corporation he will not necessarily suffer the penalty personally.

It is also true that public alarm in face of 'modern' dangerousness, as represented by the high-risk, serious corporate offender, tends to be muted by the bureaucratic impersonality of the responsible individuals, the time-lag which frequently separates the commission of the offence and the realisation of the harm caused, and the anonymity of the victim.

It would be a mistake, however, to overlook the signs of change. The consumer movement and investigative journalism between them are responsible for a better informed and more sophisticated public opinion which understands white-collar crime and reacts to it with moral indignation. The fact that such crime invariably involves a breach of trust excites strong retributive feelings, especially when the resulting physical and economic harm is widespread and is in addition publicised by the news media. Public opinion may be biased in favour of the average white-collar offender, but it is doubtful whether this is as true as it once was, and it is very doubtful whether it holds for the corporate offender, especially if he is responsible for serious physical harm to workers, consumers or members of the general public. At any rate, the powerful campaign to awaken public opinion to the nature and extent of corporate crime shows no signs of abating, more particularly in the United States.

It has become fashionable (in the United States) to compare 'crime in the suites' of corporations (so-called 'acquisitive corporate crime', by which is meant illegal activities designed to increase corporate as distinct from personal wealth) with 'crime in the streets' of cities and suburbs; and to speak of 'corporate violence' to refer to the decisions of corporate personnel which result in physical harm to employees, consumers or members of the general public. It is argued (Geis and Monahan 1976) that the category of dangerous offenders should include corporate wrong-doers, despite the relative complexity and the diffuse effects of their harmful activities which make it difficult, in many cases, to attribute to particular individuals either the potential harm or the responsibility for it, or both. The difficulty, it is said, should be met by wholehearted acceptance of the principle of strict criminal liability for corporate wrong-doing. It is the prevailing theory of criminal responsibility itself that renders the law ineffectual as a protection against the harm threatened by the impersonal corporate offender. There should be greater consistency in the treatment of offenders according to the consequences of their actions. Holmes, it is said, may have spoken truly when he remarked that even a dog distinguishes between being stumbled over and being kicked; but it is absurd that people should distinguish between being stabbed and being polluted to death.

Not surprisingly, this view does not commend itself to legal opinion. The principle of strict liability has, of course, come into extensive use; a large number of offences are enacted without reference to the essentially moral ingredients of intention, recklessness or negligence. But the principle is repugnant to the judiciary. It goes against the grain to impute blame to many, if not most, offenders convicted under the principle of strict liability. Moral stigma is thought to be misplaced and attempts are made to devise ways of protecting such offenders against criminal charges, or at least against the full implications of such charges: for example, by means of new civil penalties, which would not carry the stigma of moral culpability which accompanies a criminal sanction, or by placing strict liability offences in a lower or less serious category than 'crimes' (Law Commission 1968).

In campaigning for public enlightenment and legal and judicial impartiality, critics arguing on these lines often seem to miss an obvious point. People may indeed be suffering as much from ills caused by institutions as by private crimes, but the same measures of prevention, in particular imprisonment, do not so obviously recommend themselves; not because people feel any tenderness for large corporations or because they think it is better to be poisoned by a pharmaceutical company than by Graham Young, or even because there is less ill-intention (though all these things may be true), but because there are notable problems of controlling corporate misconduct when direct prohibitions prove to be ineffective.

Corporate offenders must be judged 'dangerous' on the same moral terms as individual offenders. In so far as a corporation which is guilty of recklessly or intentionally causing harm may be disposed and able to defy normal measures of control, it and its members can be accounted 'dangerous' in the same way as an ordinary offender. If protective measures could be effective, therefore, there is no reason why individuals in positions of authority in corporations should not come within their scope. But the questions raised here concern effectiveness rather than propriety.

Protective Sentences: a Question of Efficacy

This brings us to the arguments that focus on the efficacy of imprisonment as a protective device. Preventive confinement is said to make such an insignificant contribution to public safety that it can be dispensed with.

The plausible idea that one function served by prison is to protect the public by keeping people given to committing crimes out of circulation, away from their potential victims, has recently been put to the test in a number of empirical studies (Cohen 1978; Pease and Wolfson 1979; Brody and Tarling 1980). Investigators have tested the net effect on a given crime rate of introducing hypothetical modifications to current sentencing policy. How many of the crimes known to have been committed in a given year could not have been committed had the modified policy been in force — because those responsible for them would have been in custody? The results of this attempt to introduce precision into the argument about the protective value of imprisonment depend on how it is decided to deal with the difficulty that in order to produce estimates of the number of crimes that might have been prevented by a change of sentencing policy, account must be taken of all crimes known to have been committed, whether or not those responsible have been caught. Some assumptions are necessary about the characteristics of those responsible for the uncleared crimes and estimates of so-called 'incapacitation effects' vary within a disconcertingly wide range according to the proportion of known crimes which are not cleared up and who is assumed by the investigators to be responsible for them. (Are most crimes of violence committed by those who are eventually caught, or must a large proportion of them be attributed to offenders who are never caught? The question is strictly unanswerable, but if the latter is true, sending to prison those who are caught will not result in a significant reduction in the crime rate.)

Incapacitation studies are proliferating, but so long as there are uncleared crimes their results can never be more than approximations and they will always have to be applied to policy decisions with great caution. In any case, however, they have not so far been directed to estimating the protective value of special sentences for identified 'dangerous' offenders as such. Investigators have asked what would happen if imprisonment were abolished altogether, or they have postulated mandatory fixed-term sentences for a range of prescribed offences or, simply, longer prison sentences in general. They have not asked what would be the effect of special sentences for high-risk serious offenders.[1]

This is because they take the view that serious crimes can never be predicted with sufficient accuracy. It is true that the predictive value of assessments of 'dangerousness' is low and that if selected high-risk serious offenders are given protective sentences a number of them will be unnecessarily detained. This, however, bears on the justice rather than the efficacy of protective sentences. Their incapacitative effect must depend primarily on the extent to which those who are locked up are responsible for the harm which the measure is intended to prevent. The more narrowly this is defined to exclude all but the severest offences, the greater the chance of a high rate of cleared-up crimes and of firm evidence about the rate at which individual offenders commit their offences, and the extent to which recidivists are responsible for the risk of serious harm from which it is desired to protect the public. In any case, the argument from 'incapacitation effects' loses its force as the category of 'dangerous' offenders is defined more narrowly. When the harm is grave, the fact that preventive confinement may possibly make little difference to the rate at which it is occurring may weigh less heavily than the fact that it prevents at least some bad cases.

What about serious white-collar crimes? In general the same considerations apply. However, the more serious the offence, the more likely it is to be an instance of corporate wrong-doing and imprisonment may not be a relevant measure. It may be very difficult in such cases to locate the responsible decision-makers in a complex structure of management; but this is not the heart of the matter. Crimes of corporate acquisitiveness are, of course, perpetrated by the officers of delinquent corporations; it is appropriate that these officers should be identified and punished for their part in the corporate crime and there is no reason to suppose that imprisonment will not have its usual effects, whatever they may be, on these individuals and their colleagues. But the wrong-doer is the corporation itself and preventive measures will only be effective if addressed to this impersonal entity, the future conduct of which is not bound up with the fate of particular officers. Dangerous corporations can no doubt be deterred but they cannot be incapacitated by imprisoning their officers.

Corporations as such can be held criminally liable for their wrong-doing. Punishment takes the form of fines, which can affect profits, and notoriety, which may damage the company's goodwill. Both measures could no doubt be strengthened and rationalised: fines could be calibrated to the magnitude of the harm caused and the size of the corporation; and delinquent corporations might be required to give formal notice of a criminal conviction to the public in general or, at least, to those likely to be financially interested. But preventive confinement is hardly relevant: imprisoning officials may raise the consciousness of some corporate executives, but it will not make a direct impact on the propensity of corporations to cause harm. Corporate 'dangerousness' can only be tackled by measures such as corporate 'probation' − the establishment of a public trusteeship permitting the corporation to continue in business only so long as it continues to fulfill certain conditions; or corporate 'quarantine' − temporary suspension of the right of the corporation to engage in certain kinds of activity (Stone 1975).

It is a mistake to think, as some critics evidently do, that social prejudice and discrimination in favour of the powerful are enough to explain why preventive confinement is used more to protect the public against dangerous individuals than against dangerous institutions; and it is absurd to imply that if it is largely irrelevant to the one it ought not to be used for the other. Nevertheless, the underlying thought is an important one: that efforts to protect the public should be directed to the reform of social institutions, practices and habits.

Modifying the Environment

To look at 'dangerousness' in broader perspective is to see the need for educating public opinion to appreciate better the nature and scale of modern social hazards and to take a more realistic view of the contribution that imprisoning 'dangerous' offenders can make to public safety in an age of modern technology and corporate enterprise. It imparts urgency to the question whether it is possible to modify and control the situations that provide people in general and offenders in particular with their motives and intentions, their provocations and temptations, their opportunities and means of inflicting harm.

A wide range of more or less specific modifications to the social environment can be devised. Some modest steps are rather obvious though not, on that account, unimportant. Thus, for example, violence can be reduced in frequency by regulating the consumption of alcohol and the carrying of real or simulated weapons; armed robbery can be frustrated by attention to the design of banks, the training of personnel in security routines and arrangements for the physical transfer of money; rape can be made more difficult by the provision of street lighting and late night bus services as well as publicity directed to persuading unaccompanied women not to seek lifts. Other less obvious measures of the same kind require a better understanding of the situations in which offences occur.

Still more sophisticated measures depend on the theoretical insights and the empirical and experimental findings of the psychological and social sciences. Conflicting and inconclusive as they are, they nevertheless serve the important negative function of putting received ideas to historical and comparative test (Zehr 1976), and the positive function of suggesting new practical approaches to the problem of making preventive confinement unnecessary. These new approaches may range from ethically neutral, even praiseworthy programmes of community reorganisation and development (Silberman 1978: Chapter 12), to ethically controversial schemes and techniques of behaviour therapy directed to specific maladaptive behaviour patterns and dispensed, with or without their consent, to offenders in custody (Erwin 1978).

To do more than mention these possibilities and problems would be out of place here. There are undoubtedly more radical ways of tackling the phenomenon of 'dangerous' offenders than by protective sentencing; but whether the burden of risk they present can be eliminated by improved social arrangements or novel therapies is doubtful: in any case, the project requires time and will breed its own ethical problems. In the meantime, what emerges clearly enough from the discussion here is that preventive confinement of 'dangerous' offenders is of only marginal value as a protective device. Measured against the full range of modern social hazards its contribution to public safety is tiny, as is also its likely impact on the rates at which serious offences are committed. It serves, nevertheless, to prevent a certain number of instances of grave harm and whether there is a good case for trying to persuade the public to forgo this element of special protection is a matter left unsettled by the arguments reviewed in this chapter.

Notes

1. See, however, Brody and Tarling (1980) who assessed a large sample of English prisoners for 'dangerousness' in 1972 and in 1979 traced the criminal careers of 52 men, rated in some degree 'dangerous', who had been released in the meantime. They comment on their findings that though 'they provide good evidence in favour of careful and detailed consideration of individual cases and individual offences in discussions of dangerousness and of the dangerous offender ... they still do not encourage any idea of incapacitation policies based on predictive instruments'.

CHAPTER 2

Determining
'Dangerousness'

It is undoubtedly much harder than most people think to define and
identify dangerous offenders satisfactorily for legal purposes. Critics
argue that it is impossible to do so. They rest their case on objections
to the concept of dangerousness itself and to the notion that human
behaviour is predictable. As the term is ordinarily used in reference
to people, 'dangerousness' refers to a pathological attribute of character:
a propensity to inflict harm on others in disregard or defiance of the
usual social and legal constraints. Yet, as they rightly point out, a
'dangerous' person is not a psychological entity; nor is 'dangerousness' a
scientific or medical concept. It is not necessarily associated with
mental illness. We are all differently motivated and differently placed
to inflict harm on others; but it is not self-evident what is to count
as harmful behaviour and who is to be deemed 'dangerous'. Harmful
behaviour and unacceptable risks are socially construed and people
are socially defined as dangerous accordingly.

The notion of a 'dangerous' person as one with a disposition or
propensity to inflict harm is, therefore, empty of meaning until it is
given social content. No doubt there is a widely accepted 'common-
sense' definition of the dangerous offender as 'the repetitively violent
criminal who has more than once committed or attempted to commit
homicide, forcible rape, robbery or assault' (Dinitz and Conrad 1978);
but there is room for much disagreement and if anyone is to be justly
detained or placed under supervision in anticipation of the harm they
may do, the legal conditions must be clearly defined. What must an
offender do to place himself at risk of being deemed 'dangerous'?
On the basis of what considerations may a court find him 'dangerous'?
How could such a finding be successfully contested? The harm against
which it is permissible to provide the additional protection of a special
sentence must be specified; and legally sane offenders at any rate
must be shown to have a propensity for inflicting such harm intentionally[1] or with a degree of recklessness or neglect of the consequences
that would justify holding them in some degree culpable; and to be
likely to cause it again within the period of a proposed sentence.

It is fair to say that these requirements are nowhere fully met. There are considerable difficulties in defining 'dangerousness' satisfactorily for legal purposes; but the greater problem is to select 'dangerous' offenders for protective sentencing. The problems of assessment have given rise to a considerable literature and are often cited as reasons why we cannot with a good conscience make use of the concept of dangerousness in the administration of justice. Professor Norval Morris (1974), for example, states categorically: 'since we cannot make reliable predictions of dangerous behaviour, considerations of justice forbid us to confine people against their wishes in the name of public safety for longer periods than we can justify on other grounds'. We discuss these problems of assessment below: it will be enough at this point to say that since it is impossible to be sure how people will behave in the future, if only because of the workings of chance, any attempt to apply precautions selectively against some persons for the protection of others is bound to be more or less wide of the mark. A statistician will say how wide, by means of a statement of probability which expresses the rate at which judgments will be falsified. This makes it possible to calculate the consequences of acting upon them: so many positive judgments of *dangerous* will be falsified if no preventive measures are taken, and so many negative judgments of *safe*. By and large, it is the critics of protective sentencing who worry about the former and the public who worry about the latter: but the debate over the significance of falsified judgments of 'dangerousness' is thoroughly vitiated by the mistake, common to both sides, of identifying statistical entities ('false positives' and 'false negatives') with particular, misjudged individuals.

Statistically speaking, the most efficient method of selection is one which will minimise the sum total of falsified judgments of both kinds, positive and negative; but for the purpose of doing full justice to the individual offender, the best method is one which takes into account the maximum amount of information about his character and circumstances and that is the individualised, so-called 'clinical' method of assessment by case-study. As to efficiency, the critics point out that though actuarial methods do indeed minimise predictive error, for statistical reasons the number of falsified judgments is bound to be large in proportion if the number of offenders at risk of doing further harm is small (and the number of serious offenders at risk of repeating their serious offences is in fact small); and moreover, any attempt to reduce the proportion of falsified positive judgments of *dangerous*, by making the criteria more restrictive, simply results in increasing the proportion of falsified judgments of *safe*: 'false negatives'. And as to justice, the critics point to the results of the several attempts that have been made to validate individualised 'clinical' assessments of dangerousness which seem to show that a dismayingly high proportion of those deemed *dangerous* by this method do no harm when let free to do so.

In this chapter we review this controversy about the nature of 'dangerousness' and the methodological problems of selecting 'dangerous' offenders. It reveals inescapable uncertainties and dilemmas. It is easy to sympathise with those who argue that protective sentencing is never justified and that restraint must be justified in some other way (for instance as retributive punishment). This completely avoids the difficulties and dilemmas on which the critics rest their case, but it is the only way of doing so. Anyone who accepts the need for protective sentencing must come to terms with the issues discussed here.

'Dangerous Persons'

The idea is deeply rooted that identifying 'dangerous' persons for legal purposes is a matter of diagnosing pathological attributes of character and this is nowadays thought to be the province of psychiatry; 'dangerousness' is presumed to be something for students of abnormal psychology, even when it is not clearly associated with mental illness. This presumption has recently come under sharp attack in the United States, where the generally inadequate legal prescriptions of 'dangerousness' and the practice of referring offenders to psychiatrists, or to centres in charge of psychiatrists, for the diagnosis and treatment of dangerous propensities is alleged to have fostered a widespread misapprehension of the nature of the problem of the 'dangerous' offender. Credence is lent to the idea of a quasi-medical entity, a 'dangerous person', on which psychiatrists and associated professionals in the field of mental health are expertly qualified to advise the courts, which is an idea with serious consequences for the administration of justice (Ennis and Litwack 1974).

The falsity of any such idea is well brought out by Drs Kozol, Garofalo and Boucher, clinicians in charge of the Center for the Diagnosis and Treatment of Dangerous Persons at Bridgewater, Massachusetts. They have provided (Kozol et al. 1972) a uniquely full account of their work with legally sane offenders, in which the inadequacies of the law and the difficulties and uncertainties inherent in the enterprise of assessing 'dangerousness', as well as the essential similarity of the task to that of making commonplace judgments of innocuous qualities, are strikingly illustrated.

'What is a dangerous person? No such entity exists in the nosology of psychiatry' remark Kozol et al. and proceed to describe how they set about developing their own criteria: 'We examined the language of the Massachusetts statute and the probable intent of the legislature in the light of the tragic case which had led to the enactment of the law'. The statute in question (Mass. Gen. Laws Ann. Ch. 12.3A, S. 1 1958) was enacted following the heinous murder of two small brothers by a man who had been released from prison only a few weeks earlier, having served part of a ten-year sentence for a nearly fatal sexual assault on a young boy. It refers specifically to sexually dangerous persons but is not confined in its application to persons convicted of sexual offences. The Bridgewater team were reluctant for clinical reasons to define 'dangerousness' in exclusively sexual terms: 'It is our hypothesis that there is no difference between the person who kills to rob and the person who kills to rape', and they declined to seek among the offenders referred to them only for those motivated specifically by sexual concerns. They set out to identify those at risk of committing further 'serious assaultive crimes'; and decided, moreover, that they would not concern themselves with such crimes if they were politically motivated. They defined 'dangerousness' as 'a pathological *self-serving* potential for violence' and 'pathological' as 'a primary insistence on violence when alternatives do exist and without benevolent regard for the consequences to others'.

Having, as they explain, somewhat remedied the vagueness of the law and supplied *ad hoc* their own definition of legal dangerousness, they went on to construct their own working concept or specification of a 'dangerous person'. They focused on indications of incapacity to feel for others and to learn from experience, and paid particular attention to indications of resentment and anger as being, in their view, the principal factors governing malevolent violence associated with wilfully harmful behaviour.

> We can see the *dangerous* person as one who has actually inflicted or attempted to inflict serious physical injury on another person; harbours anger, hostility and resentment; enjoys witnessing or inflicting suffering; lacks altruistic and compassionate concern for others; sees himself as a victim rather than as an aggressor; resents or rejects authority; is primarily concerned with his own satisfaction and with the relief of his own discomfort; is intolerant of frustration or delay of satisfaction; lacks control of his own impulses; has immature attitudes towards social responsibility; lacks insight into his own psychological structure; and distorts his perception of reality in accordance with his own wishes and needs.
>
> (1972: 379)

Kozol and his colleagues depart from other standard accounts of 'dangerousness' in denying that 'anti-social psychopathy' constitutes a distinctive clinical entity. They note that it is impossible to divide people sharply into the *dangerous* and the *safe*: 'dangerousness' is a matter of degree and the spectrum is wide. Moreover, 'no one can predict dangerous behaviour in an individual with no history of dangerous acting out' and the disposition to inflict harm may be intermittent, even episodic, rather than fixed and habitual. They insist that 'dangerousness' cannot be attributed to a single factor and that it is not detectable through routine psychiatric examination; indeed, 'the terms used in standard psychiatric diagnosis are almost all totally irrelevant to the determination of dangerousness'.[2] There is no test for 'dangerousness': there are no clear-cut criteria – only clues to be gleaned from a meticulous inquiry into many different aspects of the personality and its development. No single factor is a necessary or a sufficient cause of 'dangerousness': each may become important or, alternatively, neutralised in the presence of others. Assessment must be based on an overall subjective impression or judgment which grasps the interrelatedness of many factors: 'the diagnosis is made when, all things considered, the offender clearly falls within the working concept of a dangerous person'. The assessment is a matter, in the end, of acumen sharpened by experience. Reliability, as measured by the tendency of independent assessors to agree, cannot be taken for granted even when they are equally well-informed, shrewd and practised.

Nothing could be clearer from all this than that these clinicians in case-conference (psychiatrists, psychologists and social workers), trying to decide what to say to the court about the offenders referred to them under suspicion of being 'dangerous', were engaged in a formalised version of the thoroughly familiar activity of judging character. They were entitled to the status of 'expert' before the court, not because there was much science they could bring to bear on the task but because they were practised in the art and better acquainted than any layman could be with the kind of person they were dealing with; the court could therefore properly require them to articulate and defend their reasons for whatever recommendations they decided to make.

Predictive Judgments

It also emerges clearly, however, that their terms of reference were far from satisfactory and it is tempting to argue from their experience that for sentencing purposes a man should only be judged 'dangerous' if it can be predicted that he will commit a future offence with something like the degree of particularity and certainty with which we could reckon to establish the fact that he committed a past offence. This is an unreasonable requirement, however, and in any case would simply by-pass the problem by obscuring the nature of the undertaking. For whether it be a person's benevolence or his dangerousness that is at issue, an assessment takes the form of a *predictive judgment*, not a simple prediction.

As the term implies, both evaluation and prediction are involved in predictive judgments: an evaluation of someone's character – his disposition to behave in a certain way, and a prediction – an estimate of the probability that in forseeable circumstances he will actually do so. These elements are not clearly distinguishable, however. For practical purposes they are inextricable: a predictive judgment is a prediction grounded in an evaluation. If the prediction is falsified, it does not at once follow that the evaluation was mistaken: we may say that a man acted 'out of character' which is to give him (as well as ourselves, as judges of character) the benefit of the doubt. By the same token, fair-minded persons do not jump to conclusions about a man's disposition from a single instance of relevant behaviour: they want to be sure that he is behaving 'in character'.

None of this presents great difficulty when nothing much hangs on the assessment. But predictive judgments in criminal justice are another matter. 'Dangerousness' is a matter of degree. Some offenders make their intentions very plain and will create opportunities to do the further harm they intend (in furtherance of a personal vendetta, a career of organised crime or political terrorism); others acknowledge a compulsion or impulse to do harm in certain circumstances and they are more likely to avoid opportunities than to create them. Others, however, acknowledge no such intentions or desires and they turn the truism that nobody is *certain* to do harm in the future (because something may always intervene, whether it is a change of circumstances or a change of heart) into a practical difficulty of deciding in particular cases whether we have good reason for believing we know better than the offender himself what he is likely to do in the future. A predictive judgment of his behaviour is called for and it is this type of case which gives rise to most of the difficulties and the arguments.

Judicial determinations of dangerousness must take the form of predictive judgments. Evaluations of character alone will not do: predicted harm of some specified kind must be the criterion. But making a predictive judgment is not simply a question of predicting a future event in the same sense as making a retrospective judgment is a question of establishing a past event. Assessing the 'dangerousness' of a legally sane offender does not call simply for an actuarial statement — an answer to the question 'how probable is it that a man like this will cause further harm?' It calls for an evaluation of his individual character and circumstances — an answer to the more complex question: 'In what circumstances would this person now be going to cause harm and what is the strength or persistence of his inclination to do so in such circumstances?' To which must be added the further question: 'How likely is it that he will find himself in those circumstances in the foreseeable future?'

Alternative Methods of Assessment

Broadly speaking, there are two ways of assessing 'dangerousness'. We may decide that an offender is a 'bad' risk on the basis of a study of his character and circumstances; or we may try for a more precise estimate by actuarial means. We could classify a large number of offenders into groups according to age, sex, length or other attributes of criminal records and calculate the frequency of reoffending in each group. This would enable us to decide the case of a particular offender by seeing to which group he belonged in virtue of his age, record, etc. Instead of saying, on the basis of a study of his character and circumstances, simply that he is a 'bad' risk, we could then say, more precisely, that actuarially speaking the probability of his reoffending is, say, 55%. There is nothing logically to choose between these statements: they are formally the same. When we estimate the risk presented by a particular offender we are *classing* him: it comes to the same thing, logically speaking, whether we assemble a class of 'bad' risks from a series of case-studies or from an actuarial exercise. If we deem an offender by either method to be a 'bad' risk we are, in effect, assigning him to a group of which, if it were large enough, we could expect a majority to cause further harm if we took no preventive measures. By the same token, we could expect a minority to cause no further harm and preventive measures to be unnecessary in this number of cases. These, of course, are statistical errors and it is fallacious to think of them as misjudged individuals.

Nevertheless, it is not a matter of indifference which method is used in the administration of justice. The actuarial method has great practical advantages which are widely acknowledged. It is relatively cheap and it is exact and consistent. It is efficient in selecting relevant items of information and giving them weight according to their importance. It produces optimum classifications which yield the highest probabilities with the fewest mistakes. But, of course, it derives the risk presented by any particular individual from the fact of his being a member of a statistical class; and this seems intuitively objectionable in the administration of justice. It does not pretend to explain his behaviour and leaves out of account much information that may be relevant to the probability of preventive measures being necessary in his case.

The risk that any particular individual presents diverges from that of the actuarial class to which he belongs in so far as it depends on factors which have been excluded from the overall calculation; but statisticians exclude factors if they are too rare to be given statistical weight, whether or not they have anything to contribute to explaining or understanding his behaviour. Reducing the number of mistaken predictions must, therefore, be a matter of detecting in the individual case relevant factors which the statistician cannot take into account. Of course, it may be argued that if the factors peculiar to individuals are rare, identifying them could not reduce the number of mistakes: the classification is optimal, which is to say that the rare factors have been excluded precisely because they cannot be used to raise the probability and reduce the number of mistakes. But this misses the point that, although the rare factors may be very varied and cannot each be given statistical weight, they have their rarity in common and as a class may contribute heavily to the mistakes of actuarial predictions.

Other things being equal, case-study predictions should be right more often than actuarial predictions, but this *a priori* expectation is often disappointed in practice. The case-study method has the virtues that it predicts on the basis of understanding and can take explicitly into account every possible item of relevant information about an individual offender; but it has the defects of its virtues and, in practice, the assessment is fraught with difficulty. Psychological theory is not as effective as statistical theory in selecting what is relevant and important. Practitioners of the case-study method suffer from a surfeit of information of varying quality and relevance which they find very hard to evaluate and bring systematically to bear on the task in hand.

That is not the essential problem, however. A predictive judgment takes the form of a statement of probability but it may not be arrived at by purely actuarial means, for it is not just to take preventive measures against an offender solely on the strength of his being a member of a statistical class of high-risk offenders. The assessment of the risk he presents must rest not only on evidence of a propensity to cause wilful harm, but the evidence must be specific to him and this precludes the determination of dangerousness by purely actuarial methods, whatever may be their advantages in other respects. For though a high proportion of right judgments is a necessary condition of justice, it is not a sufficient condition: it is also a necessary condition that each case should be adjudicated on its merits.

It is often implied, when methods of assessing dangerousness are being compared, that all that matters is that predictive judgments shall be as exact and consistent as possible and that the probability of their being right shall be maximised by whatever method can be devised; that to secure the highest proportion of right predictive judgments is not merely a necessary condition of doing justice generally, but is a sufficient condition of doing justice in the individual case. This, however, is not so, for the right judgment must be reached by the right means, which is to say by individual adjudication. There is a world of difference in principle between applying preventive measures in individual cases on the basis of predictive judgments, even if we know that some of them, despite all precautions, are bound to be mistaken; and deliberately incurring mistakes, to an extent calculable in advance, by applying preventive measures indiscriminately to all of a group of offenders at risk, so as to be sure of capturing a certain number known statistically to be hidden within it who will commit further serious harm. The distinction is between necessarily imperfect justice and unnecessarily rough justice; and though there may be times and circumstances when the distinction does not seem to hold up well in practice, because the number of mistakes yielded by either method is much the same, or because rough justice by some rule of thumb yields fewer mistakes on average, individual assessment is as crucial to the making of just predictive judgments as it is universally recognised to be to the making of just retrospective judgments.

How Many Right Judgments?

It is not difficult to arrange to discover how many judgments of *safe* are right judgments in the sense that they are not subsequently falsified by the offender's behaviour when placed in an open hospital or prison or released into the community. The problem is to test the validity of judgments of *dangerous*: the suggestion that prisons or secure hospitals should release their 'dangerous' inmates on an experimental basis is hardly feasible. Investigators have had to rely on the court orders which from time to time since 1966, after the famous ruling of the Supreme Court of the United States in the case of *Baxstrom* v. *Herold* (1966), have released allegedly dangerous inmates from hospitals and prisons, making it possible to follow their subsequent careers and put the assessments of their dangerousness to the test of experience.

A recent British study (Brody and Tarling 1980) adopts a less direct approach to the problem. From a substantial sample of convicted offenders in prison they selected, on the basis of case-histories, a large group whose records showed evidence of assaultive behaviour and successively eliminated by description all but those who seemed to represent the worst risk to life. A process of increasing discrimination, with reference to kinds of behaviour and circumstances which seemed to justify attention, yielded a sub-group of men who could reasonably be said to be in some degree dangerous. The judgments of dangerousness were put to the test by reference to subsequent patterns of offending, but the investigation was closer to being an experiment than an evaluation. The judgments were made for the purpose of the investigation by the researchers themselves in consultation with members of prison staffs on the evidence of an array of police, medical, psychiatric and welfare reports such as are customarily available to courts and Parole Boards. The intention was to demonstrate the practical difficulties associated with employing labels like 'dangerous', rather than to evaluate assessment procedures or to ascertain the accuracy of a sample of predictive judgments actually made and acted upon in the administration of criminal justice. Nevertheless, the results are not inconsistent with those of validation studies undertaken in the United States.

The results of five major investigations of the validity of clinical assessments of dangerousness, all undertaken in the United States, have now been published: three retrospective studies of the assessments of mentally disordered offenders released by court order, after long periods of detention, from hospitals for the criminally insane; and two studies made at first-hand of the cases of legally sane offenders referred to centres for the diagnosis and treatment of 'dangerous persons' and subsequently released by the court against the advice of the clinical staff who judged them *dangerous*. These investigations are reviewed in detail in Appendix C. No more will be said about them here than is necessary to illustrate the difficulty of reaching firm conclusions, or even an informed judgment, about the present state and future prospects of the art of making clinical (individualised) assessments of 'dangerousness'.

The studies differed in a number of respects: for example, the criteria of 'dangerousness' were different and subjects were followed up for different periods of time. However, these were small differences, incapable of accounting, even cumulatively, for the gross divergence of the results: the retrospective studies showed much higher proportions of wrong judgments of *dangerous* (80 to 86%) than the first-hand studies (54 to 65%) (Monahan 1977).

The path-breaking *Baxstrom* studies (Steadman and Cocozza 1974) are often cited as providing the most striking evidence for the gross inaccuracy of clinical judgments of *dangerous*. But the judgments that were purportedly put to the test, by the transfer of the *Baxstrom* patients out of the hospitals for the criminally insane into civil hospitals or their release into the community, could not be directly investigated. That these patients had at some time been specifically judged *dangerous* had to be inferred from their reputations and from the fact of their continued detention in secure hospitals; but this is capable of explanation on grounds, such as the exercise of administrative discretion or administrative inertia, other than a clinical assessment of dangerousness. The psychiatrists and others who were presumed to have judged them *dangerous* are said to have been hopelessly wrong on the evidence of their relatively peaceable behaviour over a period of four years after their transfer to civil hospitals or discharge from custody: but it would have been surprising if these offenders had not behaved peaceably, considering that by the time of their transfer they had been institutionalised for an average of 15 years and, at the average age of 47, were well past the peak age for violent crime.

The *Baxstrom* decision prompted a similar group of mentally disordered offenders in Pennsylvania to petition successfully for release in the case of *Dixon* v. *Pennsylvania* in 1971. The results of the follow-up of these offenders were reported in an unpublished paper by Thornberry and Jacoby in 1974[3] and are said (Monahan 1977) to be remarkably similar to those reported by Steadman: only 14% of the former patients 'engaged in behaviour injurious to another person' within four years of their release. But as a test of the accuracy of clinical assessments of dangerousness this study appears to suffer from the same crucial limitation as Steadman's, that the assessments which were the subject of the investigation were not available for inspection.

The third retrospective study (Cocozza and Steadman 1976) was free of this limitation: the investigators were able to study the reports made to the court by two psychiatrists in respect of each of a sample of defendants who were found incompetent to stand trial and assessed for dangerousness. Those evaluated by the psychiatrists as *dangerous* were no more so than those evaluated as *safe*; there was no significant difference between the two groups on any of the measures of violent behaviour that were examined, and on the basis of numerous indicators the investigators reasonably concluded that these psychiatric assessments were not at all accurate. However, the analysis of the psychiatric reports makes it evident that these were based on routine and slovenly diagnostic procedures. They provide clear and convincing evidence only of bad practice, not of the state of the art of assessing dangerousness.

The two first-hand studies were undertaken at institutions for the diagnosis and treatment of 'dangerous persons' in the United States (US State of Maryland 1973; Kozol et al. 1972). They concerned legally sane offenders referred by the courts for observation and treatment, a number of whom were in due course released against the advice of the clinical staff; and these cases were followed up for a period of five years in the one study and three years in the other. The assessments of these offenders were certainly not routine or slovenly: they were the outcome of lengthy, comprehensive and thorough case studies by teams of psychiatrists, psychologists and social workers. Nevertheless, half to two-thirds of the judgments of *dangerous* that were put to the test were not borne out by subsequent harmful behaviour on the part of the offenders concerned within the period of the investigations.

There must be some doubt whether these results are entirely trustworthy, for the investigations were not rigorously designed and executed (Monahan 1973; 1977). Nevertheless, it is difficult to avoid the conclusion that even under favourable conditions the risk of unnecessary detention imposed on offenders by a protective sentence is likely to be considerable: on the evidence of these first-hand studies, with all their weaknesses, it is at least 50 and may be as much as 66%, even when the offenders concerned have had records of serious crime accompanied by violence and the assessments of their 'dangerousness' have been carefully and conscientiously made.

Is this the best that can be done? Many take the view that it is, either because they believe that little can be done to improve techniques of assessment — that clinicians have 'taken their "best shot"' at making predictive judgments of people's behaviour (Monahan 1977) or because they believe that it is impossible to overcome the statistical constraints inherent in predicting rare events such as serious crimes. (If most people do not commit serious crimes, it is easier to be wrong than right if you predict that someone will do so, however carefully you make the assessment of his character and circumstances.) It is acknowledged that this difficulty could in theory be alleviated by confining predictions to a group of offenders among whom grave crimes were relatively common; but much is made of the fact that no one has as yet succeeded in identifying such a group of serious offenders with much more than an even chance of repeating their serious offences. A number of attempts are described in Appendix C which suggest that it could be done. It is a striking fact, however, that the reported ratios of invalid to valid judgments of *dangerous* seem to be much the same (2:1 at worst, 50:50 at best) whether they be reached by actuarial or case-study methods. To the question whether the risk of unnecessary detention could not be considerably reduced by applying improved techniques of individual assessment to members of a select high-risk group of offenders, the answer must be that as things are, some reduction could almost certainly be achieved by a combination of actuarial and case-study techniques of assessment but that in the long run the more successful the actuarial exercise of defining high-risk groups of serious offenders, the harder it must become for clinicians to improve on them by means of individual assessments; for they would be working to establish individual differences within a group so selected as to be homogeneous in the relevant respects. At least one commentator (Gordon 1977) takes the view that the offenders referred to centres in the US for the diagnosis and treatment of dangerous persons do constitute just such a homogeneous group and that the differences in individual outcomes uncovered by validation studies are almost entirely the product of chance.

As to the possibility of improving the methods of assessment themselves, there can be little doubt that the crucial weakness at present lies in the limited range of explanatory variables which can be taken systematically into account (Monahan 1977). The commonplace activity of judging character has been elaborated into a fine art grounded in the theory and practice of psychological medicine; but sociology and social psychology have done little to elaborate common-sense ideas of the influence of people's circumstances on their behaviour. If character may be pathological, circumstances may be pathogenic, in the sense that they may be abnormally conducive to disregard and defiance of constraints on seriously harmful behaviour. There is much sociological description and comparison and correlations have been established between features of the environment and kinds of behaviour and achievement. But many people living in pathogenic circumstances are not pathologically inclined to harm others and many pathological characters are living in ordinary circumstances. What are wanted are explanations of individual behaviour which link it with features of the material and social environment.

The view that the high risk of unnecessary detention which is imposed with a protective sentence cannot be reduced much below the present level may or may not be unduly pessimistic: the evidence is at best inconclusive. The task of validating predictive judgments has so far been narrowly conceived and executed. Investigators have established predictive values, compared them for magnitude and criticised them in general as unacceptably low: but they have not accounted for them in helpful terms. They have explained in general theoretical terms what depresses the predictive value of judgments of *dangerous*; and the low values of the several samples of such judgments that have been put to the test have been established. But no attempt has been made to enumerate and give specific weight to the various factors that may account for the particular values achieved by the clinicians responsible for them. Low values are flatly interpreted as 'inability to predict', even when they are plainly attributable in varying measure to factors such as routine or slovenly diagnostic procedures, characteristics of the offenders under assessment or of the sample of judgments being validated, neglect of situational or other variables and the brief period at risk, all of which are susceptible to correction or control.

In any case, so long as predictive judgments are made in the administration of justice, the moral obligation to persist with attempts to improve them and reduce the risk of unnecessary detention in protective sentencing is inescapable.

Experts and Laymen as Judges of 'Dangerousness'

Protective sentences are imposed by the judiciary and reviewed by the executive. How far should it be left to their unaided competence to decide that an offender is dangerous? If, as has been argued, deciding whether someone is dangerous is in principle no different from deciding whether he is benevolent and if, moreover, what is at issue is whether the public can reasonably be expected to accept the risks that he is judged to present, should not members of the public have an effective voice, directly or indirectly, in deciding whether a protective sentence is appropriate? Alternatively, it may be argued that assessing 'dangerousness' must be something for students of abnormal psychology, even though, as we have seen, expert assessments are subject to so much error.

A propensity to inflict intentional harm on others in disregard or defiance of the usual constraints and without the excuse of provocation or self-defence is abnormal in any sense of the word. Even serious offenders do not normally represent a risk of further serious harm and the mental state of those who do is outside the experience of most people. It seems reasonable and just to require that assessments of dangerousness should not be made without calling on the specialised experience of those whose profession it is to study and explain mental abnormality.

In the United States the courts and executive authorities administering a patchwork law of dangerousness have come to rely increasingly on expert testimony of psychiatrists as to the dangerousness of those brought before them: the mentally ill with no record of criminal conduct; defendants to criminal charges deemed unfit to stand trial; and legally responsible convicted offenders falling within the ambit of laws applying to 'habitual offenders', 'dangerous special offenders', and 'sexual psychopaths'.

In this country the same tendency is observable, though is is much less marked. The views of psychiatrists carry considerable weight in the deliberations of the Parole Board and are frequently taken into account by the courts, but psychiatrists are neither as prominent nor as influential in the administration of justice as in the United States. The Parole Board preserves its character as a review tribunal which brings to bear on the written reports of others the skills and experience of a wide range of professions and disciplines. In the courts, the calling of experts is not encouraged if there is a reasonable chance that a decision can be made without outside assistance. There has not been the same scope as in the United States for the misleading idea to take root and flourish that when psychiatrists are called as expert witnesses they are being asked to identify for the court an instance of a quasi-medical entity known as a 'dangerous person'.

Critics in the United States have impugned the competence of psychiatrists to judge the 'dangerousness' even of mentally disordered persons and have attacked their role in the civil commitment process. Some, including some psychiatrists, have drawn the obvious inference: they must be even less competent to judge the 'dangerousness' of legally sane persons and their role in the criminal process must be even more dubious. It is said (Ennis and Litwack 1974) that they are no better qualified than laymen to assess dangerousness; that laymen are well accustomed to making judgments about the mental condition of others and that the verdicts of psychiatrists about the 'dangerousness' of even mentally disordered persons have been shown to be no more valid than if they had been reached by tossing a coin. The prevailing tendency for the courts and executive authorities to defer to psychiatric judgments in criminal cases should therefore, it is argued, be checked. Strict rules for psychiatric testimony should be introduced to dispel 'the presumption of expertise'; such testimony should be limited to description without labels or reference to opinions, interpretations or predictions. The court, including the jury (if, as is said to be desirable, there is a jury), will know best what to make of these matter-of-fact observations, on a par with those proffered by other professional persons acquainted with the offender, such as social workers, the police or prison officers.

This argument exaggerates the damaging implications of the findings of attempts to validate assessments of dangerousness and may be thought in any case to go too far in underestimating the value of evidence from individuals who undeniably have wider experience than laymen on which to base an assessment of an offender's propensity to inflict harm. In English courts an 'expert' is a person capable of generalising from special experience, whether or not possessed of particular formal educational or professional qualifications: he may not testify to ordinary human nature but may be presumed to have special knowledge of any class of the population of which he has made a special study (Ormrod 1968).

The adversarial system virtually compels the expert to be a partisan for the side that calls him as a witness. Dershowitz (1973) and others have argued that defendants must, therefore, have the right to call expert witnesses on their own behalf and that the strict rules of evidence should apply; in particular, hearsay should be excluded and arrangements should be made to enable statements made on the basis of clinical interviews with the offender to be corroborated. Either the defendant should have the right to be accompanied at interview by his lawyer or other representative of his interests, or a video-taped record should be made available to the court. Von Hirsch (1972), who objects to protective sentencing, envisages the difficulties:

> In a preventive proceeding, the regular participants in the judicial process would be ill-equipped to judge the validity of the prediction. In a traditional courtroom one might imagine what predictive trials would become when they were contested: baffling arguments between prosecution and defense expert witnesses, each claiming major expertise and offering contrasting judgments. A lay judge and jury (if there is a jury) will find such evidence much harder to evaluate intelligently than evidence of past crimes.

Various solutions have been proposed: that the task of assessing 'dangerousness' should be referred to special tribunals; that a court assessor should sit with the judge; that independent psychiatrists should be appointed as court experts from panels approved by the learned societies. We found objections to each of these proposals: sentencing tribunals remove too much discretion from the judiciary; assessors may advise the court badly and 'indifferent scientific advice given into the court's ear is much worse than the worst expert evidence given from the witness box' (Ormrod 1968); independent psychiatrists are unlikely to enjoy the confidence of defendants, so that not only will justice not be seen to be done but the offender's mistrust will stand squarely in the way of a satisfactory clinical assessment of his case. There seems to be no escaping the assessment of 'dangerousness' by laymen, whether acting as judges or jurymen (if there are juries), and it seems unnecessary to deny the relevance of the special skills and experience of psychiatrists even to the cases of legally sane offenders, provided the limits of their competence are recognised, their terms of reference are explicit and the conditions under which their evidence has to be compiled are such as to enable a psychiatrist to apply the time, trouble and patience that it takes to assess criminal dangerousness properly (Scott 1977). The court must adjourn the case for a long enough period to enable the expert witness for the defence, if necessary, to acquire the kind of knowledge of his client and his circumstances that the witness for the prosecution may be presumed to have already. And the conditions under which the expert evidence is presented must be conducive to its proper exposition and comprehension by the court.

Ormrod (1968) proposed the adoption by scientific witnesses of some of the conventions that rule the Bar: 'It should be the right and duty of experts to exchange their reports before trial and, if they wish, consult together; and it should be a rigorous obligation on all experts to give the court, as clearly as they can, the limits of accuracy of their evidence, whether it is experimental or theoretical, and to disclose, if it be the fact, that other views exist in their profession. It should also be their duty to the court to indicate what inferences cannot properly be drawn from their evidence.' He further suggested that: 'All parties in civil or criminal cases should be obliged by rules of court to disclose, well in advance of trial, the reports of all scientific witnesses whom they intend to call, unless otherwise directed by the court. It should also be made clear that all expert witnesses have the right to consult together, regardless of the wishes of the parties or their legal advisers.' Most of the objections that have been raised to the calling of psychiatrists as expert witnesses when the need for a protective sentence is under consideration would be removed if these conventions were adopted.

It was put to us by respondents to our Consultative Document that the public should be involved in decisions about protective sentences: that the need for such a sentence should be decided by a jury and that the secrecy surrounding the administration of the sentence should be lifted so as to give the public an opportunity to express useful opinion, directly or indirectly, when consideration is given to the release of a prisoner on licence.

The proposal that a jury should determine not only whether a defendant is guilty but whether a protective rather than an ordinary sentence is appropriate to his case is not new. The Prevention of Crime Act 1908 provided that a jury should find for or against a defendant on a charge of being a 'habitual criminal' eligible for a sentence of preventive detention. It is said that juries disliked the task, though there seems to be no evidence to show whether they performed it well or badly. Determining whether or not an offender is 'dangerous' is a different and altogether more difficult matter, however. The case for giving that task to a jury was put to us by one respondent to our Consultative Document who argued that the question of 'reasonable fear' or 'justifiable public alarm' was too important a matter to be left to judges or psychiatrists; that juries were likely to be less inhibited than psychiatrists in expressing the fear *qua* fear, whilst some judges might not be inhibited enough; and that juries might be supposed also to have a better idea than either judges or psychiatrists of the community standards which govern fear and the acceptability of risk.

The case is supported by the distinguished American constitutional lawyer, Professor Alan Dershowitz (1973), who rests it on the principle that 'the decision to confine someone on the basis of a prediction is a social policy judgment to be made by the community'. This may be thought to smack of confusion between the making of sentencing policy and its application to individual cases: the argument for public participation cannot be the same at both stages. However, Professor Dershowitz goes on to make it clear that he is drawing on the analogy with ordinary criminal cases in which 'the legislature determines the types and degrees of harms sufficiently serious to warrant intervention; experts often aid the fact-finder in determining whether the facts meet the legislative standard; and the fact-finder should be the jury'. The same procedure, he suggests, should apply in all cases, whether civil or criminal, in which protective confinement is contemplated; and he adds, 'the need for trial by jury is particularly persuasive if the legislature had not really faced up — as is often the case when confinement is based on prediction — to the social policy issue involved in establishing standards. If these decisions about risks and freedom are to be abdicated, in a democratic society it is better that they be abdicated to a jury than to a psychiatrist or a judge.' But these arguments do not strike us as powerful enough to justify a proposal to reintroduce the jury into English sentencing practice at a time when its significance as an institution is being questioned (Jackson 1977; Baldwin and McConville 1979).

Professor Dershowitz also argues that 'trial by jury requires a judicial articulation and elaboration of the criteria for confinement. In a trial without jury judges often state their conclusions in the bare language of the statute. In a jury trial, on the other hand, the judges must instruct the jury on the meaning of the statutory criteria. These instructions are often appealed and this sets in motion the common law process of appellate consideration and construction of the statute's operative phrases. We think this point is met without the participation of a jury by our proposal (Chapter 8) that all protective sentences should be subject to automatic review by the Court of Appeal (Criminal Division); and that the strongest practical argument against involving a jury in the protective sentencing process is that it could not be expected to give reasons for its verdict. We propose in Chapter 8 that the judges should be required when imposing a protective sentence to review the evidence and give reasoned and so far as possible particularised statements of the risk represented by the offender.

Notes

1. Whether *impulsively* or not. It is often wrongly supposed that impulsive behaviour is in some sense unintentional; but that would be true only in cases of automatism.

2. Less than 7% of our patients are or have been psychotic, according to the accepted use of the term. These patients are either chronically schizophrenic or have a history of flamboyant manifestations of such a mental disorder. The incidence of dangerous behaviour among the vast numbers of persons who fall into the wide category of schizophrenic mental disease is slight, but the presence of severe psychosis *in a dangerous person* immeasurably compounds the risk that he will do terrible harm. Marked neurotic manifestations, including anxiety states and obsessive compulsive states, occur in 15% to 20% of our patients. Depressions of varying severity occur in about 24% of our patients but manic-depressive psychosis appears to play a part in no more than 2% or 3%. None of these conditions is mutually exclusive. (Kozol 1972: 303)

3. Now published in Thornberry and Jacoby (1979).

CHAPTER 3

Fundamental Objections*

It was put to us by Professor Nigel Walker that the central question is a practical one: as a matter of penal policy, should there be *any special* form of custodial sentence designed to give others greater protection against certain offenders than they would enjoy if these offenders were sentenced in the ordinary way (i.e., in most cases according to the 'tariff')? There is a trend to shorten sentences for less serious offences: already more than eight in ten sentences involve actual detention for twelve months or less, and radical proposals for consolidating this trend have been advanced by the Advisory Council on the Penal System (1978) and are under discussion. The shorter sentences become, the more difficult it would seem to be to argue that there should not be a special protective sentence for a minority of exceptional offenders likely to cause grave harm in the future. When compared with other aims, such as deterrence and rehabilitation, the protection of the public is the aim — perhaps the only one — which custodial sentences can be guaranteed to achieve; at least, during their currency. The main doubt centres round the problems of distinguishing between 'serious' and other harm and discriminating with any real degree of confidence between offenders against whom protection is needed at such a high cost in resources and hardship and those against whom it is not.

Increasingly, however, doubt is focused not only on the practical problems of defining the limits of protective sentencing and accurately identifying 'dangerous' offenders but on the propriety of the practice itself of protective sentencing. In the name of public protection psychiatrists, sentencers and parole authorities are detaining people against their will for longer periods than they can justify on other grounds alone. This practice is the subject of impassioned controversy. Fundamental objections are raised, in particular when the persons

*The Committee is heavily indebted to Professor Nigel Walker and Mr Ian White for their contributions to the discussion of the issues raised in this chapter and in Chapters 6 and 7 below. Many of the arguments advanced in these chapters are drawn from their writings, including papers prepared specially for the Committee.

concerned are of sound mind and full age to take responsibility for the consequences of their actions. The critics, for example Von Hirsch (1972), argue on the following lines.

It is a basic rule of criminal justice in a free society that a sane adult may not be deprived of his liberty except as a punishment for a crime of which he has been convicted. Protection of the public is a function of the criminal justice system, but the technique at its disposal is punishment justly related to past conduct. Predictive judgments of future conduct are out of place in criminal justice. They are, as a matter of fact, highly inaccurate: but even if they could be made as accurate as judgments of past conduct are required to be, they would not be acceptable; for preventive confinement pre-empts a man's future course of action. No one, not even the offender himself, can be certain that he will or will not reoffend. The meaning of 'beyond reasonable doubt' is not the same when applied to a future as to a past offence. Even if he declares a firm intention, one way or the other, he may change his mind or circumstances may intervene to frustrate him. To close the door on these possibilities is to infringe his right to self-determination and risk the injustice of punishing him in advance for an offence which he may not commit. Moreover, to invoke the excuse that, as a convicted offender, he has forfeited his right to be presumed harmless, is to introduce an invidious distinction between offenders and the rest of us which is alien to the spirit of our criminal justice system. Imprisonment entails a temporary diminution of a man's rights but it should not be translated into second-class citizenship; once he has served the customary sentence for his offence he must be restored to legal innocence and may not be further detained.

Professor Walker (1978) demurs; first, at the suggestion that protective measures amount to punishment for uncommitted crimes and second, at the narrowly retributive view of punishment which underlies this line of argument. He asks why the law enforcement system should be subject to a restrictive principle which we do not apply outside that system; and why the aim of protecting others should not shape sentences.

Why may the law enforcement system not take account of the harm which people *might* do? Do we not disqualify epileptics from driving and place in quarantine people who are known or suspected of carrying diseases with a high mortality rate, such as smallpox, typhoid or lassa fever? How does this differ ethically from detaining dangerous offenders for the protection of the public? Carriers of disease are dangerous to others and we do not hesitate to place restrictions on their freedom of action.

The almost universally accepted practice of quarantine seems to prove that isolating a person for the protection of others is not regarded as in itself unjust. We cannot think that public health is more important than public safety. What then distinguishes the protective sentencing of dangerous offenders from quarantine for disease carriers and makes it ethically dubious?

Lessons from Quarantine

The analogy with quarantine is persuasive; but it seems to carry the obnoxious implication that 'dangerousness' is a disease-like condition. It is, of course, nothing of the kind; as critics are quick to point out, even if it were, to advocate special sentences for dangerous offenders would be to advocate punishing them for what they *are* rather than for what they have done; and that would be, if anything, a shade worse than punishing them for what they *may* do. They argue that whereas disease-carriers, like criminally insane persons, suffer involuntarily from a condition which makes it impossible for them to lead a normal life without placing others at risk of serious harm, this is not the case of the legally sane offender, who must be presumed capable of leading a blameless life if he so chooses. Once he has served the sentence appropriate to his offence, he reverts to the state of legal innocence and must be given the same right as the rest of us to determine his own fate. To deny him this right by detaining him longer is to make of him a second-class citizen and to place ourselves on a slippery slope that, in the absence of any barrier of principle to the extension of tests of dangerousness to citizens at large, will land us in 'universal preventive confinement' (Von Hirsch 1972).

The proposition that fundamental objections to special sentences for dangerous offenders cannot be sustained by anyone who is not prepared also to reject the practice of quarantine is defended in a cogent paper by F.D. Schoeman (1979). For the purpose of argument he postulates a hypothetical practice of 'civil preventive detention' (the incapacitation of persons thought to be dangerous, whether legally innocent or not – perhaps less aptly termed 'universal preventive confinement') and concludes that 'no more serious problems arise in defending civil preventive detention, suitably qualified, than arise from defending the practice of quarantine as a measure for promoting public health'.

It is a mistake, Schoeman argues, to allow that quarantine is justified because the disease-carrier's condition is outside his control. It is true that he cannot in any way help being a carrier of disease, but it is not true that the harm that may result from his condition is outside his control. He could, after all, declare his intention to observe all the restrictions necessary to protect others from contagion: in effect, he could undertake to place himself in quarantine. However, we have good practical reasons for discounting people's sincere assertions about their intentions. Our reasons for refusing to place our faith in the good intentions of the disease-carrier may be different from and less invidious than those that make us mistrust some serious offenders; but for practical purposes this difference is irrelevant. On the assumption that, for whatever reason, neither can be trusted not to harm others in the future we detain the one in the interests of public health and the other in the interests of public safety.

According to Schoeman, two equally false arguments are in play: that dangerous offenders cannot control their dangerousness any more than disease-carriers can (because 'dangerousness' is a disease-like condition); and that the dangerousness of disease-carriers is outside their control. In fact, as he points out, the role of the law in both cases is to take control of his future conduct out of the hands of the individual 'for the protection of others'. We accept quarantine; why not, then, civil preventive detention? It infringes the principle of self-determination only to the extent that quarantine does.

This is persuasive: it looks as though the question is not whether but where to draw the line between acceptable and unacceptable preventive practices and that this is a matter of degree rather than of principle. On this view of the matter quarantine and protective sentencing are essentially similar practices: quarantine is acceptable because the sacrifice imposed on those subjected to it is strictly limited (40 days) whilst the risk of serious harm they present is accurately known and very high; in marked contrast in both respects, however, protective sentencing is unacceptable. But a vital distinction has been disregarded. Anyone who accepts the practice of quarantine must acknowledge that it may be permissible, in some circumstances, to detain legally sane and innocent persons for the protection of others from *unintentional* harm; but he is in no way committed to the proposition if it is *wilful* harm that is envisaged. Quarantine as a precaution against unintentional harm is one thing; preventive detention as a precaution against *wrong-doing* is another matter altogether.

In his *Sentencing in a Rational Society* (1972, Chapter 10) Professor Walker questions the rationality of this distinction, which as he notes, is deep-rooted in English sentencing practice, between intentional conduct which leads or is likely to lead to serious harm and conduct which is either unintentional or unlikely to lead to serious harm. 'Why should we not use long sentences to prevent serious harm which is the result of recklessness, negligence, incompetence or even accident-proneness?' In practice, he points out, it is fortunately usually possible to argue that the man who does not intend what harm he does can be prevented from doing it again by a less drastic expedient than incarceration. 'Typhoid-carriers can be prohibited from serving the public with food. Negligent surgeons sooner or later cease to be shielded by their profession, and have to practice some less hazardous form of medicine. Accident-prone drivers can be disqualified. . . .' In principle, however, the question stands and cannot be answered satisfactorily without invoking the notion of culpability which, as Professor Walker says, has no place in a non-retributive penal philosophy. This philosophy presents great difficulties, however. It harbours the idea that it might be rational, in the interests of social defence, to set about assessing the dangerousness of people in general and universalise protective measures. Of course, we do not do this; but something like it is proposed from time to time when some new piece of scientific or medical knowledge seems to make it practicable (Rennie 1978) and the slogan 'the dangerousness of "dangerousness" ' (Tomasic 1977) takes on substance.

We do not set about assessing the dangerousness of people in general: but it is important to know why not. Why pick on offenders? Why not take preventive measures against anyone and everyone likely to cause grave harm?

Our notion of the danger represented by people, as distinct from things or the elements, is firmly linked in criminal justice with the notion of an offence: that is, with an intentional past act which caused harm. The harm may include having placed others at risk; which is to say, the conduct in question may be judged to have been dangerous and the offender liable to punishment accordingly. In any event, punishment looks backward — to an offence; people are punished for what they have done if they can justly be held responsible for it. Infants and insane persons (however these social categories are for the time being defined) are not held responsible and are, therefore, not capable of wrongdoing though, of course, they may cause harm, in which case they are controlled — not judged and punished. For the rest, people are subject to the criminal justice system and liable to be punished for the harm their offences have caused, including the harm of endangering others. Nothing in all this refers to dangerous people, only to dangerous conduct. Infants and insane persons may be dangerous in themselves; but legally responsible people are punished for what they have done and not for what they may do or for what they are.

Nevertheless, selected offenders who are neither infants nor insane are deemed to be dangerous and for the protection of the public are imprisoned for longer than would be justifiable on other grounds alone. A strictly retributive penal philosophy cannot cover their cases; a non-retributive, utilitarian theory of social defence may do so, but it does not explain why, in principle, we should not look for dangerous people in general but only for dangerous offenders. The utilitarian case for restricting protective measures to offenders is an empirical not a moral case: it is that in offending they have given ground for apprehension that they will reoffend; it rests on the weak probability that having offended already they are more likely than the next man to harm in the future. But protective sentencing requires a moral and not merely an empirical justification.

If my right to be presumed harmless were to depend on the probability of my doing harm, then my being an offender who has already caused harm would be good *prima facie* evidence for such a probability. But one empirical ground for doubting my harmlessness is in principle as good as another. For a utilitarian the presumption of harmlessness is a mere presumption and no right at all. But this raises serious difficulties. Once it were granted that offenders might be deprived of their liberty by virtue of their dangerousness alone, then to confine the use of preventive measures to them would be an arbitrary restriction and the way would be opened up in principle to the extension of these measures to anyone and everyone according to the probability that they would cause harm (Von Hirsch 1972). The notion of culpability seems to be indispensable. In its absence it is indeed true, as Professor Schoeman argues, that 'no more serious problems arise in defending civil preventive detention, suitably qualified, than arise from defending the practice of quarantine as a measure for promoting public health'.

A disease-carrier who jumps quarantine and is determined to go on doing so is in the strict sense a dangerous offender: but quarantine regulations are not drawn up with him in mind, any more than the Road Traffic Act is intended to prevent people from committing homicide by motorcar. In the absence of quarantine regulations, disease-carriers going about their business would place others at risk of harm in much the same way as motorists do, which is to say unintentionally albeit sometimes carelessly or even recklessly. Quarantine imposes drastic restrictions on certain people's freedom of movement and in this respect can be said not to differ from imprisonment. No doubt there are those who object to it on just that account, that it represents an unjustified general deprivation of liberty. But it is not directed towards preventing people from doing wilful harm. Putting people in quarantine prevents them from harming others unintentionally or recklessly; but it is only an incidental consequence of their being detained that they are prevented from inflicting intentional harm. It would be only slightly more bizarre to think of quarantine as removing an individual's choice, whether or not to use his condition to inflict harm by spreading disease, than to object to the proposal to introduce indefinite disqualification for drunken drivers on the grounds that it would remove their freedom of choice whether or not to commit homicide by motorcar. Such measures are not like special sentences for dangerous offenders in being directed at protecting the public from wilful harm; they are meant to prevent people from harming each other unwittingly, carelessly or recklessly; and this makes all the difference when it comes to justifying them.

'Civil preventive detention' as a precaution against wrong-doing would be inimical to a free society in a way that quarantine as a precaution against unintentional harm is not. This is more than a matter of where the line is drawn in interfering with people's freedom of action. The crucial objection to forestalling serious offences by setting about assessing the dangerousness of people in general and confining everyone found to be dangerous is not, as Von Hirsch and others argue, that it would take the fate of responsible individuals out of their own hands – though it would certainly do that, in greater or less degree according to where the lines were drawn. The crucial objection is that such measures would entail abrogating the right to be presumed harmless which, like the right to be presumed innocent, is fundamental to a free society. In such a society people do not simply expect or hope to be treated as harmless; they have a right to be so treated, even if it is more probable than not that they do intend harm; just as they have a right to be treated as innocent even if it is more probable than not that they are guilty. These are not absolute rights: legally sane and innocent persons may be detained or otherwise prevented from doing harm they are suspected of intending to do; but infringements (e.g. police powers of arrest) are hedged about with restrictions and safeguards and in the end only wrongful actions can lead to just forfeiture of these rights, as is generally well understood in respect of the presumption of innocence.

Both parties to the argument have right on their side: those who resist the suggestion that legally sane and innocent persons may never be detained for the protection of others and point to the acceptable practice of quarantine; and those who insist that a general practice of 'civil preventive detention' would be objectionable in principle. But the objectors to civil preventive detention cannot invoke the right to self-determination in support of their position, for this exposes them to the charge of inconsistency if they fail also to reject the practice of quarantine. Not the right to self-determination but the right to be presumed free of harmful intentions would be abrogated under a system of civil preventive detention. The practice of quarantine on the other hand is acceptable in so far as it leaves this right inviolate: it is not supposed that disease-carriers in general – any more than motorists in general – intend harm but merely that they may do harm if they are not controlled. Governments may make justifiable inroads on people's freedom of action with measures of all kinds, including custody, when it is a question of preventing unintentional harm. They do not have the same scope in relation to the risk of wilful harm.

Admittedly, in this country, prohibitions are placed on the sale of offensive weapons and poisons, as though we were all potential murderers; but we accept such restrictions as underwriting rather than undermining our freedom, just as we accept in the same spirit the time-consuming and inconvenient security measures at airports. Other measures do not commend themselves as being so plainly in our individual and collective interest: for example, the requirement to leave our bags outside the counter areas of supermarkets and libraries. Such measures are irritating reminders of the decline of moral standards among the users of these institutions; but we do not resist them in so far as the suspicion cast on us is random and impersonal. It is a different matter when the suspicion is selective and personal, as for example when the police use their powers under the notorious 'sus' laws which allow a person to be arrested and charged with being a suspected person or reported thief loitering in a street or other public place with intent to commit an arrestable offence. In short, the argument is about singling out legally sane and unconvicted persons as *intending* harm and this is not entailed in the practice of quarantine, though it would be entailed in a practice of civil preventive detention and is entailed in the practice of protective sentencing.

Preventing Wilful Harm

There is, needless to say, no close analogy between the right of individuals to use protective force against an imminent threat of violent attack (whether private individuals defending their persons or their property or a policeman shooting to protect a hostage) and institutional measures for the protection of the public against a risk of future harm. Nevertheless, the individual right to self-defence has an important bearing on the justification for protective sentencing. Unlike the practice of quarantine, it does commit anyone who accepts it to acknowledging that it may be permissible, in certain circumstances, to detain or otherwise gravely harm a legally sane and unconvicted person in anticipation of the wilful harm he may otherwise do. Moreover, it establishes the very important further point that prevention and punishment may not be divorced any more than they may be confused; and this places a barrier of principle, said by critics to be missing, in the way of a slide from protective sentencing of offenders to 'universal preventive confinement', as well as carrying important implications for the form of protective sentences.

When someone exercises his right to self-defence, it is plainly a case of prevention not punishment: yet the concepts of guilt and desert are as essential to it as they are to punishment. The individual right to self-defence is acknowledged in all jurisdictions, though its extent may vary. Justifications for the use of protective force differ, but all depart from the fundamental premise that the aggressor is in the wrong; the defender is defending himself against unlawful or wrongful force. Differences of approach (for example, between Anglo-American and European jurisdictions) reveal themselves in the problem cases where the aggression, though unlawful, is excused (e.g. the aggressor is insane, or will be the innocent cause of harm to another). But these need not concern us here.[1] It is an essential part of the justification for using protective force in self-defence that the aggression, whether or not excused, is unlawful. That the aggressor uses or threatens to use unlawful force both gives me the right to act against him at all and permits me to do him more harm, if necessary for the sake of preventing him, than he would inflict by his aggression; there need be no balancing of alternative harmful consequences for he is in the wrong. In Anglo-American law, however, it is not simply a matter of doing whatever is immediately necessary to prevent the wilful harm; I must have regard to his intentions and the seriousness of the harm he threatens to inflict. The more evidently he is culpable and the graver the harm threatened, the stronger the justification for the use of protective force. The principle of proportionality applies; there are rules for the use of deadly and non-deadly force and necessary force is differently interpreted according to whether it is person or property that is to be defended. For example, I may not shoot an unarmed man to prevent him from stealing my car by driving off in it.

In short, there is no evading the issues of guilt and desert in connection with the prevention of wilful harm, whether by individuals in self-defence or, by extension, by the state in defence of the public. If guilt and desert are at the heart of the justification for individual self-defence, they must be equally central to the justification of institutional measures to prevent wilful harm; from which we infer that what justifies the imposition of preventive measures, if they can be justified, is not simply a prediction of likely outcomes but that the way they come about is such as to put the potential offender in the wrong. In other words, preventive measures against a risk of wilful harm are justifiable only against someone already justly liable to punishment for harmful conduct of the kind to be prevented; and the measures must be proportional to the harm anticipated.

'Universal Preventive Confinement'

This being so, the objection is misconceived that once preventive measures are permitted against dangerous offenders the way is opened in principle to the extension of such measures to non-offenders ('universal preventive confinement' or 'civil preventive detention'). Dangerous offenders are not detained by virtue of their dangerousness alone. It is not simply an arbitrary restriction to confine the use of preventive measures on grounds of dangerousness to offenders as a class. A man must justly forfeit his right to be presumed innocent before his right to be presumed harmless can be brought into question. The right to punish for past wrong-doing is a pre-condition of the right to prevent future wrong-doing.

Injustices of Protective Sentencing

However, this threshold requirement of justice in protective sentencing does not dispose of objections to the justice of such sentences which depend on comparisons with the principles of justice in normal criminal procedure. It is said that preventive measures amount to punishment for crimes uncommitted; that since predictive judgments are inherently uncertain the requirement of proof beyond reasonable doubt that preventive measures are necessary cannot be met; and that innocent persons are unjustly deprived of their liberty. These objections are not sound when closely examined.

To detain a convicted offender longer than is just on other grounds, because of the risk of reoffending, is said to be like detaining for the duration of that extra period someone who has as yet committed no offence at all. Dangerous offenders in custody are legally innocent like the rest of us, once they have received their just deserts and served a sentence appropriate to the offence of which they have been convicted (Von Hirsch 1972).

On the face of it, this argument is not persuasive. It requires us to take a contrived view of the position of offenders whose sentences, for whatever reason, exceed the 'tariff' or even the maximum length for the offence of which they have been convicted. It is not reasonable to equate any injustice they may suffer with the injustice that would be suffered if someone innocent of any offence were imprisoned for the same length of time. Moreover, it is worth noting that some of those who insist on this objection do not see the same difficulty in giving longer sentences to recidivist offenders (Sleffel 1977; Von Hirsch 1976). They endorse the proposal that the severity of sentences should increase with each successive conviction for a serious offence, so that a man would be punished more severely for an offence if he had a prior record. But how is a recidivist, who is in custody for longer than is just on other grounds because of his previous convictions, differently placed from a dangerous offender serving a longer sentence because of the risk of his reoffending?

More important, to speak of punishing for crimes uncommitted merely confuses the issue with rhetoric. It does not make sense to describe a sentence as punishment for the very actions that it will prevent; for in that case we would be punishing someone not for what he may do but for what, since he is prevented, he is not going to do. Prevention cannot be construed as punishing. Needless to say, this does not make it more acceptable; it still needs to be justified; but not as punishment, even though, as we have seen, it cannot be justified on other grounds except in so far as a man is justly liable to punishment for what he has already done.

Predictive judgments are inherently uncertain in a way that judgments of past offences are not. Requiring, by analogy with a trial on a criminal charge, that it should be proven beyond reasonable doubt that preventive measures are necessary implicitly judges an unnecessary application of preventive measures as incomparably worse than a mistaken release leading to a further offence. This is intuitively unacceptable; not only could the conditions hardly be met very often in practice, but preventive measures seem to be justifiable even when it is not. The trouble is with the underlying assumption, which is at fault: viz., that the mistakes that are inherent in predictive judgments relate to determinable, misjudged individuals.

Predictive judgments are inherently uncertain and mistakes are unavoidable. We may suspect that a certain person may commit a harmful offence in the future unless he is subjected to special preventive measures. We are not in a position to predict his behaviour with certainty so it is possible that, if we were not to apply these measures, he would indeed cause harm; but it is also possible that he would not, in which case if we did apply these measures we should do so unnecessarily. Whatever we do, it is likely that in a number of similar cases one or other of these risks will eventually be realised. It is disturbing enough to know, as we do, that some criminal verdicts turn out to be mistaken; despite our best efforts some innocent persons do indeed get unjustly convicted. How can we justify going into the business of protective sentencing on the basis of predictive judgments, in the certain knowledge that if we left at large all those judged to be dangerous a substantial number would not do further serious harm? How many *innocent persons,* it is often asked by those advancing these arguments, are we prepared to sacrifice for the additional protection offered by special sentences for dangerous offenders? Is not such a calculation to be rejected as indecent? Does it not amount to putting a price on the heads of innocent persons?

This argument is misconceived. Errors of prediction do not represent determinable individuals. It is not that we have difficulty in identifying the subjects of predictive error with the methods available to us; it is that they are in principle indeterminable. There are no hidden individuals identifiable in principle, but not in practice, who certainly would or would not reoffend. In this sense there are no innocent or guilty subjects of predictive judgments. Of course, the character of an offender can be misjudged. If we are dealing with a legally sane person and we attribute to him a disposition or propensity to intentional harm which he does not have, it makes sense to speak of his innocence — he is innocent of the motives or intentions which would make him dangerous. But the fact that if we were to set them at liberty, only half of those we are at any time detaining as dangerous would do further serious harm, does not mean that the other half are all in this sense innocent. For a degree of predictive error is inevitable, independently of misjudgments of the characters of individual offenders.

This line of argument from the analogy of a trial on a criminal charge misrepresents the moral choice that has to be made in considering whether protective measures may be justly imposed. The question is not 'how many innocent persons are to sacrifice their liberty for the extra protection that special sentences for dangerous offenders will provide?' but 'what is the moral choice between the alternative risks: the risk of harm to potential victims or the risk of unnecessarily detaining offenders judged to be dangerous?'

The essential nature of the problem of preventing wilful harm is misrepresented by talk of balancing individual and social interests or minimising social costs. The problem is to make a just redistribution of risk in circumstances that do not permit of its being reduced. There is a risk of harm to innocent persons at the hands of an offender who is judged likely to inflict it intentionally or recklessly — in any case culpably — in defiance or disregard of the usual constraints. His being in the wrong by virtue of the risk he represents is what entitles us to consider imposing on him the risk of unnecessary measures to save the risk of harm to innocent victims. Considerations of fault determine the allocation of risk if we cannot reduce the risk to be allocated. To that extent the choice under discussion is clear; but the problem of a just redistribution is not disposed of and we consider it in Chapter 4.

Notes

1. These cases depend on whether the claim of right to use protective force itself takes the form of an excuse or a justification (Fletcher 1978). In Anglo-American law the claim functions as an excuse, so that when the aggression is excused, the principle of lesser evil is invoked to justify the use of protective force (unless, as in the Model Penal Code, unlawful force is so defined as to include unlawful but excused aggression); and the rule of proportionality applies (Williams 1978). But in German and Soviet law, for example, the claim functions as a justification and the principle of necessity in defence of individual autonomy is invoked to justify the individual taking whatever measures are necessary to defend his person or his property against unlawful attack, whether excused or not. The rule of proportionality applies weakly, or not at all.

CHAPTER 4

The Limits of Protection

In this chapter we aim to clarify a number of issues of what may be called the practical ethics of protective sentencing. If the aim of the sentence is to protect the public against a substantial risk of grave harm, how are we to define 'grave' harm in this context and what is a 'substantial' risk? Who are 'the public' and how much protection are its members entitled to? Who should be eligible for a protective sentence? What form ought such sentences to take — must they be wholly indeterminate? What would be the elements of a fair procedure for reviewing protective sentences?

Defining 'Grave Harm.'

Dangers are 'unacceptable' risks of harm and what people are willing to tolerate is subject to all kinds of conditions and varies within wide limits. What they actually have to put up with is decided by government and the agencies of law enforcement and is in this sense a political matter. But the question whether certain ills are intolerable and should be prevented, even if necessary by measures which carry the risk that some legally sane and innocent persons will be unnecessarily deprived of their liberty, is essentially a moral one. The answer is in some sense a matter of opinion, though not in the sense that we speak of something being 'merely' a matter of opinion, nor even in the sense that it is a matter of public opinion to be democratically determined by poll or plebiscite. We want to know whether there are any limits in principle to the kinds of harm of sufficient degree against which the public may claim protection, if necessary by measures of this kind.

There are radical differences of opinion on the significance of different kinds of harm. Few people, nowadays, doubt the reality of psychological harm; but many resist the suggestion that it is as significant as physical harm. Sexual offences are almost universally given special significance, but offences against property are the subject of dispute; many people have a rooted objection to the idea that loss of or damage to property is the kind of harm that might justify preventive considerations in sentencing. Moreover, though all penal codes rely on the distinction between 'serious' and other harm, the concept of 'seriousness' is necessarily ambiguous in this connection, for it has a moral as well as a factual dimension, referring as it does to the wrongfulness of acts as well as to the injuriousness of their consequences. This seems to produce confusion when the problem is to formulate principles of protection rather than of punishment.

In *Sentencing in a Rational Society* (1972), Professor Walker recommended cutting out the ambiguity by abandoning the concept. For practical purposes in everyday life, as he pointed out, when we are forced to decide whether to take costly or troublesome precautions against some harm and 'we are not distracted by the emotions and superstitions which surround crime and punishment', we are much guided by the answer to a practical question: how difficult would it be to undo the harm if it happened? The more difficult to undo, the more seriously we regard it and the lower the acceptable risk of its recurring. Let us then by-pass all the differences of opinion that clog the issue of protective sentencing. We are agreed that the cost in resources and human suffering of imprisonment for any purpose is high; we are increasingly reluctant to use for the purpose of punishing people for the harms they have actually done; we must be even more reluctant to use it to prevent them from causing harm in the future. Instead of arguing over the artificial concept of 'seriousness' or 'gravity', let us agree that 'when the [preventive] measures involve serious and lasting hardship for the persons to whom we apply them . . . they should be used only to prevent serious and lasting hardship to other individuals of a kind which once caused cannot be remedied'.

Professor Walker was well aware that this persuasive idea is not free of difficulties. He mentioned the difficulty of classifying some harms, especially psychological harms, as irremediable; but he was at this point thinking mainly of difficulties of a practical kind which it is reasonable to expect will diminish with advances in medicine, and especially psychological medicine. However, as we agreed when we came to discuss the matter, the attempt to restate the concept of grave harm in terms of remediability solves only part of the problem of discovering a rational basis for assessing the legitimacy of claims to protection from risks of harm by means of protective sentencing. Some kinds of harm cannot be remedied by restitution or compensation; so that even when one has decided what can be remedied and what cannot, one still wants to know: Is what cannot be remedied grave enough to make it unacceptable? Theft is a seemingly clear case, for stolen objects can be restored to their owners or replaced by the insurance company. But the victims of the house-breaker or pick-pocket object at least as much to a sense of personal violation as to the loss of their belongings. That they are able to recover or replace them does not reconcile them to the offence or make them indifferent to a risk of its repetition. In other cases, for example, rape, disfigurement or kidnapping, it is more obvious that compensation could not make good the ill suffered, even though it were fair and adequate in the sense that it would be inappropriate to set it at a higher figure. We are familiar with the idea that the given compensation may do as much as compensation can do, and more compensation would do more than compensation ought to do. In any case, compensation does not touch the wrongfulness of the act which causes the ill. Offences such as theft, rape and kidnapping inflict personal injury — pain and suffering, shock and fear, injury to health, inconvenience — but their essential character is that they are violations of right and that they are prejudicial to the community. A society in which they were endemic but always duly compensated would not be preferable to one in which they were contained but never compensated. If prohibitions with sanctions are insufficient there is a *prima facie* case for prevention.

All this, of course, does not do away with Professor Walker's point that there are reasonably objective measures of physical and mental harm. If harm is construed as impairment of normal physical and mental functioning, the best way of assessing its seriousness is to use these measures to answer questions such as how extensive is the damage, can it be put right, how long will it take? But there do seem to be deeds, for example, rape or kidnapping, the peculiar wrongfulness of which cannot be accounted for in these terms and this suggests that the problem of drawing the distinction between 'serious' and other harm cannot be wholly objectified.

The distinction between physical and mental harm, which is usually taken for granted, is not free of difficulty. Physical and psychological injuries are sometimes clearly distinguishable so that the one may be identified as the cause of the other (e.g. a blow on the head as a cause of loss of memory); but the distinction is not always as easy to make: for example, loss of speech is difficult to classify in this way — or indeed pain itself; and the problem is acute in a class of instances which is being enlarged with the development of psychological medicine; for example, mental breakdown brought about by matrimonial cruelty.

Aside from difficulties of classification, some psychological injuries are notoriously elusive and intangible: an insensitive public is inclined to set them aside or, at least, to discount their significance in comparison with physical harm. The Butler Committee on Mental Abnormal Offenders remarked: 'physical violence is, we think, what the public is most worried about but the psychological damage caused by other crimes is not to be underrated'.

The fact is, however, that morally speaking the distinction is immaterial. Damage or destruction of functions, whether of body or mind, are personal harms. It is doubtful whether even the powers of walking and writing or the faculties of seeing and hearing can usefully be distinguished as physical — at least, it will be the non-physical aspects of them that make them morally significant; and the same is true of disfigurement. Bodily harm of lesser degree, which does not amount to loss or invasion of personality, can have the same moral significance if, for example, it damages an individual's health or his capacity to follow his normal occupation. The wrongfulness of such harm is not measured by the extent of the injury in physical terms but by its effect on the person.

Rape and kidnapping are harms which consist wholly in the lack of consent, the violation of right. Their peculiar wrongfulness cannot be explained or measured in terms of pain or hardship, though of course they may entail both. They are harmful only against the background of a certain value and respect for the person. The wrongfulness of rape does not depend on its causing mental distress — on the painful consciousness and unhappy remembrance of the victim; nor upon its resulting in lasting psychological damage — though these harmful effects would bear on the seriousness of the particular offence. The fact that, nowadays, the trauma can sometimes be relieved by psychiatric treatment and the hardship represented by an unwanted child removed by an efficient abortion does not mean that rape is less wrongful than it was: though its consequences in terms of pain and hardship may be on average less serious than in the past, the case for protecting people against it is in no way weakened.

Harms to the person are *sui generis.* Our attitude to them, in principle, is not affected by the possibility that injuries may be successfully treated or that those who suffer them may receive compensation — even fair and adequate compensation; for there is no sense in which the remedy can remove or the good of the compensation can equal the mischief or the harm done to the victim.

The distinction between offences against the person and offences against property is also not clear-cut. When Professor Walker suggested that preventive measures should be used only against offenders likely to cause irremediable harm to others, he drew the inference that 'since most loss of or damage to property can be remedied by compensation, this rule excludes all or nearly all property offences'. He did not, of course, mean to exclude offences against property which carry significant risks of harm to persons, for example, aggravated burglary or arson. But such risks are inherent in a great many lesser property offences which would be excluded by his proposed rule. The theft of items of no intrinsic value can have far-reaching physical consequences; for example, the theft of a battery from a railway warning device[1] or the theft of a railway signal wire.[2] Burglary and theft may occasion a great deal of personal injury to victims who seek to restrain the offender even though he is carrying no weapon. The psychology of ownership imparts a special significance to people's dwellings and other personal belongings which are commonly experienced as extensions of the personality; so that loss of, or damage to, goods and chattels is assimilated psychologically as an attack upon the person. Fraud, blackmail and obtaining by deception are property offences which may ruin victims with a mixture of indirect attacks on physical and mental well-being. Evidently, whilst there are the usual differences in the seriousness of particular instances, measured by the actual or intended hardship caused to victims, there is no clear line demarcating offences against the person and offences against property. It is difficult to argue that property offences always result in a distinctive and inherently less significant kind of harm or that they always cause harm of a lesser degree than offences against the person.

Yet some people are unwilling to acknowledge that it may ever be justifiable to impose a custodial sentence to prevent, as well as to punish, offences against property. They argue that society should require a level of tolerance from victims of property offences which puts such offences outside the category of those against which the public may be given special protection. As to the difficulty of drawing a clear distinction between offences against property and offences against the person in terms of the kind and degrees of harm they cause, they sometimes argue that the difficulty is not central to the institution of property in the modern world. The victims of the most serious offences against property today, measured in terms of the value in money of losses and damage sustained, are impersonal institutions, not individuals. In so far as private individuals are involved, they suffer financial loss — an injury that is compensable in principle. Offences against property of the kind that cause harm to individuals that is not compensable in principle represent lesser violations of the personality. Since we are agreed that protective sentences which carry the risk that offenders may lose their liberty unnecessarily should be used only to prevent serious harm, it would follow that property offences should never make an offender eligible for a protective sentence of imprisonment.

The force of this argument depends on the presumption that the harm caused by major offences against property will be confined to institutions or, in any case, will take the form of compensable financial loss. But it seems unnecessary to import an empirical assumption about the consequences of particular classes of offence into a classification of harms, and arbitrary to prescribe that protection against grave harm of a particular kind may not be provided when it is caused by offences of one kind rather than another.

In short, harms to the person are *sui generis* and enjoy special moral status. They range in degree from deprivation of life, through destruction and impairment of functions of body and mind; restrictions on personal freedom of longer or shorter duration, by coercion or threat, to lesser violations of personality, such as assault occasioning actual bodily harm or loss of, or damage to, personal property. We concluded that any of these harms are candidates for prevention in certain circumstances, except that when the preventive measures carry the risk that the persons to whom they are applied will be deprived unnecessarily of their liberty, they should be used to prevent those of lesser degree only when their gravity is enhanced because they expose victims to the risk of unusual hardship (pain and suffering, shock and fear, injury to health or beggary).

'Substantial' Risk

We are talking of two risks and the problem of making a moral choice between them: the risk that an offender may be unnecessarily deprived of his rights and his liberty; and the risk that innocent, unknown persons may suffer harm in the future. Obviously we should not contemplate the former unless the latter entails grave harm. But this requirement of justice is sometimes twisted in the public mind to mean that so long as the anticipated harm is serious enough, potential victims are entitled to be relieved of the risk even at the cost of hardship to others. This view of the matter invites the reproachful reminder (see Chapter 1) that when the hardship of preventive measures, including the risk that they may be unnecessary, would fall on members of the public themselves they find the risk of serious harm acceptable enough (for example, the risk of death and serious injury on the roads), and that it is manifestly inequitable to impose the real and immediate hardship of such measures on identifiable persons to obtain protection for persons unknown against risks of harm of no greater gravity than are readily tolerated in other circumstances.

However that may be, the justice of claims to protection from risk of harm cannot be compared simply in terms of its gravity. Even if the harm envisaged be grave, people are not entitled to be relieved of the risk at the cost of hardship to others, unless it can be justly shifted according to fault. If, however, it can be so shifted and if the harm is indeed grave, then they may have a just claim, even if the risk of their suffering it is low.

It is true that anyone's claim to protection is stronger or weaker in proportion to the risk he bears; and that the larger the population at risk from a particular offender, the smaller the risk to any particular potential victim. Nevertheless, it would be paradoxical to infer that the strength of the case for a protective sentence varies inversely with the size of the population at risk; for though the risk is diffused the cause of it is not and there would seem, *prima facie*, to be no justification in the circumstances for refusing to take preventive measures.

The claim is a communal or collective one and the risk to particular individuals need not be 'substantial'.

Yet collective claims are not unproblematic: they run to abstraction and they invite the fallacy of misplaced concreteness. Though the claims of groups to protection (neighbourhoods, cities, states, industrial and occupational groups, consumers, etc.) are no more than logical constructions out of the claims of the individual members severally, not all harms to the public can be easily construed as particularly affecting individuals or attributed to particular offenders.

Who exactly are the victims of espionage, tax fraud or the destruction of major works of art or other items of cultural importance? They are not only anonymous, like the victims of manufacturing fraud or environmental pollution, but because the harm they suffer — though unquestionable and not necessarily less serious in itself — is very indirect it is virtually impossible to establish and assess. We are driven to speak in more or less unpersuasive and easily abused abstractions: the harm is said to be to 'the state', 'the nation' or even 'the fabric of society'.

The problem is different when the communal claim cannot be laid at the door of a particular offender, for in this case protective sentences are out of place and not merely difficult to determine justly. Crimes not in themselves in the first rank of seriousness, if prevalent in a community, can place its members at exceptional risk of harm and may give rise to widespread and socially paralysing fear. The offenders are individually responsible for the harm suffered by their victims but (unless they happen to be persistent, notorious or organisers of marauding gangs) they are only marginally responsible for the cumulative consequences of their collective activities — for the damaging consequences for the life of the community of diffused and prolonged public alarm. Street robbers and burglars may be collectively responsible, though not necessarily to any significant extent individually so, for grave harm to the community. But only if an offender is himself at risk of causing grave harm in the future may protective considerations enter into the determination of his sentence. How 'substantial' need *that* risk be? The answer is frequently given in terms of a misleading comparison with the level of proof required for conviction on a criminal charge.

In a trial on a criminal charge we require the court to be convinced beyond reasonable doubt that the defendant has committed the offence in question; the verdict must 'leave nothing to chance' and even a slight doubt that he is indeed the offender drastically undermines the justification for punishing him. This requirement is misplaced in relation to predictive judgments, not because the requirements of justice need be less stringent, but because in the nature of the case they cannot be exactly the same. It is not open to us to 'leave nothing to chance' in predicting an offender's future behaviour. The aim must be to leave nothing — or, realistically, as little as possible — to any factor other than chance. Each offender's chances of reoffending are peculiar to himself; the outcome of the dynamic interaction of his character and circumstances. If *per impossibile* we perfectly understood the dynamics of human behaviour and were in possession of and could handle all the relevant facts about him and his circumstances, we could predict his behaviour with a probability of being right equal to 1 minus the probability of our being wrong on account of the workings of chance. But this would still not bring us close to certainty, for the element of chance must be very large.

The correctness of a predictive judgment cannot depend on our being justifiably certain that an offender will actually reoffend, as the correctness of a retrospective judgment depends on our justifiable certainty that he committed an offence in the past. It depends primarily on the soundness and reliability of an assessment of his disposition to inflict harm. Whether, if he is left at large, he will actually do harm is very much a matter of chance, and doubt on this point is less damaging to the justification for protective measures than is doubt whether he has committed a past offence to the justification for punishing him. Only the probability that he intends or has a wilful propensity to inflict harm need be anything like as high as the probability of the facts required for a conviction on a charge.

Individual assessments of propensity to inflict harm are a requirement of justice in protective sentencing and the quality of these assessments is the true test of a predictive judgment. However, the judgment contains a prediction — a statement of the probability that, taking into account his circumstances as well as his character, an offender will or will not cause harm if left at large. Needless to say, if there is little likelihood of his actually doing harm in the future, the case for preventive measures is weakened no matter how likely it is that we are right to believe the assessment of his character or intentions. To this extent the emphasis laid by critics on the validity of predictions that harm will actually result from leaving particular offenders at large is justified: it is the validity of the prediction of his future behaviour which determines the degree of risk that a protective sentence will deprive an offender unnecessarily of his liberty. However, the case for a protective sentence must rest on both probabilities taken together: that we are right to believe in the assessment of the offender's character; and that he will actually do serious harm if left at large. If a man who is not given a protective sentence turns out not to do harm it does not follow that to have imposed the sentence would have been unjust. To impose a risk of being unnecessarily detained is not in itself an injustice since preventive measures are not in themselves illegitimate and may be justified in certain circumstances.

There is a good deal of evidence, discussed in Chapter 2, to suggest that as matters now stand Parole Boards and similar bodies are, on average, at best as likely to be wrong as right in thinking that the offenders they decide to detain as *dangerous* would actually do further harm if left at large. Whatever may be the prospects for improvement, in the present state of the art of making predictive judgments it is likely that at least two persons are detained for every one person who is prevented from doing further serious harm: which is to say, each dangerous offender in protective custody probably suffers at least a 50% risk of being unnecessarily detained.

The fact is that most serious offenders do not repeat their serious offences and this presents a purely statistical difficulty. Supposing that as many as half of them will do so, no matter how carefully we make the individual assessments we are, on average, as likely to be wrong as right if we select some to be detained on the ground that they will cause further serious harm if left at large. If the fraction is smaller than one-half, we are more likely to be wrong than right and we would make fewest mistakes by treating all serious offenders as good risks. But if we could define a sub-group of whom more than half will commit a further serious offence, we would make fewest mistakes by treating the members of this sub-group as bad risks.

So long as such relatively high-risk sub-groups of serious offenders have not been identified we are in a dilemma: we must either treat all serious offenders as non-recidivists, suspecting, nevertheless, that there are among them high-risk individuals against whom it would be justifiable to take special measures; or we must decide that certain types of offence are so harmful that it is justifiable to act on the best predictive judgments possible in each case, knowing that the chances of being right are at best fifty-fifty at the moment and that we risk imposing special measures unnecessarily in the majority of cases, or failing to impose such measures on a minority for whom they would be necessary. Current practice in this country rests unavoidably on the second horn of this dilemma.

There is as yet no definable category of relatively high-risk serious offenders. Nevertheless there are individuals who have committed offences such that even a low risk of their repeating them is unacceptable. We concluded that substantial justice is done so long as the class of eligible offenders is severely restricted and each case is painstakingly adjudicated on its merits. Since there is no truth of the matter and an offender's dangerousness, so far as it can be ascertained, is a matter of degree and there is a large element of chance in the outcome, it is more important to hedge the making of predictive judgments with safeguards than to stipulate precisely what level of probability that an offender will actually reoffend must be established before such a sentence can be imposed.

Ethical Requirements

Investigations to determine an offender's dangerousness may not be imposed on him without regard to the nature of the offence of which he stands convicted. He does not lay himself open by the mere fact of offending to general assessments of his dangerousness: his criminal conduct must have manifested the grave harm which is to be prevented.

This is an important principle which is generally but not consistently observed by the courts when invoking protective considerations in sentencing (Chapter 5). It is not easy, without frustrating the purpose of protection, to make statutory provision for its strict application: we considered but rejected the device of restricting the protective sentence to particular offences or offence-categories (Chapter 8). We agreed with Professor Walker (1978) that the principle would be safeguarded if the scope of the protection to be provided by the sentence were defined in terms of categories of grave harm to which the courts were required to refer in determining the eligibility of an offender for a protective sentence: in judging the seriousness of the harm done, attempted, risked or intended at the time of the offence of which he stands convicted; and in determining whether he had committed on some separate occasion an act of a similar nature, which would constitute the *prima facie* case for supposing that his offence was not an isolated incident resulting from an unusual situation which is unlikely to recur but is part of a recurring pattern.

Professor Walker (1978) also offered an extension of the uncontroversial principle that if it can be reasonably argued that the circumstances which provided the offender with his incentive have ceased to exist (for example, through the death of his enemies) or that for some other reason (such as incapacity) he is unlikely to repeat his behaviour, this argument must operate in his favour. He proposed, and we agreed, that by the same reasoning it should also operate in his favour, notwithstanding the grave harmfulness of his most recent and past conduct, if he had never served a sentence of imprisonment for a serious offence. If he is to receive such a sentence for the first time in his life, it should not normally be a protective sentence: other things being equal, he should be given an opportunity to disprove the reasonable argument that the experience of imprisonment under an ordinary sentence will make him less likely to repeat his behaviour.

Protective sentences are an instrument of social policy; but they are not to be administered as such, any more than are sentences of any other kind. If a protective sentence is imposed it must be only because in the circumstances it is not unjust. The aim of the proceedings is not to prevent future harm but, given the availability of the special sentence and the conditions attaching to it, to deal justly with the offender.

As we have seen, a predictive judgment is not simply a forecast of what is likely to happen; it is a judgment, not a simple prediction, of an offender's future behaviour and it takes due account of his likely responsibility for the harm he may cause, as well as of the likelihood of his causing it. This point may be brought out by the example of two offenders equally likely to cause further harm: the same measure may not be equally just for both. One of them may have a standing intention to go out of his way to cause harm (e.g. as a professional robber or member of a terrorist organisation), while the other may be the sort of person who is liable to cause harm only if he falls into certain situations of strain, provocation or temptation. In the latter case, justice requires us to see whether the anticipated harm cannot be prevented by changing his likely circumstances, rather than by imprisoning him. Supposing, however, that it is not in our power to change his circumstances; then we shall be thrown back on depriving him of his liberty as the only means of prevention open to us. But even then we may still hesitate: if there is a case, given his circumstances, for regarding him as likely to be less than fully culpable (because the pressures on him seem more than we have a right to expect him to endure) we must consider whether we ought not, after all, to accept the risk of the harm he may do and reject a protective sentence in his case.

The mere fact of a future outcome is not what determines the justice or injustice of preventive measures. The objective in dealing with 'dangerous' offenders is to find the just course and not simply the practical way out of the difficulty they present.

Special sentences are meant to provide additional protection for members of the public by means of a just redistribution of certain risks of grave harm; they are not the means to a policy of indefinite incapacitation of dangerous offenders.

It follows that such sentences should not be wholly indeterminate. They should be imposed for a fixed term, with provision for review and release. These stipulations are the cause of some difficulty. The idea of fixed-term sentences, even when they are semi-determinate because they are reviewable, is widely felt to be incompatible with the idea of protection. If the process of ageing or the experience of prison have changed a dangerous offender's disposition whilst he has been serving his sentence, well and good; he may be released at once. But supposing he is not judged fit for early release and serves his time with no change of disposition; he must be released at the end of his sentence though, as the Butler Committee put it, he may be as dangerous as he ever was. The Committee remarked that this possibility constituted 'a serious defect in society's defences which ought, so far as possible, to be put right'. For mentally unstable offenders who are not committed to hospital but seem dangerous, they proposed an indeterminate but reviewable sentence, of which the essential feature is statutory insistence on regular review, at which the case for further detention rather than the case for release has to be made by the authorities.

Are determinate sentences really incompatible with the aim of protection? Is it so, that either we should continue to detain a man so long as his disposition remains unchanged — if necessary, for life — or should he never have been given a protective sentence at all? This objection is misconceived for it depends on forgetting that though preventive considerations are valid in themselves, they are not sufficient by themselves to justify the detention of a legally sane person. A protective sentence depends for its justification, as we have seen, as much on our having the right to continue to punish the offender as it does on our having good reasons to continue to detain him because he remains dangerous. Protective sentences are longer than would be justifiable on other grounds alone, but they are not exempt from the proportionality rule.

Another objection to determinate protective sentences is that to detain a man for a short additional period on preventive grounds is either inequitable or pointless or both. It is argued that if a special sentence is not very much longer than an ordinary sentence, the brief period of additional protection it provides is bought at too high a cost to the offender: but this is fallacious. The offender's sacrifice of his liberty and the protection afforded the public vary together; the relationship between them must be the same whether the difference between the protective and the ordinary sentence is two years or twenty years. The argument that it is pointless to provide some fraction rather than the whole of the protection needed to eliminate a risk to the public is not persuasive as it stands. There is no general obligation to impose protective sentences; each case must be decided on its merits and whether the amount of protection provided by a just sentence in a particular case is worthwhile is not a matter that can be decided in general terms.

Underlying these unsatisfactory reasons for rejecting the limited protection afforded by determinate sentences may be detected another, more complex, cluster of considerations which, in various ways, take into account the rate at which offenders commit their crimes. Suppose a man is likely to reoffend once in ten years, is it not pointless to impose a protective sentence which is no more than two or three years longer then the ordinary sentence for the offence, since two or three years fall so far short of the ten years after which the man may be expected to reoffend? The answer to this objection must depend on what is meant by saying that someone is 'likely to reoffend once in ten years'. He may indeed be a man whose disposition to commit, say, arson or rape lies dormant over long periods during which it would be pointless to detain him (Soothill and Pope 1973; Soothill et al. 1976): if he really is unlikely to reoffend during the next nine years but is expected to become dangerous again thereafter, he poses a problem which cannot be met by a period of protection shorter than ten years. But if 'he is likely to reoffend once in ten years' states a *rate* of re-offending for a class of offenders, it does not mean that such offenders repeat their offences periodically — i.e. at ten-yearly intervals; it means that the *average* interval between offences is ten years and possibly, also, that an interval between offences of about ten years is more likely than any other. It would be fallacious to draw from these rates and patterns of offending conclusions about the behaviour of a particular offender in a particular year — to conclude, for example, that he will not reoffend next year but only after an interval of nine years; or, by the same token, that a sentence affording only nine years of special protection would be pointless, since he would be bound to reoffend in the year immediately following his release. The rates at which classes of offenders repeat their offences are no guide to the particular value of protective sentences of shorter or longer duration. They are no guide, either, to the justice or injustice of preventive measures as such. They could, however, be used to provide a very rough indication, if this were wanted, of the amount of protection on average that special sentences would be likely to provide, on certain assumptions about their average length as compared with the average length of ordinary sentences for the same offences.

Review and Release

Any long sentence creates problems, among which is the decision when to release the offender from prison. This is not avoided by a system of determinate sentences unless the release date is rigidly calculated by reference to their length (as is remission for good conduct), and the longer the sentence the less acceptable this is. Yet any system of parole has to face the problem of the offender who is regarded as dangerous. If the length of the sentence is intended as a protection for others (rather than as a deterrent or retributive penalty), it follows that it should be regularly reviewed in order to consider whether the need to protect others still requires the prisoner to be detained in custody; and the review procedure must be fair and effective, providing adequate safeguards both for the rights of the offender and for the safety of others. The aim must be to secure that the offender is not released so long as there is good reason to believe that he is likely to do serious harm if he were at large, but that he is detained no longer than is necessary for that purpose.

In deciding what the elements of a fair and effective review procedure should be, the main questions that call for consideration are: how often shall reviews take place and shall their frequency be determined by statute? What should be the character of the review

THE LIMITS OF PROTECTION

procedure — judicial, administrative, or *sui generis*? Who shall carry out the review and who shall be responsible for taking the decision for or against release?

The arrangements for the review of the life sentence, which comes closest in English sentencing practice to being a protective sentence, are discretionary in character. There is no fixed time after which the case must be reviewed; the date upon which the case is first referred to the Local Review Committee in the prison in which the prisoner is detained is fixed by the Home Secretary in consultation with the Parole Board; the dates of any subsequent reviews are fixed by the Board itself.

If the frequency of reviews is left to the discretion of the executive or of some other reviewing body, there must always be some danger that the prisoner's case will be overlooked or will not be reviewed as early or as frequently as is desirable in his interests. The only safe course seems to be to confer on the prisoner a statutory right to a review of his case at stated intervals: a review at which the protection of others would be the only consideration and at which the onus would lie on those who thought the prisoner should be detained longer to show why this should be so.

Doubts have been expressed about this proposal; it is said that if the intervals between reviews are fairly short — and the prisoner's rights will be empty if they are not — the reviews may sometimes have little meaning in cases where it is evident that the prisoner will have to be detained for a very long time, and that the effect on the prisoner in such cases is likely to be disturbing and frustrating. This is undoubtedly a disadvantage of mandatory reviews at fairly short intervals; but account must also be taken of the abundant evidence of the adverse effects on prisoners of the uncertainty inherent in the present discretionary arrangements. However that may be, it is difficult to deny the paramount necessity of guaranteeing to every prisoner serving a protective sentence the unqualified right to regular and frequent review of the need for his continued detention. This is accorded to dangerous mentally abnormal offenders who are detained in secure hospitals with restrictions on discharge; the Home Secretary is obliged to refer the case of such offenders to a Tribunal for review within two months of being so requested after the end of the first year of detention and thereafter at various specified intervals. Admittedly, punitive considerations are entirely absent in these cases; the purpose of the review is to decide whether or not it is safe to lift the restrictions on discharge. But the possibility that to extend the right to review to legally sane offenders could lead to the early release of some heinous offenders, because they were regarded as being unlikely to do serious harm again, can be avoided by stipulating that the first review of a protective sentence may not take place before the end of a specified period in custody or that the recommended date of release on licence may not be earlier than it would have been had an ordinary sentence been imposed for the offence in question.

The crucial question, on which opinions differ widely, is whether the form of the review should be based on a judicial or an administrative model. Those who favour a judicial model take it as self-evident that any proceedings in which issues affecting the rights and liberties of individuals are determined ought to follow as closely as may be the well-tried principles and practices of judicial procedure, which are designed to ensure that the evidence and arguments are fairly presented and examined and that justice is done in the interests of both the individual and the community, or that a reasonable balance is struck between them. Thus the onus of proof is placed on those who wish to depart from a judicial model.

Those who favour some more informal and less rigorously objective procedure, based on an administrative model, point to the prime requirement that the procedure should be such as may be expected to produce the most reliable (or least unreliable) assessment of the prisoner's dangerousness. Given that the purpose of a review is to decide whether the time has come when the prisoner may be released without unacceptable risk to the public, it is of primary importance that reviews shall be carried out in a way which is most likely to yield a soundly based result. Since predictions of a prisoner's future behaviour must nearly always be hazardous and uncertain and, in the last analysis, largely intuitive, it seems that the right approach is to entrust the review to a tribunal which by its composition and experience is well-qualified to examine the widest available range of information about the prisoner and to place a proper value upon pieces of evidence of unequal value and reliability (for example, to give no more weight than they deserve to reports on the offender's conduct in prison). The free-saying discussion of such a many-sided body, approximating to the spirit and procedures of a case conference, would be most likely to reach a fair predictive judgment of an offender's behaviour.

It is probable, however, as is often pointed out, that a reviewing body of this kind will err on the side of caution whilst the characteristics of a judicial procedure must in general inure to the benefit of the prisoner. Personal appearance or legal representation will give him the opportunity to challenge unfair statements contained in prison or other reports. The application of rules of evidence will tend to exclude adverse allegations which are based on hearsay or second-hand information. An obligation for the Tribunal to give reasons for its decision will help the prisoner to challenge an unfavourable decision, either by appeal if that is provided, or by less formal methods. Although these opportunities will not always help the prisoner's case, the exclusion or rebuttal of unfavourable evidence must sometimes weaken the case for further detention and lead to earlier release. The hope is that this result would in most such cases not only give satisfaction to the prisoner but be objectively justified. However, there must be a risk that in some cases prisoners will be released prematurely and the public interest will be ill-served.

If protective sentences are admitted to a system of criminal justice, they must be administered with due regard for their avowed purpose, which is to relieve the public of an unacceptable risk of grave harm. If a court fails to convict a guilty person, no real harm is done in the sense that the harmful consequences may be diffused and largely intangible: encouragement of crime and a blow to the reputation of the law; but the same cannot be said of the mistaken release of a dangerous person. On the other hand, such sentences must also be administered with due regard for the rules of natural justice as they apply in the circumstances.

All reviewing bodies have the duty to act fairly, that is to say, in accordance with the rules of natural justice; but to speak of 'rules' conveys a spurious precision, for the concept of fair play is necessarily flexible and the scope and context of the 'rules' will vary according to the circumstances in which they are to be applied. Thus, it is arguable, and indeed has been so decided in the High Court,[3] that in circumstances in which parole is a privilege rather than a right, and in the context of practical procedures which ensure thorough consideration of all cases and embody the statutory safeguards of the prisoner's rights to make written and oral representations on his own behalf, the administrative practice of withholding from him an account of the specific reasons for refusing his application for parole is not in breach of the rules of natural justice. There can be little doubt, however, that when detention is dictated by protective rather than punitive considerations release, whether unconditional or on licence, is to be considered a right to be claimed in certain circumstances rather than a privilege to be earned and that in this case entirely discretionary arrangements for reviewing the sentences of dangerous offenders could not be held to meet the requirements of natural justice.

A fully judicial procedure implies, *inter alia*, personal appearance and legal representation of the prisoner, judicial standards of evidence, the giving of reasons for the decision of the Tribunal, the acceptance of its decisions as binding, and a right of appeal. Such a procedure would be inappropriate to the review of protective sentences, primarily for the reason already indicated, that it would risk doing less than justice to the case for continuing to detain the offender for the protection of the public. It is possible, however, to devise a range of procedures which, while departing in varying degrees from these comprehensive standards, would preserve enough of them to justify the description of 'quasi-judicial'. For example, the prisoner might be entitled to representation but not to be present himself, there might be some relaxation of the normal rules of evidence, the powers of the Tribunal might be only advisory and not issue in a binding decision or, if binding, not subject to appeal.

There would seem to be a strong case for granting a prisoner serving a protective sentence the direct right of access to an independent tribunal of a quasi-judicial kind, charged to review and report on his case to the Home Secretary. This need not entail any constraint on the Home Secretary's discretion to permit his release on licence, with or without further advice from a suitably constituted panel of advisers sitting privately as a case-conference to assess the prisoner's 'dangerousness' in the light of all the evidence, including the report of the quasi-judicial tribunal to which the prisoner himself had the right of access. The arrangements for reviewing the cases of dangerous offender-patients committed to secure hospitals with restrictions on their discharge offer a model which, with certain modifications, would meet the requirements for the review of the cases of prisoners serving protective sentences and we discuss these at length in Chapter 10.

Notes

1. *R.* v. *Holmes,* [1966] Crim. L. R. 457.
2. *R.* v. *Yardley,* [1968] Crim. L. R. 48.
3. *Payne* v. *Petch,* 30.vii.1979, Queen's Bench Division, High Court of Justice (unreported).

PART II

The Dangerous Offender in England Today

CHAPTER 5

The Law and Practice in the Courts

Nowhere on the English statute book, in dealing with the penalties that can be imposed by the courts on convicted offenders, is there any mention of, or meaning assigned to, the words 'dangerous' or 'dangerousness'. Certain criminal offences, it is true, do import into the elements of a crime a statutory definition for the purpose of determining criminal responsibility; thus the legislation on road traffic and on the misuse of drugs provides respectively for offences of 'dangerous driving' and of the possession, manufacture and supply of 'dangerous drugs'. But elsewhere the law is silent on this important aspect of penal policy.

In successive legislative attempts during this century to prescribe appropriate penal measures for the 'dangerous' offender, the draftsmen have studiously avoided either using that term, or specifically identifying those offenders to be dealt with by protective measures otherwise than by criteria related to age and previous criminal record, or providing a formula identifying with any degree of precision the 'dangerous' offender. The task has been left to the courts; and they have not been much more forthcoming in deciding on what basis they should proceed to sentence appropriately the 'dangerous' offender. The jurisprudence is sparse and unhelpful towards any formulation of who is a 'dangerous' offender. Instead, the courts have characteristically trodden the path of pragmatism and eschewed any kind of theoretical underpinning for their sentencing practices. The result may not, however, be as unsatisfactory as the absence of any rational definition would suggest.

Practice of the Courts

The concept of the 'dangerous' offender comes closest to legal recognition through judicial practice in the use of the sentence of life imprisonment for those few serious offences that carry the life sentence as the maximum penalty. It also manifests itself in the use of the determinate sentence for a handful of 'abnormal' crimes whose perpetrators are assumed to be dangerous and, albeit in covert form, in some of the sentences of determinate length passed on offenders thought to present a risk of committing or repeating serious offences. Ordinary determinate sentences, selected by the judges primarily with reference to the seriousness of the offence and previous criminal convictions, may reflect the normal range of sentences for offences of that type, yet still may be longer in duration than they would otherwise have been. This is because the sentencer perceives the need to provide the public with protection beyond what might be provided by a sentence within the normal range.

Two statutory provisions, while not explicitly invoking the concept of dangerousness, are designed specifically to permit the courts to exercise protective powers in the interests of safeguarding the public. These are (i) the extended sentence and (ii) the power, in lieu of imprisonment, to attach a restriction order to a hospital order under the Mental Health Act 1959.

Within certain non-custodial measures there is also discernible a strongly protective component. Disqualification from holding a driving licence and the seizure and confiscation of substances or objects used in crime – offensive weapons, drugs or pornography – are examples.

Life Imprisonment*

Following the Criminal Justice Act 1948, the life sentence became the maximum sentence for manslaughter and a number of serious non-homicidal offences – robbery, rape, arson and other serious violent offences against the person.[1] Until the 1960s courts confined the use of discretionary life imprisonment almost exclusively to manslaughter convictions; rarely did the courts impose indeterminate sentences for the non-homicidal offences. Thereafter there was a change of policy. As a proportion of all life sentences passed by the courts, the percentage relating to non-homicidal offences rose from 3% in 1962 to 16% in 1976, in which year 49 life sentences were imposed for offences other than murder. In 1979 the courts passed 157 life sentences, of which 47 were for offences other than murder.

Two quite separate justifications have been advanced by the judges for the use of the life sentence for those offences other than murder for which it is available. One has been that the sentence is sometimes given in mercy to the offender. Judges have explained that the seriousness of the offence might dictate a lengthy determinate sentence but that the offender's recovery from some mental or personality disorder might justify an early release. In that situation it would be to the prisoner's advantage that his period in custody should be left to be

*Mr David Thomas of the Cambridge Institute of Criminology generously provided us with working papers on the use of life sentences and detention orders. We wish to record our appreciation whilst exonerating him from responsibility for any mistakes and misinterpretations in what follows.

determined by the Secretary of State on up-to-date advice as to his progress while in prison. Some of the force of this approach was lost with the advent in 1967 of parole, which enables the release on parole licence of an offender sentenced to a determinate period in excess of eighteen months, after he has served one-third of his sentence. Nevertheless the 'merciful' life sentence continued to be resorted to by judges in recent years. The Advisory Council on the Penal System in its report on *Sentences of Imprisonment* (1978: para. 234) rejected the practice on the ground that experience had shown that those subjected to 'merciful' life sentences in fact tended to stay longer in prison than they would be likely to stay had they been given the alternative penalty, a determinate sentence. Following that recommendation, the Court of Appeal (Criminal Division) has consistently disavowed the 'merciful' life sentence.

The other justification for the life sentence is that it enables the court to impose indefinite detention upon those who supposedly present a danger to the public. The principal criteria governing the selection of those offenders who qualify as a danger to the public seem now to be well-established by the Court of Appeal (Criminal Division) and have been stated in many cases. They relate to the gravity of the offence, the mental condition of the offender and the risk that he will commit serious offences in the future. The practice of the Crown Courts in their use of the life sentence remains problematical; since, however, life sentences are almost invariably reviewed on appeal, the problem of disparity is not as great as in other areas of sentencing practice.

Although the criteria for the imposition of a life sentence have been stated in many cases they have never been reduced to very precise terms and the policy of the courts has changed from time to time in the interpretation and relative emphasis given to them. The Advisory Council studied the decisions of the Court of Appeal over the past 30 years and concluded that there had been a distinct shift in policy. The results of their study are set out in their Report (1978: Appendix P). They suggest that towards the end of the 1960s the criterion that the offence must be of a grave kind was relaxed and that this led the courts to resort to life imprisonment where in earlier days they would not have countenanced it. They suggest, also, that there has been a tendency to broaden the criterion that the offender must be shown to be suffering from a mental disorder that indicates he should not be released before successful psychiatric treatment has been undertaken, and that this requires decisions from the doctors which would be assisted by the indeterminacy of the life sentence. That criterion was extended to cover not only the offender who might be suffering from some recognisable, treatable mental condition but also the offender whose unstable character indicated a likely repetition of his offence. The Council regretted these changes: they declared in their Report (1978: para. 234) 'we prefer the case-law evolved by the courts in the 1950s and 1960s. That earlier jurisprudence accords with our view of the proper use of life imprisonment. Accordingly, we propose that the courts should consider uniform adherence to that jurisprudence.' Their view seems to have been heeded by the Court of Appeal; recent decisions reveal a shift of policy in the direction they advocate.

The criterion that the offence or offences must themselves be grave enough to warrant a long sentence, has been rendered somewhat ambiguous by recent cases. It is unquestionable that the instant offence does not have to be of the most serious kind to justify a life sentence.[2] But the level of seriousness which must be reached is uncertain. The increased use to which the life sentence has been put by the courts suggests strongly, as noted by the Advisory Council, that the judges have been prepared in recent years to entertain life sentences for offences that would previously have been regarded as insufficiently serious to attract the indeterminate sentence. In the earlier decisions the courts, while regarding offenders as a danger to the public, felt that the offences were not sufficiently serious to justify the indefinite period of protection afforded by a life sentence.[3]

The modern approach is illustrated by two cases — *Ashdown*[4] and *Wheal*[5]. Ashdown was convicted of robbery after threatening a man in the street with an air pistol and stealing £2. The Court admitted that on the facts of the case a fixed-term sentence of no longer than five years would have been appropriate, but nevertheless upheld a life sentence in view of evidence of his abnormal sexual drives and the likelihood that he would, without treatment, commit violent or sexual offences in the future. In *Wheal* the Court established the principle that the seriousness of the instant offence and the risk of repetition were related factors which must be weighed together:

> The Court has to bear in mind not only the gravity of the particular offence but also the risk to the public of any repetition of the offence. It would seem on the authorities that life imprisonment may be justified in a case where, although the facts of the offence themselves were not of the gravest, nevertheless the likelihood of repetition was strong. On the other hand, where the risk of repetition is very remote, then life imprisonment would only be justified if, on a balancing exercise, the gravity of the offence was of the gravest.

The balancing exercise required by these cases is by no means clear; the evidential material necessary to establish dangerousness in cases of different levels of gravity is not indicated; it is not made clear what must be the nature and degree of the likelihood that the offender will commit further offences in the future to justify a life sentence.

It was said in 1968 that the anticipated offences must be 'specially injurious',[6] and that a life sentence was appropriate only if the risk of the offender being at liberty at the end of a fixed term sentence was one which the public ought not, in all the circumstances, to have to bear. But what type of harm, and what degree of risk the public should bear, has been left open to question; the issue appears to be determined very much on an *ad hoc* and pragmatic basis. Thus in 1977, for an offence of arson, which was 'on the face of it . . . a trivial matter', the trial judge imposed a sentence of life imprisonment 'as a protection to the public against the risk of a repetition of an offence of this nature'. On appeal, the Court did not think that the evidence pointed to a very high risk of repetition, and reduced the sentence to a simple probation order. There was, however, little discussion of the degree of risk or the nature of the anticipated harm.[7] The anticipated harm apparently need not be related to the nature of the instant offence. Where an offender who had pleaded guilty to robbery, burglary and going equipped for burglary had a history of indecent assaults on small boys, and had been in the past subject to imprisonment, hospital orders and restriction orders, it was permissible to impose on him a life sentence because of his abnormal sexual instinct, although this was related only indirectly, if at all, to the nature of the instant offences.[8] In 1980, however, in the case of *Kelly*[9] the court has taken a conservative view of the degree of protection to which the public is entitled, and in the case of *Hercules*[10] a liberal view of the chances that an offender would cease to be dangerous within the period for which he would be detained under a fixed-term sentence proportionate to his offence.

The Court of Appeal has from time to time reiterated the view that where there is 'no question of mental disease or anything requiring mental treatment at all', such a sentence is 'quite wrong in principle'.[11] But the courts have been reluctant to define too precisely or narrowly what constitutes mental instability for the purpose; nor have they indicated precisely (or at all) what evidence is required to prove it. In one case in 1977 it was held that alcoholism alone did not constitute mental instability.[12] Apart from this, however, instability of character appears to have included a wide range of personality disorders, including emotional immaturity and impulsiveness. The Court of Appeal, in one case in 1976 involving a 22-year-old convicted of inflicting grievous bodily harm with intent after a bout of drinking, said that the fact that there was no evidence of mental illness, and no available treatment, was irrelevant to the appropriateness of life imprisonment. The offender's emotional immaturity was sufficient evidence of his dangerousness: if he were released he might again go out drinking, 'and then there is every prospect that he will commit some extremely violent and dangerous crimes'.[13]

Some offences appear intrinsically to warrant a finding of mental instability, especially if they reveal abnormal sexual proclivities. A life sentence in one case in 1973 was upheld for two offences of buggery, one of attempted buggery and two of indecent assault on males, without any discussion of the offender's mental condition other than a finding that there was no mental disorder.[14] Similarly, in another case in 1976, the court stated that, apart from the offender's propensity to indecent assault on boys aged 10 to 14, he was 'a responsible, highly intelligent, law-abiding individual'.[15]

Now, however, the court is showing signs of being critical of the use of the life sentence and will not uphold it unless a clear case for life imprisonment is made out with substantial medical evidence of mental instability in support. A finding of mental instability, imprecise and unrefined as the concept is, is felt to be integral to dangerousness: the one exhibits the other. Thomas (1979: 302) has described the Court's policy:

> What is important is not whether the offender's condition can be accurately described by a recognized psychiatric term, but whether it can be predicted with a sufficient degree of confidence that the offender will, unless restrained, commit further grave offences in the future, and that his propensity to do so will not decline within a foreseeable period.

Two cases in 1980 bear out this statement of the position. In the case of *Kelly*[16] the Court rejected life imprisonment for a young man of 20, convicted of two offences of wounding with intent and with several previous convictions, including two for wounding in which the victims had been stabbed. There was no medical evidence indicating a mental or medical condition and the Court decided that a determinate sentence would give the public the degree of protection to which it was entitled. Accepting that the offences were grave and that the offender was a danger to the public, the sentence would be varied to eight years' imprisonment, consecutive to other sentences to which he was already subject. In the case of *Hercules*[17] the sentence was rejected for a man of 40 convicted of wounding with intent and with three previous convictions for violence. The medical evidence was that he was not suffering from mental illness: he had a prolonged history of alcoholism and a deep-rooted personality problem, but his condition was not amenable to treatment. The Court decided that he was approaching an age when his aggressive tendencies might be expected to die down; although he was a danger to the public while he still had those tendencies, time itself would cure them. The Court would take the risk of substituting for 'life' a sentence of seven years' imprisonment.

The following principles probably underlie the present use of the life sentence when it is not mandatory:

1. The offender must have committed an offence of considerable seriousness; but its seriousness is not the primary consideration. If the risk of a future grave offence is substantial, 'life' may be used even if the current offence would not justify a long fixed term.

2. 'Life' should not be imposed where the offender is not 'dangerous'. With an occasional exception[18] the discretionary life sentence has not been used for offenders merely because they have committed very grave offences. Dangerousness is at most a subsidiary factor in deciding the length of a fixed-term prison sentence, and does not justify a greater length than the facts of the current offence warrant.
3. The offender must be either suffering from a mental disorder or in some other way of unstable character so that there is a likelihood of his committing further grave offences.

As a protective device against the exceptional, 'dangerous' offender the sentence of life imprisonment has not established itself as a satisfactory instrument of penal policy. Though it is imposed sparingly and the Court of Appeal does not hesitate to take a cool view of the degree of protection to which the public is entitled and a hard look at the case for an indeterminate sentence, the established criteria justifying its imposition have lacked clear exposition. So there is absent from the jurisprudence any discussion about special procedural safeguards in the presentation of evidential material establishing any one or more of the criteria; the courts have not provided any guidance as to the type and quality of evidence required for the purpose of ensuring a proper application of the criteria. In short, the discretionary life sentence lacks appropriate legal prescription.

Detention Orders upon Children and Young Persons

For juvenile offenders who are deemed dangerous, the courts have used s. 53(2) of the Children and Young Persons Act 1933 as the equivalent of the sentence of life imprisonment for adults. As a result of the Criminal Justice Act 1961, the section can now be applied in respect of any offence punishable in the case of an adult with imprisonment for fourteen years or more; and it has been held to apply to common law misdemeanours. It allows the court to order the detention of a child or young person, in any institution or other place specified by the Home Secretary, for any period within the maximum which could be imposed upon an adult convicted of the same offence. Where the offence, therefore, is one which carries life imprisonment, the order for detention under s. 53(2) can be for life. The Court of Appeal has stated, however, that detention for life should only be imposed when it is impossible to predict how the offender will develop in the future. More commonly, the period of detention will be limited by the court to a specified period, typically between about 6 and 20 years.

In one well known case,[19] an order for 20 years' detention under s. 53(2) was imposed upon a sixteen-year-old youth who admitted charges of attempted murder and robbery of a man who was attacked, knocked to the ground, repeatedly kicked and beaten about the head with a brick and then left unconscious after being robbed of 30p, some keys and five cigarettes. His two co-defendants, also juveniles, received detention orders of 10 years. The Court of Appeal, in upholding these sentences, stated that there was clearly a risk of repetition of offending by the youths concerned and that the protection of the public had to be the paramount consideration; in such a case an order under s. 53(2) was the only appropriate sentence. The court stated that the length of the sentence should be fixed according to the length of time during which the offender might remain a danger, and that in cases of doubt a longer rather than a shorter period should be preferred. In this case, the court considered that the principal offender might well remain dangerous until he reached his early thirties and that a period of twenty years' detention was therefore appropriate. The basis for selection of this length of sentence was apparently the court's belief that the defendant would by that time have 'fully matured'.

The child or young person subject to a detention order, whether or not it is for a determinate period or for life, may be released by the Home Secretary at any time subject to the recommendation of the Parole Board. In this sense the offender is in a position very like that of a prisoner serving a long determinate or life sentence, and indeed will often be well into adulthood by the time he is seriously considered for release.

The use of s. 53(2) does appear to differ from the sentence of life imprisonment, however, in the principles governing its use. The criteria for determining 'dangerousness' for the purposes of s. 53(2) appear to be looser and more vague than those formulated by the Court of Appeal for life imprisonment, and it is doubtful whether any of the three defendants in the case just referred to would have satisfied the criteria for a sentence of life imprisonment. To qualify for a detention order a youth must have committed a serious offence, usually involving grave harm or risk to life, and must be thought likely to act in a similar way in the future. Beyond that, no firm criteria have been established. In particular, there does not seem to be a need for evidence of mental instability as required for a life sentence. This is, perhaps, because the alternative of a fixed-term sentence of imprisonment is not available when the offender is under the age of 17.

Restriction Orders

Closely allied to the sentence of life imprisonment as a protective device is the provision in the Mental Health Act 1959 which empowers the Crown Court to impose a restriction order upon mentally disordered offenders. Section 65 of the Act provides that whenever a Crown Court deems it expedient to make a hospital order under section 60 in lieu of imprisonment,[20] it may additionally make a restriction order. The restriction order is appropriate if 'having regard to the nature of the offence, the antecedents of the offender and the risk of his committing further offences if set at large' the Crown Court Judge thinks it is necessary to impose the restriction for the protection of the public. The restriction order may be limited or unlimited in time. The normal practice of the courts has been to make restriction orders unlimited in time. Only if the medical evidence indicates with confidence that recovery from the mental disorder will take place within a defined period does the court sanction a limited duration to the restriction order under section 65;[21] but such cases are rare.

The primary legal effect of a restriction order is that while it remains in force the mentally disordered offender can be released (or transferred to another mental hospital, or given leave of absence) only under the authority of the Secretary of State.[22] The Home Secretary, either on his own initiative or at the request of the offender-patient, may refer a case to the Mental Health Review Tribunal for its advice.[23] Following the recommendations of the Aarvold Committee on the release procedure for restricted offender-patients, there has been established extra-statutorily an Advisory Board which advises the Home Secretary on the propriety of release in any case where the mentally disordered offender may present a particular risk on release. The ultimate decision whether to release rests with the Home Secretary in his unfettered discretion. Any discharge of a mentally disordered offender subject to a restriction order that remains in force — the order itself may be revoked by the Home Secretary — may be made conditional, in which case the person remains liable to recall until such time as the restriction order either expires or is revoked.

The Act does not include any definition of the kind of harm against which the public is entitled to protection. The Court of Appeal (Criminal Division) has said that:

> It is very desirable that they [restriction orders] should be made in all cases where it is thought that the protection of the public is required. Thus, for example, in the case of crimes of violence, and of the more serious sexual offences, particularly if the offender has a record of such offences, or if there is a history of mental disorder involving violent behaviour, it is suggested that there must be compelling reasons to explain why a restriction order should not be made.[24]

The Court did not, however, say that these were the only types of cases which would justify a restriction order; its scope is in practice wider. In several cases a restriction order has been upheld by the Court of Appeal even when the offence and past history of offending have been neither violent nor especially serious; for example, a restriction order was held to be proper for one offender before the court on two counts of burglary, because he persistently absconded from open hospitals and might therefore obtain his ultimate freedom unless a restriction order was made.[25]

The Butler Committee was critical of the use to which restriction orders were put, and of the lack of stringency in the statutory criteria for imposing them:

> Evidence given to us by the Home Office has indicated the probability that these orders are imposed in numbers of cases where their severity is not appropriate. . . . There is no indication of the seriousness of the offences from which the public is intended to be protected by the restriction order provisions, and some courts have evidently imposed restrictions on, for example, the petty recidivist because of the virtual certainty that he will persist in similar offences in the future.[26]

They therefore proposed 'that the wording of s. 65(1) should be more tightly drawn to indicate its true intention, namely to protect the public from serious harm', remarking that 'A more restrictive wording of the section would help the courts in making the difficult decision whether it is appropriate to impose this severe form of control.' In 1978, 126 restriction orders were imposed; of these, 78 (62%) were made in respect of offences against the person; 6 (5%) for robbery and burglary; 18 (14%) for sexual offences; 17 (14%) for arson and other criminal damage; and all but one of the remainder (4%) for various property offences.

The distinguishing feature of the restriction order is that it may be imposed only in respect of offenders suffering from a definable mental disorder which brings them within the mental health system. It is not available in the case of offenders who, although they may display some degree of mental disorder, are ineligible for a hospital order under the Mental Health Act 1959, either because their mental condition is insufficiently severe or because a place in a hospital cannot be found for them, or because their offence is trivial. But once the criminal court decides to commit the offender to a mental hospital it applies a test of potential dangerousness, when deciding whether to impose a restriction order, that is no more satisfactory than that employed in the passing of a sentence of life imprisonment.

Extended Sentences

The extended sentence, introduced by the Criminal Justice Act 1967,[27] is the third and last memorial to successive legislative attempts to identify and apply preventive measures to the dangerous offender. The history of these attempts to provide preventive detention for selected offenders has been related in the recent report of the Advisory Council on the Penal System on *Sentences of Imprisonment*; we have found it unnecessary to traverse the ground adequately dealt with there.

For our purposes the most important feature of the first two legislative essays in this intractable area of penal policy — the Prevention of Crime Act 1908 and the Criminal Justice Act 1948 — has been the absence of any clear statutory distinction between the persistent (and often petty) offender and the dangerous offender — the social 'nuisance' and the social 'menace'. The 1908 Act, while explicitly catering merely for the 'habitual criminal', was nevertheless proffered optimistically as an important means for dealing with offenders who were a danger to society. A Home Office memorandum laid before Parliament on 17 February 1911 stated:

> Only the great need of society to be secured from professional or dangerous criminals can justify the prolongation of the ordinary sentences of penal servitude by the addition of . . . preventive detention. . . . It was repeatedly stated by Lord Gladstone in the course of the Debates that the Bill was devised for the 'advanced dangerous criminal', for 'the persistent dangerous criminal', for 'the most hardened criminals': its object was 'to give the State effective control over dangerous offenders': it was not to be applied to persons who were 'a nuisance rather than a danger to society', or to the 'much larger class of those who were partly vagrants, partly criminals, and who were to a large extent mentally deficient'.

The Dove-Wilson Committee (Home Office 1932), while reproducing the 1911 memorandum, perpetuated the confusion between the menace and the nuisance. It regarded persistence in crime *per se* as a form of dangerousness. It singled out for particular comment the professional criminal who deliberately makes a living by preying on the public, those who practise thefts or frauds on a small scale, and those who repeatedly commit sexual offences against children and young persons.

There were two reasons for this reluctance to recognise a clear distinction between persistent and dangerous offending. First, it was believed that persistent offending itself might give rise to the need for special measures of protection, if necessary by long periods of incarceration: petty thefts or frauds might inflict more serious injury on victims of slender means than major thefts or burglaries committed against persons of wealth. Second, serious offences in themselves justified long sentences of imprisonment as punishment within the normal range, so the question of protection did not arise. Not surprisingly, therefore, the courts tended to restrict the use of imprisonment for protective purposes, for a period longer than punishment of the instant offence would allow, to repetitive offenders convicted of comparatively minor offences. Protection against offenders convicted of serious offences against the person could be adequately dealt with under the ordinary arrangements.

Preventive detention was available under the 1908 Act. Wherever a person with three previous convictions resulting in penal servitude was found by a jury to be an 'habitual criminal', the courts were empowered to pass an additional sentence of not less than five nor more than ten years for the protection of the public. This 'double-track' system was not greatly liked by the Director of Public Prosecutions and the courts, and fell into disuse. From 1922 onwards an average of only about 30 offenders a year were sentenced to preventive detention. Following the recommendations of the Dove-Wilson Committee of 1932, the Criminal Justice Act 1948 repealed the previous preventive detention legislation and substituted two new provisions. For the younger recidivist, between the ages of 21 and 30, who might still be reformed, a new sentence of corrective training of between two and four years, as specified by the court, was created. For the confirmed recidivist who would not be responsive to a short period of corrective training, a new form of preventive detention was provided. A single sentence, in length between 5 and 14 years, was fixed at the discretion of the judge; as such it was passed instead of, rather than in addition to, the ordinary prison sentence. As a result of the emphasis upon repetitive offending as the primary qualification for preventive detention, this too failed to discriminate between the nuisance and the menace. Petty, inadequate offenders whose crimes involved property of very little value became all too often the prime candidates for preventive detention (Hammond and Chayen 1963). Under the influence of the Lord Chief Justice, Lord Parker, in the 1960s it too declined in use.

The Report on Preventive Detention by the Advisory Council on the Treatment of Offenders (Home Office 1963) was the first to draw a clear and unambiguous distinction between the dangerous and the persistent offender, and to suggest that only certain forms of persistence constituted a danger. But it went on to argue that society needed to be protected from both, if necessary by special sentencing measures:

> It must, we think, be recognised that the community ought to be protected, by some means or other within the penal system, both from the dangerous criminals, who are fortunately comparatively rare, and from the more numerous offenders who practise thefts or frauds on victims who may be severely afflicted by the loss of a small sum or seriously distressed by what may rank as very minor housebreakings.

The White Paper, *The Adult Offender*, (Home Office 1965), on which the extended sentence in the 1967 Act was based, endorsed this view. It recommended a new sentence for the persistent offender 'whose character and record of offences are such as to put it beyond all doubt that they are a real menace to society, and to exclude the petty criminal who commits a series of lesser offences'.

The result was the extended sentence. For an offender satisfying the criteria of eligibility the court may impose, for the protection of the public, an extended sentence of up to five years for an offence carrying a maximum of two, three or four years, and of up to ten years for an offence carrying a maximum of five to nine years. If the maximum for the offence is more than ten years, the length of the extended sentence must remain within that maximum.[28] This sentence is designed to provide protection in two ways. It may provide for a longer period of imprisonment than that which would have been appropriate for the offence itself; it ensures that the offender can be made subject to licence whenever he is released from his sentence, and that the licence period will last until the end of the nominal sentence rather than until the expiration of the normal two-thirds of the sentence when he would be entitled to release with remission.[29] In other words, it may be used cumulatively as a custodial and non-custodial protective sentence.

Although the intention was to draw a distinction between the 'menaces' and the 'nuisances', no criteria were inserted in the legislation, nor have any emerged in judicial practice, to define the types of persistent offending which constitute a 'menace'. Instead, eligibility has continued to depend almost exclusively upon aspects of previous record. The offence for which the extended sentence is given must be punishable with imprisonment for two years or more; it must have been committed within three years of liberty after a prison sentence for a previous offence punishable with at least two years' imprisonment; the offender must have been convicted or sentenced by a Crown Court on at least three previous occasions since his 21st birthday of offences punishable with at least two years' imprisonment; the total length of imprisonment to which he was sentenced on those occasions must be at least five years (including suspended terms of imprisonment); and at least one of the sentences must have been for at least three years (or at least two for at least two years).

The definition of the sort of offender who is eligible for the extended sentence is restrictive and complex. Like its precursors it lacks any direct reference to the degree of seriousness of the risk of the harm which the offender might present in the future. As the rubric to the statute itself indicates, it is a measure which applies to the 'persistent' rather than to the 'dangerous' offender. Predictably its use, like that of its predecessors, has steadily declined, from a peak of 129 sentences in 1970 to only 14 in 1976. Moreover, it is used primarily for property offenders. Of the 75 extended sentences imposed between 1974 and 1976, only 12 (16%) were in respect of offences against the person. The Advisory Council on the Penal System in 1978 accordingly recommended its abolition without specific replacement.

Unlike the early history of preventive detention, therefore, the experience of recent years has exhibited a growing distinction between dangerousness and persistence. By the explicit terms of the legislation the extended sentence concentrated upon persistence. Judicial practice, by contrast, has indicated a persistent unwillingness to resort to preventive confinement on the grounds of the offender's mere persistence in committing crime. Since offenders who might present a risk of inflicting serious harm in the future will often not qualify for the extended sentence in terms of previous record, its value as a protective device against serious offending has been, and will continue to be, minimal. Persistence refers to the past; dangerousness to the future. Persistence in offending against the criminal law undoubtedly provides some evidence of dangerousness, but it does not and cannot of itself amount to dangerousness. None of the legislative attempts has, moreover, provided any substantive criteria for establishing who is a dangerous offender.

Determinate Sentences

The majority of offenders sent to prison receive determinate sentences if only because, for all but a few serious offences, the available sentences are restricted by maximum penalties of determinate length. Some offenders, however, undoubtedly receive sentences greater in length than would be applied were it not for the fact that the court considers them to be dangerous, either on account of the special nature or circumstances of their crime, or because they are thought more likely than others to commit or repeat serious offences. In such circumstances one component in the sentence reflects a desire to provide additional protection to the public. Sometimes the additional protective element is openly declared by the sentencer; often it is covertly applied.

There are some crimes of which the perpetrators are deemed *ipso facto* dangerous: crimes against the State; and crimes (dubbed by the Court of Appeal 'abnormal'[30]) carried out with exceptional determination, ruthlessness and skill and accompanied by unusual violence. What may be termed, by contrast, 'normal' crimes may attract sentences with a protective element if the court believes that the offender, by reason of his record, is more likely than others to offend again.

The classic example of an *offence against the State* is treason, rare in times of peace; more commonly, the offence of espionage, which may include the more serious instances of breaches of official secrets laws. Betrayal of one's country is a crime which arouses both a punitive and a protective reaction in extreme form. The sentence of 42 years' imprisonment passed by the Lord Chief Justice, Lord Parker, on George Blake in 1961, is the longest determinate sentence passed in English penal history. Not only were three of five separate counts in an indictment charging espionage for the Soviet Union, carried out when Blake was employed by the British Secret Service, punished by three consecutive maximum penalties of 14 years' imprisonment; there was also, notably, a departure from ordinary sentencing policy. The Court of

Appeal, in upholding the sentence for a case that was 'one of the worst that can be envisaged in a time of peace', concluded that the sentence had a threefold purpose. It was intentionally punitive; it was designed and calculated to deter others; and it was meant to be a safeguard to the country.[31]

Other criminal activity against the State, in the shape of kidnapping of politicians and terrorist offences, has attracted similar judicial responses. Sentences on those who have taken hostages with threats to kill them if demands — whether political or personal — are not met by the agencies of law and order have reflected the presumed dangerousness of the offenders. In the 'Spaghetti House' siege case (not a case of political terrorism but a case of armed robbery aping the technique of terrorists) the Court of Appeal declared that anyone who starts out on an enterprise of violence for political purposes should be left in no doubt that if he is caught and prosecuted to conviction, the court will inflict very severe punishment.[32] And the legislature, in the Prevention of Terrorism Act 1978, has adopted a like posture in including in the list of extraditable crimes a wide range of violent crimes that might otherwise have qualified for exemption from surrender to another country, on the grounds that they were offences of a political character.[33]

The Court of Appeal in 1975,[34] when dealing with lengthy sentences passed on a number of men involved in the series of skilfully executed armed robberies on banks that had plagued the country in the late 1960s and early 1970s, referred to the growing public menace of a class of crime that they described as 'abnormal' in contrast to those offences exemplified in the instant appeal which they dubbed as 'not wholly abnormal'. 'Abnormal' crimes, in the view of the Court, comprise not only offences of political treachery and fanaticism, but also crimes marked by sophistication, that is to say, technical and organisational ingenuity in defeating security devices, as evidenced by the Great Train Robbery in 1961; or by 'great and horrid violence', as revealed in the Kray and Richardson trials of the 1960s. Crimes that are ideologically unmotivated, relatively unsophisticated in conception and only incidentally violent in execution were referred to by the Court as 'not wholly abnormal' crimes, for which sentences would reflect the normal range for serious offences of the kind.

Every day, however, judges pass sentences longer than they would otherwise be on the express or implied ground that the offender has shown by his record that the public needs to be protected against him. While the offences for which these sentences are given are sometimes against the person, they are far more often offences against property: burglary, theft, dishonest handling or obtaining by deception.

The practice of introducing a protective element into a determinate sentence is subject to one important limitation. Sentences must obey the rule of proportionality; they must bear some relation to the offence for which the offender is being 'punished' and must not exceed the upper limit of the 'tariff' for that offence. But as the maximum sentences provided by law are very high and as the 'tariff' ranges for the particular offence are accordingly also high, and at the upper end of the range very high indeed, this limit on the sentencing power is, in practice, of not much importance. A man may still receive a sentence 'for the protection of the public' which, but for that consideration, would seem to a rational sentencer to be immoderately severe.

The courts in this country recognise the existence of dangerous persons — they distinguish in their sentencing practice the ordinary from the exceptional, dangerous offender; but they are frequently enabled to do so without breaching the rule of proportionality by the existence of very high maximum sentences which bear little relation to the normal range of sentences passed on 'ordinary' offenders.

When the Court of Appeal has detected a sentence longer than that appropriate for the particular offence, it has usually reduced its length. Even though the offender is considered a danger to the public,[35] even if the court forms the view that an offender is 'an enemy of society', the correct principle for sentencing is to sentence for the offences charged and on the facts proved or admitted. As the court remarked in the case of *King and Simpkins,*[36]

> the learned judge increased the sentences . . . because of his view, for which there was ample evidence, that these young men were enemies of society. But the court has to bear in mind that in our system of jurisprudence there is no offence known as being an enemy of society. The court is concerned with the offences charged in the indictment. It may well be that at a trial the evidence establishes that those who have committed the offences charged are dangerous men. When the evidence establishes that, the court has no reason for mitigating the penalties in any way. If the evidence does establish that the accused are dangerous men, then it is no good their saying that they have no previous convictions or that they are still young men. The evidence cancels out such mitigation as there is. But the fact remains that the correct principle for sentencing is to sentence for the offences charged and on the facts proved or admitted.

Nevertheless, there have been occasions when the Court of Appeal has acknowledged the propriety of a protective element in an ordinary determinate sentence. For example, a woman with a long history of disturbed, impulsive and aggressive behaviour (but only one minor previous conviction) was sentenced to three years' imprisonment for an offence of criminal damage causing loss valued at £18. The Court of Appeal accepted that three years was too long for the offence, but nevertheless upheld the sentence because of the need to protect the public from her.[37] In similar vein, the Court of Appeal upheld a total of ten years' imprisonment on a persistent burglar, and stated:

In fixing the length of a man's sentence it is permissible to take account . . . of the risk of his offending again if he regains his liberty. If that risk is great, and if the harm likely to be caused by the repetition of the offence is serious, a long sentence may be justified. The Appellant's history shows that if he were released from prison it is as sure as anything can be that he would burgle again and go on burgling until he was caught. The harm he would do to others would be very serious. These considerations justified giving him a longer sentence than might be appropriate for another man convicted of similar offences.[38]

In another recent case the defendant, who was a 'confirmed congenital pederast', received concurrent four-year prison sentences for two 'trivial homosexual indecent assaults' (and a consecutive sentence of one year for a separate offence). Medical evidence indicated that he had 'homicidal fantasies with regard to small boys and the consequence of that is that there is a very great danger that this man, if at liberty, might inflict serious harm or might indeed kill'. The Court of Appeal admitted that the sentences 'were plainly determined primarily in order to protect the public and less with regard to the nature of the offences', but upheld them on the basis that 'all we can do is to pass a sentence which is not unjustly long but will serve to protect the public longer than a sentence solely passed to meet the gravity of the assault'.[39]

This approach, even in the limited and exceptional cases, has now been disavowed by the Court of Appeal in *Gooden*.[40] In that case a 50-year-old pederast, convicted of a series of not very serious indecent assaults on a number of male teenagers, was sentenced to a total of eight years' imprisonment. The trial judge, with some reluctance, considered it his duty to pass such a long sentence in order to provide a substantial period during which the offender would be unable to molest young boys. In reducing the sentence to four years' imprisonment the Court of Appeal declared that if the offender did not qualify for an extended sentence — the only sentence statutorily providing for a protective element — it was wrong to pass a sentence containing any element of protection beyond that provided by a term of imprisonment appropriate to and commensurate with the offences for which the offender was being sentenced. The Court reaffirmed the principle, not invariably adhered to, that unless the court is imposing an extended sentence under section 28 of the Powers of Criminal Courts Act 1973, it should sentence solely on the basis of the offences charged and on the facts relating to the offences proved or admitted.[41] By the time the appeal was heard (leave to appeal having been given out of time) the offender had completed the equivalent of a sentence of three and a half years with full remission. The Court declined to accede to the submission by counsel that a protective element could be provided by substituting a sentence of two years' imprisonment coupled with a suspended sentence supervision order. The Court did not think it just or appropriate to tack on to the period of custody a further two-year suspended sentence with supervision by the probation and after-care service.

Notwithstanding the alertness of the Court of Appeal, it is clear that determinate sentences are being passed in greater length than they would otherwise have been, because of an estimated likelihood that the offender will commit or repeat a serious offence. Although some sentences are not markedly in excess of the normal range they may nevertheless incorporate an additional protective element; and such sentences may not even reach the appellate court, on the basis that legal advice indicates that, while the sentence is in excess of the norm, it is not sufficiently excessive to warrant any optimism that it will be reduced on appeal. Since the recent practice direction from the Lord Chief Justice, that after 15 April 1980 the power to order loss of time in the case of a hopeless appeal will be more vigorously applied, the potential for the covert protective element in sentencing is all the greater.[42] The covert protective element might, moreover, cover cases where there is not only a risk of future serious harm but also a high degree of probability of repetition of less serious harm. This unsatisfactory state of affairs stems from the lack of any statutory criteria or judicial guidance upon which the addition of a protective element can properly be based.

Ancillary Orders

A hint of a development in the sentencing process towards the explicit provision of a protective sentence comes from an unexpected source. Whenever a criminal court convicts an alien liable to deportation it may proceed to make a recommendation for deportation under s.6 of the Immigration Act 1971. The jurisprudence has exclusively concentrated upon aliens other than EEC nationals, and has merely declared that the recommendation must be justified on the grounds that the alien's continued presence in the United Kingdom is to its detriment. The more serious the crime and the longer the criminal record, the more obvious it is that the court should recommend deportation.[43] But the application of this power to EEC nationals, protected generally against any restriction on the freedom of movement of workers within the member states, is making its impact upon the courts' attitude towards the 'dangerous' offender.

Article 48(3) of the Treaty establishing the European Economic Community permits measures being taken to restrict such freedom of movement which can be justified on grounds of public policy. And a recommendation for deportation on conviction by a criminal court has been held to be a measure within the Article.[44] That case, involving a conviction by the Metropolitan Stipendiary Magistrate for possession of a dangerous drug, prompted the European Court of Justice, in a preliminary ruling requested by the Magistrate, to explain the circumstances where public policy justified a measure taken in the form of deportation. Without explicitly declaring the precise limits of such public policy, the European Court's decision proceeded along the path towards a definition of dangerousness that alone would justify the imposition of a deportation order.

The Court noted that Article 3(2) of Council Directive 64/221 of 25 February 1964 (which it held had a direct effect, so as to confer on individuals rights that a national court was bound to protect) provides that a previous criminal conviction of the alien could not be a sufficient ground in itself to justify a member State taking the measure of deporting him. (Article 3(1) provides that measures taken on grounds of public policy must be based exclusively on the personal conduct of the individual concerned.) The Court stated that this Article presupposed the existence, in addition to the disturbance of the social order that any infraction of the criminal law necessarily involves, *of a genuine and sufficiently serious threat* to the requirements of public policy. The existence of a previous conviction could, therefore, be taken into account only in so far as circumstances which gave rise to that conviction were evidence of personal conduct constituting a present threat to the requirements of public policy. Although, in general, a finding that such a threat exists implied the existence in the individual concerned of a propensity to act in the same way in the future, it was possible that past conduct alone might constitute such a threat to the requirements of public policy.[45]

This ruling precludes measures being taken against the EEC worker on the grounds of mere persistence in criminal activity, and it diverts attention away from past conduct (except in so far as it indicates a future propensity). It focuses instead on the contemporary behaviour that discloses a 'sufficiently serious threat', without actually stating that such conduct constitutes dangerousness. But the implication is clear. Only a serious threat to the social order, tested by criteria of actual propensity disclosed by past behaviour and contemporary evidence of an existing threat of serious harm, will suffice to justify a protective order. Furthermore, the Articles of Council Directive 64/221 impose procedural safeguards that are absent from English legislation dealing with the deportation of aliens through the route of the criminal courts. But this deficiency is likely to be remedied nationally as a result of the ruling of the European Court of Justice in *R.* v. *Secretary of State for Home Affairs, ex p. Santillo.*[46]

The European limitation upon the hitherto unbridled power of English courts to recommend convicted EEC nationals for deportation will inevitably spill over into the same power as is exercisable against

DANGEROUSNESS AND CRIMINAL JUSTICE

other non-patrials liable to deportation. The European concept of 'a present, genuine and sufficiently serious threat to the requirements of public policy', imported into the English jurisprudence, may eventually come to be adopted generally into the sentencing policy of the courts.

Notes

1. A breakdown of the number of life sentences passed, and the offences for which they were imposed, for each year from 1958 to 1976 is to be found in Appendix O to the Report of the Advisory Council on the Penal System on Sentences of Imprisonment, June 1978, pp. 217–21.
2. *Beagle* (1976), 62 Cr. App. R. 151 *per* Scarman L.J., is the only case which appears to hold differently.
3. *Scott*, 15.v.1970; *Williams*, [1974] Crim. L. R. 376.
4. (1974), 58 Cr. App. R. 339.
5. 7.v.1974.
6. *Hodgson* (1968), 52 Cr. App. R. 133.
7. *Ainsworth*, 6.iv. 1977.
8. *Hildersley*, [1974] Crim. L. R. 197.
9. *Kelly* [1980] Crim. L. R. 27.
10. *Hercules*, [1980] Crim. L. R. 27.
11. *O'Connor*, [1960] Crim. L. R. 275; *Picker* (1970), 54 Cr. App. R. 330; *Beever*, [1971] Crim. L. R. 402.
12. *Johannsen* (1977), 65 Cr. App. R. 101.
13. *Chaplin*, [1976] Crim. L. R. 320.
14. *Skelding* (1973), 58 Cr. App. R. 313.
15. *Watson*, [1976] Crim. L. R. 698.
16. *Kelly*, [1980] Crim. L. R. 27.
17. *Hercules*, [1980] Crim. L. R. 27.
18. *R. v. Trusty, Chard and McCarthy*, 8.iii.1977.
19. *Storey, Fuat and Duignan* (1973), 57 Cr. App. R. 840.
20. A hospital order may be made in respect of an offender convicted of any imprisonable offence (in some cases before a magistrates' court even without the court proceeding to convict) if the court is satisfied on the evidence of two medical practitioners registered under the Mental Health Act that the offender is suffering from a mental disorder susceptible to treatment, and that the most suitable method of dealing with the offender is by way of a hospital order.
21. *Gardiner* (1967), 51 Cr. App. R. 187, 193.
22. A mentally disordered offender under a hospital order without the addition of a restriction order is treated as if he were a patient compulsorily admitted under the civil process under Part IV of the 1959 Act; as such he may be released by order of the Physician Superintendent or on the order of a Mental Health Review Tribunal.
23. Section 66(6), Mental Health Act 1959. Under section 66(7) the mentally abnormal offender has a right to ask periodically for his case to be referred to the Tribunal.
24. *Gardiner* (1967), 51 Cr. App. R. 187, 193.
25. *Eaton*, [1976] Crim. L. R. 390; *Toland* (1974), 58 Cr. App. R. 453. By virtue of s.40(3) of the Mental Health Act 1959, if a person subject to a hospital order without a restriction order is absent without leave and not taken into custody within 28 days, or, in the case of persons aged 21 or over, suffering from subnormality or psychopathic disorder, within 6 months, the hospital order automatically ceases to have effect.

26. Committee on Mentally Abnormal Offenders 1974: para. 14:24.

27. Now sections 28 and 29, Powers of the Criminal Courts Act 1973.

28. *D.P.P.* v. *Ottewell*, [1970] A.C. 642.

29. The extended sentence prisoner becomes eligible for parole in the normal way after one-third of his sentence. If he is released on parole, however, the period of licence runs until the end of the nominal sentence. In addition, if he is released on or after the expiration of two-thirds of his sentence, the Home Secretary may and invariably does order that the licence period shall run until the end of the nominal sentence.

30. *R.* v. *Turner and others* (1975), 61 Cr. App. R. 67.

31. [1962] 2 Q.B. 377. George Blake escaped from Wormwood Scrubs in 1966 and safely reached East Germany. Cf. *R.* v. *Fuchs*, 2 March 1950, who received the maximum of 14 years' imprisonment on several counts in an indictment for espionage, in revealing the allies' nuclear power secrets at the establishment at Los Alamos, USA.

32. *R.* v. *Termine* (1977), 64 Cr. App. R. 299, 301–2; *R.* v. *Al-Mograbi and Cull* (1980), 70 Cr. App. R. 24.

33. See also Internationally Protected Persons Act 1978, section 1(3).

34. *R.* v. *Turner and others* (1975), 61 Cr. App. R. 67.

35. *Rose*, [1974] Crim. L. R. 266; *Coombs*, [1973] Crim. L. R. 65 and *Robson*, 6.v.1974, cited by Thomas (1979:37).

36. *R.* v. *King and Simpkins* (1973), 57 Cr. App. R. 696.

37. *Arrowsmith*, [1976] Crim. L. R. 636.

38. *Lightbody*, [1977] Crim. L. R. 626.

39. *Corner*, [1977] Crim. L. R. 300; and *Jason*, 20.ii.1976, where the risk of repetition and the possibility of mental illness were held to justify a long sentence. These two cases, together with *Arrowsmith*, [1976] Crim. L. R. 636 and *Lightbody*, [1977] Crim. L. R. 626, would appear to be contrary to the principle enunciated in *Gooden*, [1980] Crim. L. R. 250.

40. [1980] Crim. L. R. 250.

41. Following *Lundbech*, 4.vi.1970.

42. Widgery (1980).

43. *R.* v. *Caird* (1970), 54 Cr. App. R. 499; *R.* v. *Nazari and others*, 14.iii.1980.

44. *Bouchereau*, [1977] E.C.R. 1299.

45. *Bouchereau*, paras. [28], [29] and [35].

46. [1980] and C.M.L.R. 308.

CHAPTER 6

In Detention

Once in detention, whether for a fixed term or for an indeterminate period in prison or in a secure hospital, the dangerousness of an offender is assessed for administrative purposes: in the first instance to determine the degree of security necessary in his case; and subsequently to decide whether it would be safe to grant parole or release him on licence or conditionally discharge him from hospital.

Security in Prison

To be detained under conditions of maximum security is to be classed unambiguously as 'dangerous'. The present practice of classifying prisoners for security purposes dates from 1967 and follows the recommendations of Earl Mountbatten of Burma's Report of an inquiry into prison escapes and security (Home Office 1966). The classification turns on a judgment of the seriousness of the harm that would result from a prisoner's escape. There are four categories, of which the first, category 'A', comprises the prisoners whose escape would be 'highly dangerous to the public, police and the security of the state' and who are, therefore, detained under conditions of maximum security. This formulation is taken from the Summary of Recommendations in Appendix C of the Report and is notably more inclusive than the definition proposed in the body of the Report which describes category 'A' prisoners as 'those who must in no circumstances be allowed to get out whether because of the security considerations affecting spies or because their violent behaviour is such that members of the public or the police would be in danger of their lives if they were to get out' (para. 212). This definition which has passed into administrative practice takes into consideration not only the risk that a prisoner might, if he escaped, do violent harm or endanger the security of the state but also the risk that his escape may arouse public alarm and lower the reputation of the police and prison service.

Prisoners are classified for security purposes by the Prison Department of the Home Office. The 'highly dangerous', category A, prisoners are selected by a special and separate administrative procedure, for an account of which we are grateful to the Prison Department of the Home Office.

The selection of category A prisoners is in the hands of a Prison Department Headquarters Committee, consisting of officials most closely concerned with the management of such prisoners, attended by an experienced governor of a prison holding prisoners under conditions of maximum security. Prisons are required to notify the Prison Department Headquarters of the reception of any prisoner who is charged with or convicted of murder (except 'domestic' murder), an offence against the Official Secrets Acts, robbery that features violence, a violent sexual assault or terrorism; or who is indicated by the police as 'exceptionally dangerous' and likely to be eligible for inclusion in category A. A preliminary scrutiny of available information from Prison Department files or police records leads to the provisional allocation of a number of such prisoners to category A. Any prisoner so allocated before conviction who subsequently receives a sentence which indicates that the trial court took a less serious view of his offence than seemed warranted on the evidence available to the Prison Department is removed from the category. The rest, still provisionally in category A, are placed in an Allocation Centre where detailed reports are prepared for the assistance of the Committee, which must give full consideration to each case and reach a firm decision on whether or not the prisoner shall remain in category A, and, in either case, to which prison he should be allocated. Allocation Centre reports provide formal and informal assessments of the prisoner's character and reaction to his sentence. They are supplemented by police descriptions of the prisoner's offence and antecedents; his notoriety; the publicity and public alarm which would arise if he escaped; the effect of his escape on the reputation and morale of the prison service; and the likelihood of his escape (with particular reference to the assistance available from his associates who are capable of aiding his escape and the funds available, perhaps from the proceeds of his crime, which could be used for the purpose). The most important consideration, however, is the likelihood that, if at large, the prisoner would commit a further serious offence. The risk is, of course, difficult to assess and the Committee must rely largely on the details of the offence, together with the assessment of the prisoner by police, doctors, probation officers and prison staff who know him primarily from their dealings with him. The Committee also takes account of any opinion expressed by the judge at the prisoner's trial or in any letter he might write to the Home Secretary. Their recommendations are thus based on a number of subjective judgments from a variety of sources.

The outcome of this selection procedure was described in a recent Home Office publication as follows:

Only about 1% of all sentenced adult male prisoners and a handful of women and young prisoners are currently placed in the highest security category: those whose escape would be highly dangerous to the police or the public or the security of the state. Almost all convicted category A prisoners are serving sentences of 10 years or over and about 40% are serving life sentences. They are not a homogeneous group in other respects. They include one or two spies and a considerable number of professional criminals, most with violent records, some of whom have associates outside who might be willing to help them escape. About one third are dangerous sexual offenders, whose escape would endanger the public but who may present no particular threat while in custody.   (Home Office 1977: 117)

Following the recommendations of the Radzinowicz Committee (Advisory Council on the Penal System 1968) on the regime of long-term prisoners in conditions of maximum security, category A prisoners are held in a small number of prisons known as dispersal prisons. In addition, there are two special security wings in which those who combine the dangerousness of category A with great resources for escape may be held. A variety of considerations are taken into account in deciding to which prison any prisoner should be allocated. These include the need to avoid dangerous combinations of prisoners by separating co-defendants or associates from previous prison sentences, the nature of the regime in each prison,[1] and the need to place a prisoner as near as possible to his home, in order that he may maintain links with the outside world, or for other considerations of a compassionate nature.

Category A prisoners are defined as 'highly dangerous', but their dangerousness is held under close review. Each case is reconsidered at least annually and special reviews may be undertaken at any time on the request of a prison governor. The Committee looks for evidence that time spent in custody since his conviction has eroded a prisoner's dangerousness to a point where he no longer falls within the definition contained in the Mountbatten Report. The length of time spent by prisoners in category A is governed by no norm; but it would be totally exceptional for a man to be held in category A up to the time of the expiry of the sentence. The Committee seeks to ensure that category A prisoners are given adequate time in a less restrictive regime to prepare themselves for release.

Parole and Release on Licence

Prisoners detained under conditions of maximum security (like mentally abnormal offenders detained in secure hospitals subject to special restrictions) are clearly labelled 'highly dangerous'. In addition, there is a less well defined group of offenders in prisons or in secure hospitals, whose dangerousness is a reason for the refusal of the authorities to grant parole (or, in the case of those serving a life sentence, to release them on licence) or to discharge them from hospital. Parole, or release on licence, is a privilege, not a right of prisoners and no reasons are given for the decisions taken. However, the more generously the privilege is granted, the more likely it is that serious offenders whose applications are refused are being detained because they are regarded as dangerous.[2]

The Home secretary is the final judge in every case of whether a dangerous offender may be safely released. His discretion is unfettered in the case of those who are detained in mental hospitals; however, he may not disregard the advice of the Parole Board that a prisoner should not be released.

The considerations to be taken into account in reviews of fixed or life sentences are not laid down by the law. A certain amount has been said about them in the Annual Reports of the Parole Board.[3] But the most concrete statement of policy is contained in the latest edition of *Notes for the Guidance of Local Review Committees* which are reproduced in the Annual Report of the Parole Board for 1975. The Report quotes the remarks of the Home Secretary in announcing an extension of the use of parole:

> It remains important that the grant of parole should not expose the public to serious danger during a period when the prisoner would otherwise be serving his sentence in prison. If a prisoner has previously committed crimes such as serious offences of violence or major professional crimes, parole is justified only if there is good reason to believe that he will avoid crime in future. . . .

The *Notes* for Local Review Committees took up this point, and said

> Common sense and general experience will best guide committee members in identifying cases where the danger is grave. The following are no more than fairly obvious examples:
>
> a. A person concerned, usually as a member of a gang, in a sophisticated crime intended to produce a large reward and accompanied by the use, or readiness to use, lethal weapons. Only one conviction of such a crime is sufficient to classify a person as a grave offender.
> b. A person concerned in an act of terrorism, such as the placing of bombs or the hijacking of aircraft. Only one conviction of such a crime is sufficient to classify a person as a grave offender.
> c. A person convicted of more than one sophisticated crime intended to produce a large reward, committed on different occasions, even if violence has not been used or contemplated.
> d. A person convicted of more than one act of violence (including sexual assault) or arson, commited on different occasions, leading to prolonged suffering, disability or stress for the victims.
> e. A person convicted of only one such act of violence (including sexual assault) or arson if owing to his mental condition there is a substantial risk of repetition.

Offenders not falling into any of the above categories are unlikely
to present a grave threat to the public. But the operative word is
'unlikely'. The infinite variety of cases defies simple classification
and members of committees, like members of the Parole Board,
must make their own judgments in unusual or borderline cases.

The *Notes* went on, however, to add that even prisoners who had committed what was clearly the one offence of their lives, and for whom
early parole would normally be justified, would include a few exceptions: '. . . for example, notorious cases of fraud or breach of trust and
cases which, though not nationally notorious, have given rise to serious
local concern. Each case must be considered in the light of the peculiar
circumstances.' These *Notes,* prepared in the Home Office, indicate a
policy for the exercise of administrative discretion in determining a
prisoner's dangerousness which is close in spirit and substance to that
adumbrated by the judges of the Court of Appeal in the same year,
1975.[4] Offenders are treated administratively as 'dangerous' when they
are refused parole or release on licence because they present what is
deemed to be an unacceptable risk of serious harm, either because of
the nature of their crime or because of their record as serious offenders.
The risk of harm is taken for granted when the offender stands convicted of a crime of the kind described by the judges of the Court of
Appeal as 'abnormal' and well illustrated in the *Notes.* Offenders
convicted of such crimes are *ipso facto* 'dangerous'. The ordinary run
of serious offenders, whose crimes are not of this 'abnormal' kind,
are not normally to be treated as presenting a special risk of future
harm unless they have been convicted of at least two serious offences,
committed on separate occasions, notwithstanding that they may be
serving long sentences which have been fixed with protective considerations in mind, or even a life sentence.

Discharge from Secure Hospitals

Offenders admitted to hospital (without restrictions) under section 60
of the Mental Health Act have a right to apply to a Mental Health
Review Tribunal for their discharge.

The Mental Health Act provides for Tribunals to be established for
each health region in England and for Wales. The Lord Chancellor
appoints individuals to the panels for each region and also appoints
the chairman, who must be a lawyer, who has responsibility for selecting
from the panels the three or more members who will constitute the
Tribunal to hear a particular case. A legally qualified member always
sits as president of the Tribunal and it must also contain a medical
member (a consultant psychiatrist holding appropriate professional
qualifications) and a member chosen as having qualities or experience
which are likely to be useful to the Tribunal. The primary question for

the Tribunal in ordinary cases is whether the offender is suffering from mental disorder and if the answer is 'no' they must discharge him. The question of his dangerousness does not arise unless he is found to be still suffering from mental disorder; but even if he is still disordered they are nevertheless bound to order his discharge if his detention does not seem necessary 'in the interests of his health or safety or for the protection of other persons' (s. 123. Mental Health Act 1959).

An offender placed under special restrictions for the protection of the public has no right of application to the Tribunal and the Tribunal has no power to discharge him. The Home Secretary, however, is obliged to refer his case to a Tribunal for advice within two months, if so requested, after the end of the first year or thereafter at stated intervals.

The Mental Health Review Tribunals are governed by procedural rules made under statute which give them a quasi-judicial character. At present few of these rules apply to the cases of restricted patients, though in practice the procedures followed in these cases are similar in most respects and, in particular, the restricted patient may be legally represented at the Tribunal hearing if he so wishes.

After hearing the case the Tribunal does not take a decision but, instead, forwards its conclusions to the Home Secretary as advice and he is the final judge of whether the patient can safely be released. The Tribunal's advice to the Home Secretary is regarded as confidential. Recommendations are often wide-ranging and apart from addressing itself to the question of immediate discharge of the patient from hospital, the advice might for example suggest that the Home Secretary shall consent to the transfer of the patient from a special hospital like Broadmoor to a less secure hospital nearer the patient's home, as a first step towards discharge into the community. We are informed that, in the experience of the Home Office, Tribunals when advising the Home Secretary on the cases of restricted patients do so mainly from the point of view of the patients' interests. In the cases of restricted patients the Home Secretary does not, in practice, look to the Tribunal for advice on whether or not a particular offender is dangerous, though Tribunals do sometimes comment on a patient's dangerousness and no doubt the Home Secretary sometimes takes this advice into account. The ordinary Home Office procedures for deciding whether to discharge a restricted patient seem to be informal. Advice is always sought from the doctor in charge of the case and may be sought also from other persons who are thought to have knowledge of the patient and his circumstances. An extra safeguard is provided in a few cases judged to present a special risk. On admission to a secure hospital the doctor in charge, either of his own motion or on the advice of the Home Office, may 'star' a patient-offender as needing, if his discharge is under consideration, to be referred to the Advisory Board on Restricted Patients.

This body was set up in 1973 following the report of the Aarvold Committee on the Review of the Procedures for the Discharge and Supervision of Psychiatric Patients subject to Special Restriction (Home Office 1973). The Home Secretary will not release a 'starred' patient against the advice of the Advisory Board. This procedure does not have the force of statute, but the Home Secretary has imposed it on himself to safeguard against disasters such as the release of Graham Young[5] which led to the Aarvold review in the first place. The proceedings of the Advisory Board on Restricted Patients are private and unregulated, like those of the Parole Board; and its power to prevent the release of a dangerous offender is effectively the same. The Butler Committee proposed a substantial enlargement of its scope.

The procedures of the Mental Health Review Tribunals are quasi-judicial in character. The Rules governing their work deal, *inter alia*, with the following matters: representation of the offender; his appearance before the Tribunal and presence during the hearing of his case; disclosure to him or his representative of evidence before the Tribunal; the admissibility of evidence; the administration of the oath and the power of subpoena; privacy of Tribunal proceedings; hearing procedure; decisions and the giving of reasons to the offender. Few of these Rules apply in the cases of restricted patients referred to the Tribunal by the Home Secretary, though in practice the procedures followed are similar in most respects. The Committee on Mental Health Review Tribunal Procedures expressed the view in their 1978 Discussion Paper that the absence of procedural rules in these instances was wrong in principle and also led to some confusion and uncertainty. They thought that the hearing of all cases before the Tribunals should be governed by similar procedural rules, with differences only when necessary to cover the special circumstances of restricted offenders.

No procedural rules govern the work of the bodies charged with reviewing the sentences of prisoners: the Parole Board and the Local Review Committees in the prisons in which prisoners are detained. This difference in the treatment of the cases of legally dangerous offenders according to whether they are detained in hospitals or in prison, reflects the deep reluctance in the English criminal justice system to give explicit and distinctive recognition to the practice of protective sentencing.

Notes

1. The regime of prisoners detained under conditions of maximum security in dispersal prisons includes, *inter alia*, searches, close supervision of visits and letters and restrictions on the activities in prison in which such prisoners may take part. It is worth noting that Lord Mountbatten made a number of humane suggestions for what he called 'social and psychological aids to security' which would 'make it easier for the vast majority of prisoners to accept their sentences' (para. 318). The following examples show what he had in mind:

The closer the relationship between prisoners and staff, and the more the majority of prisoners accept the fairness of their treatment, the easier it will be to detect symptoms of unrest which often indicate the planning of an escape attempt.

(para. 332)

In the newest prisons it would be possible, by slightly reducing the cell space to provide additional water closets and a much needed shower bath, to bring the arrangements up to a reasonable standard.

(para. 323)

Where a prisoner has a reasonably stable marriage and is serving a sentence of any length, there should be the possibility of home visits . . . at regular intervals in the course of the sentence . . . I make this recommendation primarily because I believe it would contribute towards the stabilisation of prisoners for whom there are good hopes of rehabilitation, and because I believe it would add to the other psychological and social measures discussed in the preceding paragraphs which might reduce the incentives to escape.

(para. 324)

The policy of giving very long sentences up to and including the full life of a prisoner introduces a new type of imprisonment bringing with it human problems which will have to be faced. Among these is the question of family contacts, and I hope consideration will be given to this question for prisoners who cannot, for security reasons, be allowed home on parole.

(para. 325)

A liberal, and what may seem a permissive regime, if it is carefully introduced and controlled and if a few determined escapers are prevented from taking advantage of it, so far from increasing risks to security can help positively.

(para. 326)

2. In August 1975 the Home Secretary announced the extension of the use of parole to 'more than 60% of prisoners who are eligible but do not receive it'. The figures for 1979 indicate that about 39% of prisoners who apply for it fail to get parole at some time before their due date for release; but no separate account is given of those convicted of serious offences and the figure may be higher for them. In 1979 the Parole Board considered the cases of 282 life prisoners of which 63% were refused release on licence.

3. See the Reports of the Parole Board for England and Wales for 1968: 58–62; 1969: 39–43, 54; 1970: 47; 1972: 3; 1973: 14–16.

4. *R. v. Turner and others* (1975), 61 Cr. App. R. 67. See Chapter 5, pp. 82–5.

5. Graham Young was originally committed to Broadmoor at the age of 14, after he had intentionally poisoned more than one member of his family. His detention was under a restriction order with a 15-year limit. Nine years later he was conditionally released, but within a few months had poisoned several of his workmates, two fatally. He was sentenced to life imprisonment in 1972; and it was his case which was largely responsible for the setting up of the Aarvold Committee, whose recommendations now govern the consideration of the release of patients subject to restriction orders.

CHAPTER 7

For and Against Change

The concept of 'dangerousness' in English criminal justice is elusive. It is not used with any precision and the nature of the risk to which it refers is never defined in terms so as to make it contestable. It is possible, as we have seen, to piece together an account of what it is that the English public is thought to need protecting against; of what, in this country, a man must do to place himself at risk of being judged *dangerous*; and in broad terms, how much protection the courts will afford the public by means of exceptional sentences of one kind or another. But these matters are far from explicit.

This account of current policy and practice raises certain closely connected questions concerning, on the one hand, the extent and adequacy of the protection afforded to the public against the 'dangerousness' of certain offenders; and on the other, the scope of judicial and administrative powers of judging offenders to be 'dangerous' and of dealing with them accordingly.

The ethical concerns upon which controversy in the United States is mainly focused have, until very recently (Bottoms 1977), attracted little attention in this country. These relate to the nature of the concept of human dangerousness; the scientific pitfalls and practical difficulties in the way of assessing it for legal purposes; and the moral objections to making use of it in the administration of criminal justice. We considered these fundamental questions in Part I. Here we are concerned with criticisms of the present arrangements in Britain which have been directed, in the main, to the question of public safety; in particular, to the limitations of ordinary custodial sentences for dealing with 'dangerous' offenders, but also to the scope given to judicial and administrative discretion in sentencing practice.

Protection of the Public

The protection afforded by ordinary custodial sentences is incidental to their primary retributive and deterrent purposes. Their length is related to the seriousness of the offence of which an offender stands convicted, rather than to his dangerousness in terms of the probability that he will inflict grave harm in the future.

The Scottish Council on Crime in their Report (1975) noted with concern the rise in recorded violent crime in Scotland. Being convinced that 'there is within society a small but important group of individuals who are violence-prone and who are potential perpetrators of serious crimes of violence', they recommended the introduction in Scotland of a new form of court disposal, a 'public protection order' which would be available, under an extensive range of safeguards, to secure the continued detention of a violence-prone offender 'until it is safe for him to be released'.

The criminal process, the Council argued, looks back rather than forward and in this it contrasts with compulsory measures under the mental health laws, which are based on the need for future protection:

> If all offenders were suffering from mental disorders of a nature and degree which warranted detention in hospital, the protection of the public would (in theory, at least) be adequately achieved. There are, however, dangerous offenders whose condition does not warrant their detention in hospital under a hospital order and whose dangerousness, moreover, is not closely correlated with the seriousness of the offence of which they stand convicted before a court. [Thus:] A man may commit an act of extreme violence – say, murder his wife and family – because of a domestic situation which is highly unlikely ever to recur; and that man may not be a future danger. Another may be before the court for his second pub brawl – perhaps charged only as breach of the peace – and yet there may be strong circumstantial and psychological evidence that he is a dangerously violent person, and that it has been the result of chance or the intervention of other people that his past aggressive behaviour has not resulted in death or serious injury, [in which case] the criminal court at most only imposes a short prison sentence, with a short period of protection of the public, leaving the public unprotected thereafter until a more serious crime is committed on one of its members and the longer prison sentence is imposed.

In England, the Butler Committee in their Report on the Mentally Abnormal Offender (Home Office 1975) reported that they had received a memorandum, prepared jointly by officials of the Home Office and the Department of Health and Social Security, which drew attention to the same problem of 'the legal obligation to release at the end of a fixed prison sentence a small number of men who are probably dangerous but who are not acceptable for treatment in hospital'. The Committee acknowledged a 'defect in society's defences' and recommended that it should be made good by means of a new form of indeterminate sentence: the 'reviewable sentence' for offenders 'who are dangerous, who present a history of mental disorder, who cannot be dealt with under the Mental Health Act and for whom a life sentence is not appropriate'.

Neither committee offered an estimate of the size of the problem, though both were clear that the number of such offenders was small. Dr B. D. Cooper, Senior Medical Officer, H.M. Prison, Parkhurst, told us that, in his opinion, they numbered fewer than three hundred.[1]

The limitations of ordinary custodial sentences for protective purposes are thrown into sharper relief with the decline in the use of the penalty of imprisonment and the trend to shorter sentences for less serious offences. When the Advisory Council on the Penal System in their report on *Sentences of Imprisonment* (1978) proposed that this trend be consolidated and rationalised, they necessarily confronted the problem. They acknowledged that in recommending a drastically scaled-down structure of maximum ordinary sentences, which would narrow the present wide gap between the maximum permissible and the normal range of ordinary sentences, they were largely eliminating the discretionary power of the court to deal with the exceptional case of the offender judged likely to cause serious harm in the future. They, therefore, provided for a special sentence which might exceed the permissible maximum in such cases, its length to be left entirely to the discretion of the court without the constraint of a statutory maximum. Thus they accepted the need for the distinction, made in practice by the courts, between the 'ordinary' and the 'dangerous' offender and proposed, in effect, that it be formalised.

The Report did not say, however, what the Council expected or intended to be the effect of their recommendations on the size and composition of the group of offenders (other than those committed to mental hospitals) who are at present effectively classed as *dangerous* and sentenced accordingly. It may be presumed that few of those now given a discretionary life sentence (53 in 1978) would escape the proposed new special sentence; but the effect of the proposed reduction of the gap between the permissible maxima and the normal range of ordinary determinate sentences is hard to estimate. There is no means of discovering the number of determinate sentences which are at present fixed with protective considerations in mind. It seems likely that they are often imposed for offences against property, which are largely excluded from the range of serious harms for which the Advisory Council reserve the protection of their special sentence. However that may be, the longer the determinate sentence, the less likely it is that it will have been fixed with protective considerations in mind. Since such considerations in determinate sentencing are disavowed by the Court of Appeal, a large proportion of the longer sentences — say, those of more than seven years (191 in 1978) — are likely to reflect only the gravity of the crime together with the offender's record. Moreover, the history of preventive detention and of extended sentences shows how reluctant English judges are to make use of special precautionary measures — though, no doubt, they would be readier to do so if their discretionary powers were circumscribed.

All in all, it is probably realistic to estimate that not more than half of the annual total of long determinate sentences *plus* most discretionary life sentences could be expected to be replaced by the proposed special sentence: if so, the total in 1978 would have been about 140.

Discretionary Powers

A large part of English sentencing practice is determined by judges and administrators in the exercise of their discretionary powers and only a small part by legislation. In their report on *Sentences of Imprisonment* (1978), the Advisory Council on the Penal System pointed out that the maximum penalties prescribed by Parliament for specific crimes have little or no influence upon the level of judicial sentencing and do not provide a valid guide to sentencing policy or practice, because they are fixed with reference to the 'worst possible cases' and hence bear no relation to the vast bulk of cases dealt with by the courts. Parliament in its penal legislation has impinged only marginally on the sentencing powers of the courts; it has understandably been much more insistent in circumscribing the release powers of the Executive.

The English system gives a great deal of scope to judicial discretion in the choice of offenders for protective measures and no doubt most judges, at any rate, regard this as a strength rather than a weakness of the present arrangements. However, the view that a sentence intended, even if only in part, to protect the public by forestalling harmful conduct represents a more serious infringement of rights than an ordinary retributive sentence and should not be freely available to the courts, is not foreign to the English system. It clearly underlies the elaborate statutory conditions which must be met before an offender may even be considered for the extended sentence. The objection to leaving the court with complete discretion to choose offenders for special treatment because they are judged to be dangerous seems to apply equally to the covert protective element in many of the longer determinate sentences passed under the present system; and as we have seen, the introduction of protective considerations into the fixing of ordinary sentences is disavowed by the Court of Appeal.

Whatever view be taken of the case for greater legislative control of the ordinary sentencing powers of the judiciary, there cannot be much doubt about the desirability and importance of restricting by statute the scope of protective sentencing, by specifying the kind of harm to which it may apply and the characteristics of the offenders on whom protective sentences may be imposed.

There is more room for debate over judicial discretion to determine the length of protective sentences. Wholly individualised and indeterminate sentences are anathema to many penologists as representing arbitrariness and injustice. On the other hand, the 'fixed' sentence provided, for example, in the recent Californian law (Uniform Determinate Sentencing Act 1978), is open to equally strong objections of the same kind: it is arbitrary and unjust in practice, insofar as it allows only the minimum discretion to the judge to deal with the question of aggravation or mitigation and no discretion to the Executive in terms of early release. The Advisory Council sought a middle course between these two extremes. They took the view that judicial discretion was insufficiently circumscribed by statutory law. They sought to restrict the wide discretion now permitted to the courts by the practice of fixing a maximum sentence for each offence which would be high enough for the worst cases. At the same time they chose, in making their recommendations, to confer on the courts what they described as a 'useful breadth of discretion in dealing with serious cases'. A maximum penalty of life imprisonment means in effect that there is no statutory limit to the length of the determinate sentence which may be imposed. The Council made clear their objection to the wholly indeterminate life sentence. They recommended only with great reluctance its retention for certain non-homicidal offences for which it is currently imposed. They nevertheless rejected the option of providing that all other protective sentences of determinate length exceeding the maximum should be subject to either a uniform limit or one fixed for the offence in question. They 'found the rigidity of a fixed limit unattractive as a means for dealing with cases which would have widely ranging characteristics' and decided to recommend that where the maximum was to be exceeded there should be no statutory limit to the length of any determinate sentence.

As to the administration of the sentences imposed by the courts, the uncertainties and discriminatory implications of the present discretionary system of parole and release on licence are productive of much dissatisfaction among prisoners and are the subject of much criticism of the discretionary powers of the Executive. These criticisms apply with particular force to the administration of protective sentences. In recommending new forms of protective sentence both the Butler Committee and the Scottish Council on Crime proposed that the new sentence should be subject to obligatory review every two years, a review at which the protection of others would be the only consideration. The Scottish Council went further in recommending that at the review the onus should lie on those who thought the prisoner should be detained longer to show why this should be so; detention would be renewable at the two-yearly review only if a positive case were established and the prisoner would have a right of appeal to a court of law against the decision to continue his detention.

Other Approaches

The laws of most, if not all, western countries make provision for the sentencing of offenders against whom the public requires special

FOR AND AGAINST CHANGE

protection. We have not made a comprehensive survey of other approaches to the problem, but it is clear that the availability and scope of protective sentences vary a great deal and that there are wide variations also in the extent to which judicial and administrative discretion determines sentencing practice. It seems fair to say that nowhere is the legislative framework satisfactory and nowhere is discretion appropriately regulated.

Some penal codes limit protective sentences to a short list of specified offences. Thus in Denmark *forvaring* ('protective custody') is confined by statute (s. 70 of the 1973 Code) to homicide, robbery, rape and other serious sexual offences, kidnapping, menaces, arson or attempts at any of these offences. This is the approach recommended by the Butler Committee for its 'reviewable sentence'; but the list of offences which they recommended was more extensive, chiefly because English law sub-divides offences into more groups.

At the other extreme are codes which appear to give wide discretion to the sentencing court. An example is the Swedish Penal Code of 1965, of which Chap. 30 provides that 'internment may be imposed if the crime . . . is punishable by imprisonment for two years or longer and in view of the defendant's criminality, mental condition, conduct and other circumstances, a long-lasting deprivation of liberty, without duration fixed in advance, is deemed necessary to prevent further serious criminality on his part'. Under this chapter the court can fix a *minimum* term of at least one and not more than 12 years, after which he may be detained longer or transferred to non-custodial supervision. (In 1974 only 37 such sentences were imposed, with very low minima, and on petty offenders.)

Some codes limit the availability of protective sentences to special categories of offender defined with reference to their past record rather than to the instant offence of which they stand convicted. The habitual criminal statutes in the United States (and the provision for the extended sentence in this country) are of this kind. Yet others take account also of special features of the instant offence which seem indicative of a wilful disposition to inflict harm. For example, the United States Federal Criminal Code provides for an extended sentence of imprisonment for 'a dangerous special offender' (Sleffel 1977: 29–32). A 'special offender' is one who satisfies one of the following criteria:

(a) he has at least two previous convictions for offences punishable by death or imprisonment in excess of one year, and was imprisoned for one or more of these previous offences, and has committed the present felony offence within 5 years either of release from such a sentence of imprisonment or of the commission of one of these previous offences;

(b) he committed the present offence as part of a pattern of criminal conduct, constituting a substantial source of income and manifesting special skill or expertise;

(c) the present offence was, or was committed, in furtherance of, a conspiracy, with 3 or more other persons, and the defendant did, or agreed to, initiate, organise, plan, finance, direct, manage, or supervise all or part of such conspiracy or conduct, or give or receive a bribe or use force as all or part of such conduct.

These complex criteria for determining an offender's eligibility for a protective sentence are not matched when it comes to the determination of the threat he presents to public safety: an extended sentence of imprisonment may be imposed 'if a period of confinement longer than that provided for such felony is required for the protection of the public from further criminal conduct by the defendant'.

Few codes, in fact, specify the nature of the harm against which the public need to be protected. The so-called sexual psychopath statutes in the United States are directed specifically against sexual offenders but are notoriously vague when it comes to determining the content of an offender's dangerousness. Apart from a finding that the offender has a mental disorder or disability and a propensity to commit sex offences, they merely require a determination that he is, or is considered to be, a danger to others (Sleffel 1977: 89–100).

The American Law Institute's Model Penal Code is no more precise in this respect. Its 'criteria for an extended term of imprisonment' (ss. 7.L3, 7.O4) rely heavily on the phrase 'protection of the public', but without indicating what it is that the public needs protection against. The criteria are that

(1) the defendant is a persistent offender whose commitment for an extended term is necessary for protection of the public (the section goes on to specify a minimum age and previous number of convictions).

or (2) the defendant is a professional criminal whose commitment . . . is necessary for protection of the public. (The section goes on to define professionalism as devoting oneself knowingly to criminal activity as a major source of livelihood, or having resources not accountable as derived from a source other than criminal activity.)

or (3) the defendant is a dangerous mentally abnormal person whose commitment . . . is necessary for protection of the public. The Court shall not make such a finding unless the defendant has been subjected to a psychiatric examination resulting in the conclusion that his mental condition is gravely abnormal: that his criminal conduct has been characterized by a pattern of repetitive or compulsive behavior or by persistent aggressive behavior with heedless indifference to consequences: and that such condition makes him a serious danger to others.

or (4) the defendant is a multiple offender (sc an offender simultaneously convicted of several offences ?) whose criminality
was (sic) so extensive that a sentence of imprisonment for an
extended term is warranted (Note the absence of any mention
of the protection of the public) . . . (the section goes on to
specify restrictions).

or (5) (in the case of a misdemeanour) the defendant is a chronic
alcoholic, narcotic addict, prostitute or person of abnormal
mental condition who requires rehabilitative treatment for a
substantial period of time . . . (the section goes on to insist
on commitment to an appropriate institution).

Note that criterion (3) actually uses the adjective 'dangerous' although
in an apparently redundant way (since the effect of the criterion would
be the same without the adjective). But why is the adjective used only
in connection with mental abnormality, and not in connection with the
other criteria? Is it implied that while the public needs protection
against offenders of types (1), (2), (4) and (5), they are not dangerous?

Another American proposal 'for the protection of the public' was
contained in the Model Sentencing Act of the National Council on
Crime and Delinquency in 1963:

s.5 *Dangerous offenders*
Except for the crime of murder in the first degree, the court may
sentence a defendant convicted of a felony to a term of thirty years,
or to a lesser term, if it finds that, because of the dangerousness of
the defendant, such period of confined correctional treatment or
custody is required for the protection of the public, and if it
further finds . . . that one or more of the following grounds exist:
(a) the defendant is being sentenced for a felony in which he
inflicted or attempted to inflict serious bodily harm, and the
court finds that he is suffering from a severe personality
disorder indicating a propensity towards criminal activity;
(b) the defendant is being sentenced for a crime which seriously
endangered the life or safety of another, has been previously
convicted of one or more felonies not related to the instant
crime as a single criminal episode, and the court finds that he
is suffering from a severe personality disorder indicating a
propensity toward criminal activity;
(c) the defendant is being sentenced for the crime of extortion,
compulsory prostitution, selling or knowingly and unlawfully
transporting narcotics, or other felony, committed as part of
a continuing criminal activity in concert with one or more
persons.

(This is followed by procedural requirements as to psychiatric reports
and other evidence necessary for such findings.) Note that this draft
also uses the word 'dangerousness', redundantly. In this case, however,
it is implied that all three types of offender are dangerous.

It is harder to formulate a satisfactory definition of grave harm for the purposes of protective sentencing than it is to delimit the category of eligible offenders and it is not surprising that the task has been so frequently shirked by the legislature and left to the courts. The apparently straightforward approach to a definition in terms of legal offence-categories will not serve: the specification must be in more general terms. Moreover, the difficulties are political as well as conceptual. There are wide differences of opinion as to when protective measures are justifiable, as well as problems with the classification of harms by kind and degree.

There are, however, a few statutes which do provide a substantive definition of dangerousness by specifying the harm against which the public is entitled to special protection. For example, the new Canadian Criminal Code, which embodies many of the proposals of the Canadian Committee on Corrections (1969), is more specific. It provides for the indeterminate detention of an offender who has committed a 'serious personal injury offence' (restrictively defined in s. 687 of the Act) if it is established to the satisfaction of the court that:

> the offender constitutes a threat to the life, safety or physical or mental well-being of other persons on the basis of evidence establishing:
>   (i) a pattern of repetitive behaviour by the offender, of which the offence for which he has been convicted forms a part, showing a failure to restrain his behaviour and a likelihood of his causing death or injury to other persons, through failure in the future to restrain his behaviour,
>   (ii) a pattern of persistent aggressive behaviour by the offender, of which the offence for which he has been convicted forms a part, showing a substantial degree of indifference on the part of the offender as to the reasonably foreseeable consequences to other persons of his behaviour; or
>   (iii) any behaviour by the offender associated with the offence for which he has been convicted, that is of such a brutal nature as to compel the conclusion that his behaviour in the future is unlikely to be inhibited by normal standards of behavioural restraint.

As to their form, protective sentences vary widely. Perhaps three basic forms can be distinguished: the wholly indeterminate sentence (i.e. indeterminate in respect of the length of time spent both in custody and in the community under licence); the semi-determinate or 'reviewable' sentence; and the 'renewable' or extendable sentence.

The wholly indeterminate sentence seems to be most common; but there is a variety of methods of review and release. Some provisions resemble the arrangements for the review of the English life sentence and merely provide for administrative review without statutory safeguards: several sexual-psychopath statutes in the United States embody provisions of this kind (Sleffel 1977). Other arrangements require review at specified regular intervals by an administrative review body, perhaps with certain evidential and procedural safeguards. The new Canadian Criminal Code requires review after three years, and not later than every two years thereafter. A few provisions require review by a court as well as, or in preference to, an administrative body. For example, the Canadian Committee on Corrections (1969: 262) recommended that, in addition to an automatic annual review by the Parole Board, a person sentenced to preventive detention as a dangerous offender should be entitled to a hearing every three years to determine whether he should be further detained. And the sentence of indefinite detention in Denmark can be changed or rescinded only by the court (upon an application by the public prosecutor, the director of the institution, the guardian of the offender, or the offender himself) (Lønberg 1975: 26).

The semi-determinate sentence, with a maximum and a minimum, or simply a maximum, fixed by statute, or fixed by the court within statutory limits, leaves the actual date of release to be determined by an administrative body within the maximum specified. It is the form of sentence most commonly adopted in habitual criminal statutes in the United States which allow the permissible maximum sentence of imprisonment for an offence to be extended for offenders who meet the specified criteria of eligibility (Sleffel 1977: 1–18).

The renewable sentence, that is, a sentence of a length fixed by court or by statute with the express proviso that before its termination an application can be made to the court to extend it for a further fixed period, appears to be the least common form adopted. It is characteristic of sentencing statutes in Sweden and the Netherlands. In Sweden the sentence of 'internment' is effectively an extended sentence which may be lengthened by a review body for three to five years beyond the minimum term set by the judge. Thereafter it becomes a sentence renewable by the court for three years at a time upon the request of the internment board. In 1976, as we were informed by Professor H. Thornstedt, of Stockholm University, no such request had ever been made. The sentence of 'detention at the Government's pleasure' in the Netherlands, for offenders who at the time of their crime had 'defective development' or 'impairment of their mental faculties', also takes a renewable form. It is for a fixed period of two years but may be extended by one or two years any number of times by the courts as required.

Conclusions and Proposals

Having reviewed the present arrangements for safeguarding the public from the risk of serious harm from certain offenders, the arguments for change and some other approaches to the problem of protective sentencing, we found that we were not, on balance, of the opinion that a strong case had been made for the introduction of any new form of protective sentence whilst the present general structure and level of maximum sentences remains unchanged. It did not seem that the alleged weaknesses in these arrangements had been established clearly and convincingly enough to justify proposals, such as those of the Butler Committee or the Scottish Council on Crime, for an extension of the inherently objectionable practice of wholly indeterminate sentencing. Nor, on the other hand, did it seem that the manner in which judicial and administrative powers to declare and treat certain offenders as dangerous are at present exercised could be shown to be productive of such injustice as to call for immediate radical reform outside the framework of a general reform of sentencing practice. However, we were unanimously of the opinion that sentences of imprisonment should be much reduced in length and that were this to come about or be brought about – for example, by means of a drastic reduction in the maximum permissible lengths as recommended by the Advisory Council on the Penal System – a special protective sentence would be needed for a minority of exceptional offenders who, if left at large, would give rise to justifiable fear for the safety of the public.

As to the need for a new form of indeterminate sentence, the scale of the problem had not been demonstrated, though it was said to be small. It was alleged that there were at any time a number of prisoners who, on account of their mental condition or history of violent conduct, were highly likely to cause further grave harm when released at the end of their determinate sentences; but no arrangements had been made to follow the post-release careers of such offenders and there was in fact no evidence to show that determinate sentencing had actually resulted in serious harm which could have been prevented by the delayed release of certain offenders. The problem was too hypothetical, and possibly too small in any case, to justify incurring the increased risks of unnecessary detention which an extension of indeterminate sentencing would entail.

We were not in a position to assess the extent of the practice, disavowed by the Court of Appeal, of taking protective considerations into account in passing determinate sentences, though we noted that this was frequently done in cases of offences against property which were likely to fall outside the categories of grave harm to prevent which we thought it would be justifiable to impose a protective sentence. Like the Advisory Council, we rejected wholly indeterminate sentencing and we regretted the shift in policy which has led to a marked increase in the use made of the life sentence for non-homicidal offences in the last 10 years. However, though undoubtedly the decisions of the Parole Board are fallible, there appeared to be no substantial evidence that conclusions are reached which are ill-founded or unjust to the life-sentence prisoner; or that mistaken releases are indicative of a less than proper regard for the safety of the public.

We were left with the conclusion that while the present sentencing structure remains unaltered, the reform of the piecemeal and largely discretionary arrangements for protective sentencing might have little purpose or effect. If, however, a two-tiered structure, as proposed by the Advisory Council, were to be introduced the case for reform would not be in doubt; and we reached agreement on what would be necessary to deal justly and effectively with the minority of exceptional offenders who present an unacceptable risk of harm to the public. In such a system it would be necessary to remedy the lack of legal prescription which at present characterises the English arrangements for protective sentencing. Its scope and application would need to be precisely defined and delimited. The statutes should state clearly against what harms and which kinds of offender the public may be given the protection of a special sentence; what the form and length of such sentences may be and how they should be imposed and administered so as to satisfy the need to protect both the offender's right to challenge his sentence and the public claim to reasonable protection against the risk of serious harm from him in the future.

In general, we were disinclined to the view, sometimes advocated in relation to ordinary sentencing practice, that the less discretion permitted to the courts the better, allowing only for a necessary degree of flexibility in applying the law in practice. The problem with protective sentencing seems to be to achieve a right blend of statutory requirement and discretionary power. Individualisation and some degree of indeterminacy are essential to justice in protective sentencing: in this context they afford some guarantee that the risk of unnecessary detention, which is inherent in protective sentencing, will be kept to a minimum. We agreed upon the categories of harm against the risk of which we thought it right that the courts should be able to provide the protection of a special sentence for certain offenders and the criteria to be applied in selecting such offenders; and we formulated proposals for a semi-determinate form of protective sentence and arrangements for imposing and administering it which we believe would meet the requirements of justice better than present arrangements can be shown to do. The nature of these proposals is indicated here; they are fully described in Chapters 8, 9 and 10. They are meant to be the practical expression in the English context of the principles elicited from the discussion in Part I of the ethical and related problems of protective sentencing.

The difficulty of arriving at a satisfactory statutory framework for protective sentencing was not lost upon us when we considered the American and Scandinavian laws. They seemed mostly to provide for protective sentencing far wider in scope than we envisaged ourselves proposing, reluctantly and hesitantly, for adoption in the context of a new sentencing structure in which the maximum sentences for ordinary offenders would be drastically reduced; and they were directed to the selection of offenders without defining or specifying the harm against which the public was entitled to a measure of special protection.

As a preliminary to defining the categories of anticipated harm which would in certain circumstances justify a protective sentence, we attempted a clarification of the notion of 'grave harm' for this purpose which is reported in Chapter 4 and which is the basis for the categories we propose in Chapter 8. These categories are intended to be precise enough to become statutory law, acknowledging the right of members of the public to special protection against certain offenders if they are judged to present an unacceptable risk of grave harm to their lives, safety, or physical or mental well-being: either direct and specific harm from actions resulting in serious physical injury, serious psychological effects of exceptional personal hardship; or indirect and generalised harm from actions which damage the environment or the security of the state. Our classification is similar in its intended scope to that proposed by the Advisory Council, though it is formulated in somewhat more precise and concrete terms. Thus, we propose that the elements of grave physical and psychological harm should be specified (death; serious bodily injury; severe or prolonged pain or mental distress) and that serious sexual assaults, which we take to be harmful *sui generis*, should be given separate mention. We have added to the category of indirect, generalised harm represented in their classification by serious damage to the security of the state, another, viz., damage to the environment resulting in serious damage to public health or safety. We rejected the category 'damage to the general fabric of society' as being either redundant or too inclusive in its vagueness.

As to the selection of offenders, we propose that the statutes should restrict protective sentences to offenders who are at least 17 years of age at the time of the sentence and are ineligible for a hospital order under the terms of the Mental Health Act 1959 or, if ineligible, without a place in a secure hospital. We gave careful consideration to the problem of defining the *prima facie* case for a protective sentence. The requirement must be, as the Advisory Council conclude, that the offender should have done, risked, attempted, threatened or conspired to do serious harm, and this suggests that protective sentences should be limited to specified offences as proposed by the Butler Committee. On closer consideration, however, the attraction of this device proved to be spurious: it would meet the essential requirement that the harm to be prevented by the sentence should be present in the offender's criminal conduct; but its effect would be too restrictive for the purposes of providing protection. We propose that the difficulty be met by a provision in more general terms that the nature and circumstances of the offence of which the offender stands convicted should be such as to give rise to a reasonable fear that he will cause grave harm in the future; and that he should have been convicted (or found guilty as a juvenile) of at least one other act of a similar nature, committed on a separate occasion, leaving to the court the interpretation in this context of the evidence concerning the nature and circumstances of the relevant offences.

We did not think that the statutes should prescribe tests of dangerousness: for example, the pattern of behaviour or mental condition which would justify the conclusion that an offender was all but certain, more likely than not, or more likely than others of similar age and circumstances, to inflict grave harm on someone in the foreseeable future, and the evidence that should be required to prove the case in these terms. We reviewed the extensive literature devoted to the problem of assessing dangerousness and reached the conclusions set out in Chapter 2. The nature of predictive judgments, the limited scope for precision and certainty in such judgments and the widely varying characteristics of the relatively few offenders likely to meet the qualifying conditions which we propose for a protective sentence, call for the exercise of a broad discretion rather than the application of statutory tests. Given clear statutory indications of the harm to be averted and of the duty of the court, in general terms, to have regard, in forming an opinion on the need for a protective sentence, to the nature of the offence of which the offender stands convicted and his character, conduct and antecedents, we felt that criteria and consistency in their application could be left to emerge from the exercise of discretion guided by case-law and practice directions from the Lord Chief Justice. It seemed more appropriate, and more likely to meet the requirements of justice, to hedge the making of predictive judgments with procedural safeguards than to attempt to regulate their scope and content; for example, as we propose *inter alia* in Chapter 8, to require the court to receive reports from a psychiatrist and a social worker, to provide for the defence to call their own expert witnesses, to make the assessment contestable and to require the court to give reasons for the sentence imposed.

We understood the reluctance with which the Advisory Council recommended the retention of the wholly indeterminate life sentence for murder and certain other serious offences for which it is currently imposed. In our view, all such sentences should be determinate. That they would be long sentences and not merely a slight stretching of the normal range of sentences we did not doubt: but we thought, for the reasons given in Chapter 4, that the protection afforded to the public should be proportional to the anticipated harm as well as related to the estimated duration of the risk. We saw no need, however, to fix either a general maximum length for protective sentences or limits specific to particular kinds of anticipated harm, provided that such sentences were automatically referred to the Court of Appeal as we propose they should be.

We agreed that protective sentences should entail the minimum curtailment of the offender's liberty compatible with their purpose and that, other things being equal, non-custodial measures are therefore to be preferred to custodial measures and specific to general curtailments of liberty. Our discussion of the practical problems of replacing custody by control through supervision in the community is reported in Chapter 9.

We favoured the introduction of quasi-judicial procedures into the review of protective sentences (Chapter 10); but we thought that the discretion of the Executive to release should be retained for the duration of the determinate sentence imposed by the court. This reflected our view that while protective sentences must not be freely available to the courts, once imposed they must be administered so as to do proper justice to the public interest as well as to the rights of the offender; and that there is a risk, if the responsibility for the decision to release is removed from the Executive, that less than justice may be done to the public interest. Our proposals make provision for regular and frequent reviews throughout a protective sentence, whether or not the offender is in custody, and thereafter for a period of up to three years of extended licence, at the discretion of the Executive. It may be necessary to provide a transitional period of supervised adjustment to life in the community, in cases where unconditional release from custody at the end of a determinate sentence would otherwise be unduly abrupt. We propose that the Home Secretary should be required to take account in reaching his decisions of the advice of a statutory Advisory Board for Special Offenders, as well as of the recommendations of the quasi-judicial Review Tribunal. The Advisory Board, its composition and procedures modelled on those of the Parole Board for dealing with the cases of life-sentence prisoners, would, in our view, be best suited to the requirements of the task of assessing the risk represented by an offender, whilst the Review Tribunal would secure his right to contest the decision to keep him in custody.

Notes

1. Brody and Tarling (1980) state that 9.5% of a 1 in 10 sample of adult men serving sentences in English prisons in the South-east in 1972 could, from all available descriptions of them, reasonably be described as 'dangerous'. A small number of serious cases among them had, by 1979, been released at the end of determinate sentences (ten long; four medium). Only one of these men had committed a seriously assaultive offence. The group of released 'dangerous' men as a whole had been responsible for nine such offences — half the total number recorded against all the released prisoners whose subsequent careers could be followed up.

PART III

Protective Sentencing

CHAPTER 8

A Statutory Framework

We come now to describe our proposals for sentencing the minority of exceptional, high-risk serious offenders in the context of a general reduction in the maximum permissible length of ordinary sentences. Such a reduction would severely curtail, if not for practical purposes exclude, the discretionary power of the judiciary to deal with them other than by means of a life sentence when it is available. We foresee the need in such a situation for a statutory framework for protective sentencing which would, in effect, rationalise and make explicit the existing practice. We are far from envisaging any expansion in its scope and for the reasons we have given in Chapter 7, in discussing the Advisory Council's Report on Sentences of Imprisonment, we would expect the introduction of a special sentence, under the conditions we propose, to result in some retrenchment, notwithstanding the modest extent of present practice.

Our general objective is to bring protective sentencing under statutory control, while leaving ample scope for the necessary exercise of judicial discretion. As we have said, the English system leaves a great deal of scope to judicial discretion; but where long sentences are concerned it limits this discretion by statute. Thus the life sentence is confined by statute to a limited range of offences; and extended sentences for persistent offenders are circumscribed by elaborate statutory requirements which have to be satisfied before an offender is even eligible for consideration for such a sentence. The history of these sentences in the hands of the judiciary does little to encourage the fear that with more comprehensive provision the courts would seek to extend the practice of protective sentencing; but the case for statutory control of protective sentencing does not rest primarily on mistrust of the judiciary.

Most of the necessary control of protective sentencing should be statutory in form; but there will be a need for auxiliary controls of a less formal kind. Home Office circulars have occasionally been used, especially at magistrates' court level, to give advice about sentencing procedure: for example, about the need for social inquiry reports before sentencing certain categories of offender to imprisonment. But protective sentencing is a matter for the higher courts and the alternative device of a practice direction by the Lord Chief Justice would probably be more appropriate. This device has been used to guide courts on specific issues; for example, a practice direction was issued to guide the courts in the use of preventive detention and corrective training (Parker L.C.J. 1962), and similar guidance was given on the use of 'restriction orders' under the Mental Health Act 1959 (Parker L.C.J. 1967). Such a direction would have the decided advantage over a statute that it could offer procedural advice and give examples of the types of offenders who might or might not be suitable for particular types of protective sentences. In the past, practice directions have not usually been issued until experience has indicated that courts are misusing a power or a procedure. Moreover, they have not in the past been issued as a result of the recommendations of committees, although they have sometimes followed consultation with other bodies such as the Prison Department. However, there is no reason why the Lord Chief Justice should not feel able to give some initial guidance to sentencers on points which could not be included in a new piece of legislation and we have indicated below a number of points on which we think such guidance would be needed.

Scope and Limitations of Protective Sentencing

The passing of a protective sentence is a serious matter. The public is entitled to the protection of such a sentence only against grave harm; furthermore, no offender should be eligible for a protective sentence unless grave harm is manifested in his criminal conduct.

Grave harm

The interpretation of grave harm in this context is clearly of prime importance and should be prescribed by statute. Our first thought was that it should be as specific as possible. We considered whether we should follow the example of the Danish legislature (among others) and the Butler Committee and draw up a list of offences, using their legal definitions, which would serve both to define the harms against which the public is entitled to the protection of a special sentence and the sort of offences which would make it permissible for a court to consider imposing such a sentence. We appended to our Consultative Document (Appendix A) a list of offence-categories, each of which covered actions which might be thought to involve harm against the risk of which the public needs to be protected. They ranged from those that everyone agrees cause harm of this sort, in all or most cases, to those about which some would say that they rarely or, perhaps, never would do so. Certainly, the list went well beyond what we ourselves were inclined to think it should include. Respondents were invited to use this list to indicate their own view of what a schedule of qualifying offences for a protective custodial sentence should comprise. Unfortunately, the request was ineptly formulated; it smacked of circularity and was misunderstood in this sense by a number of people. Past and present members of the judiciary among our respondents were unanimous in rejecting the suggestion that judicial discretion to invoke protective considerations in fixing the length of determinate sentences should be limited. Nevertheless, all were willing to indicate which offences they thought should qualify an offender for a sentence wholly or partly designed to protect the public.

There were marked differences of opinion among the informed and interested persons who compiled qualifying schedules from the list. They included past and present members of the judiciary, the Parole Board, the Prison and Probation Services, the Police Forces, psychiatrists and criminologists as well as members of the general public. These differences turned on different attitudes to offences against property, sexual offences other than rape and offences of neglect and violence against children. A few persons thought that serious offences under the Road Traffic Act (e.g. causing death by reckless or dangerous driving) should be included on the list and a few others wished also to include offences such as keeping unsafe factories or polluting the environment by tipping toxic waste. No respondent referred to the discussion in the relevant paragraphs of the Report of the Butler Committee, or to the schedules of qualifying offences drawn up by that Committee in connection with their proposal for a reviewable sentence for certain mentally disordered offenders outside the terms of the Mental Health Act (1959) and ineligible for a life sentence.

In the event, our own view of the nature of the problem changed. On closer consideration the attraction of a list of qualifying offences turned out to be spurious. There is, to begin with, the difficulty that a list of offences will not readily serve to delimit the scope of the protection against future harm to be afforded by a special sentence. There are many ways of causing grave harm, however it be defined. A protective measure cannot sensibly be tied to a classification of criminal offences which has been devised for the purpose of attributing criminal responsibility to individuals in terms of their acts and intentions and not as a means of defining the types and degrees of harm which result from their acts.

Then there is the difficulty that though a list of qualifying offences appears to protect offenders against the imposition of long sentences when the offence of which they stand convicted is not itself very harmful, the compilation of such a list creates an immediate dilemma. If it is a fairly short list restricted to very harmful offences it excludes offences of a kind which occasionally bring to light offenders very likely to cause grave harm. It would exclude the sort of case in which it is clear from the evidence, taken together with the offender's previous history and other information about him, that he is quite as likely to cause grave harm as an offender who is convicted of a very harmful offence, but the evidence alone leads to conviction for a lesser 'wide spectrum' offence (for instance, malicious wounding as distinct from intentionally causing grievous bodily harm). If, on the other hand, the list is long enough to include all such lesser offences, it may suggest to courts that they should automatically consider a protective sentence whenever someone is convicted of any such offence (and is otherwise eligible), which is by no means what we intend. It would be necessary to add the requirement that the behaviour should fulfil certain other requirements which are not necessarily part of the legal definitions of the offences; and if so it seems necessary to have two lists, one a lengthy list of offences, the other a list of the things against which protection should be provided and which can be more easily and clearly defined in other terms.

We took note of the experience of the Butler Committee which had sought to define an 'offence condition' by listing the offences which could, other conditions being satisfied, lead to a special sentence but had eventually found it necessary to distinguish: A. offences which would qualify an offender irrespective of previous convictions, if any; B. offences which would qualify him if he had previously been convicted of an offence on list A. In other words, list A proved to be not wide enough (though it included what might be regarded as the 'wide-spectrum' offence of arson); but the Committee did not feel able to add the offences on list B unconditionally. Yet the condition attached to list B offences overlaps with the requirement that in considering the need for a protective sentence the court should have regard to the offender's previous history; and it is, in any case, too restrictive a solution of the dilemma.

We abandoned the attempt to use legal offence-categories, either to delimit the scope of the protection to which the public was entitled or to restrict the class of eligible offenders by defining an 'offence condition' for the protective sentence. We did our best to clarify the concept of grave harm, as reported in Chapter 4, and agreed that a model statute should provide: (i) that the public shall be entitled to the protection of a special sentence only against grave harm; (ii) that certain other conditions being satisfied, any offence which has caused or was intended to cause grave harm could lead to a protective sentence; (iii) that *grave harm* shall be interpreted in this context as normally comprising the following categories: death; serious bodily injury; serious sexual assaults; severe or prolonged pain or mental distress; loss of or damage to property which results in severe personal hardship;

damage to the environment which has serious adverse effects on public health or safety; serious damage to the security of the state. We compared this proposal with the recommendations of the Advisory Council on the same matter in Chapter 7.

The definition of grave harm in these terms gives the courts the task of determining whether a particular offence comes within it and, if it does, whether it gives rise to reasonable anxiety about the future. Were the harmful consequences the result of an improbable contingency? (Was the victim's death the result of violence or the effect of alarm on his weak heart?) Might they well have been worse — was there an inherent risk of grave consequences? (Was the offender carrying a loaded shotgun though it was not brought into use on the occasion?)

Restricted eligibility

We think that the class of eligible offenders should be further delimited. Not only should it be defined with reference to the nature of the offence but it should be restricted to certain legally definable categories of offender. We considered the categories which have been used to restrict sentences in this way:

1. *age* (e.g. extended sentences are confined to offenders aged 21 or older). The Scottish Council on Crime adopted the age of 16 (when Scots become eligible for adult sentences). We agreed to recommend the age of 17, which is the corresponding age for England and Wales. Special arrangements exist (under s. 53(2) of the Children and Young Persons Act 1933) for young offenders who are thought to present a grave risk to the public to be detained for a long period and, in the case of offences which are punishable in the case of an adult with life imprisonment, indefinitely. But our proposals are concerned with young adult and adult offenders only.

2. *sex* (e.g. women cannot be sent to detention centres). But, obviously, there are women as well as men offenders who present a high risk of grave harm (e.g. terrorists) and it would be in any case inappropriate to reserve the protective sentence for men.

3. *previous convictions* (e.g. extended sentences require at least 3 previous convictions). But this is as evidence of *persistence*. As evidence of a risk of grave harm we think it reasonable to require that the offender shall have been convicted (or found guilty as a juvenile) of one other act of a similar nature to the instant offence, indicating a willingness to cause or risk causing grave harm within the statutory definition. The act should have been committed on some separate occasion from the present offence, though the convictions may be simultaneous.

4. *previous custodial sentences; and time since the end of the last custodial sentence* (e.g. the extended sentence has elaborate specifications

on these points). We agreed with Professor Walker (1978) that it is difficult to assert that nothing but a special sentence would prevent an offender from repeating his offence, unless the deterrent effect of at least one ordinary custodial sentence has already been tried. Obviously the possibility of exceptions must be considered. There might be cases in which (even in the absence of a previous custodial sentence) the pattern of a person's offences convinced the court that he was undeterred by the almost certain prospect of a substantial prison sentence; for instance, if he was convicted on the same occasion of more than one act of serious violence committed with obvious disregard of the likelihood of detection, or if he declared a fixed intention to commit further grave harm within the meaning of the statute. Such cases would be rare, but neither the principle nor the exceptions to it could easily be made statutory. The desirability of taking experience of imprisonment into account would be an appropriate matter for a practice direction to the Court from the Lord Chief Justice.

5. *ineligibility for hospital orders* (e.g. psychiatric probation orders are thus restricted in theory by s. 3 of the Powers of Criminal Courts Act 1973). It was proposed by both the Butler Committee and the Scottish Council on Crime, and we agreed, that a protective sentence should not be imposed on an offender who is eligible by reason of his mental condition for a hospital order under the Mental Health Act 1959; unless, though eligible, he cannot be found a place in a secure hospital.

Limited availability

We considered, as a further limitation on the use of the protective sentence, the device of limiting its availability either to a particular court or courts, or to a special tribunal. Just as the trial of some types of offence (e.g. murder) can take place only in courts presided over by a judge of a certain rank, so it would be possible to confine to such courts the power to impose a protective sentence. This would not necessarily mean that the trial of the offence would have to take place in such a court; the convicted offender could be committed to one for sentence. There are objections, however, to this idea. Committing for sentence involves delay and also obliges two judges instead of one to familiarise themselves with the case. We agreed that the same result — the confirmation by a high-ranking judge of the need for a protective sentence — could be achieved by reliance on the Court of Appeal.

We considered the suggestion (Walker 1972; 1978) that such cases might be committed to a special tribunal which would include not only a judge but also 'experts' of other kinds. A court which had convicted an offender in circumstances which seemed to point to a protective sentence would be permitted — not obliged — to commit him to the special tribunal. If the tribunal agreed that a protective sentence was needed it would so decide; if not, it would remit him back to the court for an ordinary sentence. The offender would have the right of appeal, either on the ground that his case did not call for committal to the tribunal, or that the tribunal's sentence was longer than was necessary. (Release would not be a matter for the tribunal.)

There would be clear advantages in such an arrangement. The responsibility for a rather specialised task would rest with one body which would be in a position to maintain a consistent policy on the basis of experience; and it would bring to bear on the difficult task of protective sentencing knowledge and experience not possessed by the judiciary. There are a number of possible objections, however. To give a power to sentence to such a tribunal would be a major breach with tradition (but this is not an objection based on merit); it would not command the confidence which a judge commands and its decisions might be undermined by the Court of Appeal. We found more persuasive the objection that it would be very difficult in practice to give members of the tribunal access to all the evidence needed for sentencing without imposing on them the unreasonable requirement that they should attend the trial throughout (supposing that it could be known in advance that it would be necessary for them to do so); and more persuasive still, the objection that retributive as well as protective considerations must enter into protective sentencing, that protective measures cannot and ought not to be sharply distinguished from ordinary sentences and that it would be inappropriate to remove the decision from the court to a non-judicial tribunal, albeit one which would include a judge among its members or even would sit under a presiding judge.

We have therefore concluded that the best solution is to allow any Crown Court (but not magistrates' courts) to impose a protective sentence, but to provide that in *every* case there should be an *automatic* review by the Court of Appeal (Criminal Division). Thus the actual task of imposing the protective sentence would rest with the trial judge, but there would be an opportunity for a single body (the Court of Appeal) to formulate a consistent policy for protective sentencing, and to apply it to every case which, in the view of the trial judge, warranted a protective sentence.

Under the present appellate procedure as it applies to sentencing, an application for leave to appeal, with accompanying papers, is first considered by a single judge of the Court of Appeal. If the application is granted, the appeal is heard by a full court of two or three appeal judges. If it is refused, the offender is notified and has 14 days within which to renew his application, which has the effect of bringing it before the full Court for hearing as an application regardless of the single judge's refusal of leave.

In our view it would be desirable in principle for every protective sentence to be reviewed by the full Court. This would not only give weight to the rights of the individual in judicial consideration of the case, but it would also allow the use of the sentence to be thoroughly documented and the principles governing it laid down. This could be secured by entitling the offender to legal aid for an application for leave to appeal, with the effect that his application can be heard direct by the full Court, before whom he will be legally represented.

It may be suggested that this would overburden the full Court. There is no way of knowing how many cases there might be; but we have arrived at a figure, admittedly somewhat speculative, of 140 a year.[1] Many, if not most, of these could be expected to appeal on their own initiative. The additional burden of making appeal automatic should not be very great; but if the proposal be resisted, we suggest as an alternative that every protective sentence should be reviewed by one Lord Justice of Appeal, as if it were an application for leave to appeal, and thereafter should follow the present sequence of events. As with the present life sentence, cases would no doubt proceed to the full court if they appeared to pose an important question of principle, even if there was no evident injustice to the individual offender.

In addition to automatic review, we propose a provision that the sentencing judge and the Court of Appeal should in their discretion have the right to call in an assessor or assessors to sit with them in an advisory capacity only. The Supreme Court rules already empower a judge in civil cases to call in an expert on his own motion to advise him on any matter; there would not seem to be any problem in extending this to criminal cases. Courts should make use of this power not in a generalised way, but for the purpose of calling an individual with special knowledge of some aspect of the case in question. It might be an appropriate ground of appeal that an assessor had not been called to advise on an issue relevant to the need for a protective sentence.

A Single Measure

In defining the class of offenders eligible for the protective sentence by reference to criteria such as the nature of the offence, age, etc., we made no reference to suitability for custodial or non-custodial measures. However, we debated at length the desirability of providing for a separate non-custodial protective sentence (a 'community control order') which might or might not be preceded by a period in custody. It was argued that there might be cases in which it would be just to impose a non-custodial but not a custodial sentence; and that, in any case, the courts should be given every encouragement to minimise the length of sentences of imprisonment even for the exceptional, dangerous offender. Some of us felt strongly that there should be written into the arrangements for protective sentencing, a presumption, other things being equal, in favour of non-custodial measures of control; and the availability of a separate non-custodial protective sentence would make it possible to lend weight to the presumption by instructing the courts that, in the absence of good and specific reasons for believing that a non-custodial sentence would not provide the necessary degree of protection, they must prefer it to a sentence of imprisonment.

However, our prime objective was to ensure that the protective sentence would be used as infrequently as possible. Having proposed restrictive qualifying conditions with this objective in view it became unrealistic to pursue further the idea of a separate non-custodial sentence. We could not envisage any of the high-risk serious offenders, who would alone be eligible for the protective sentence under our proposals, failing to attract a relatively long sentence of imprisonment within the normal range. If a protective sentence were considered necessary for such an offender it would be unwise and in any case impractical for the court to determine that it should at some point in time take a non-custodial instead of a custodial form. We agreed that, in the circumstances, there was no case for proposing a separate non-custodial protective sentence. The aim of minimising the length of time spent in custody by prisoners under protective sentence must be achieved within the frame of a single measure.

A semi-determinate sentence

We had rehearsed the arguments for the view that a protective sentence must take a wholly indeterminate form. If there were no other consideration than the protection of others they would be incontrovertible and the English life sentence would be the appropriate model. However, we were agreed that protection can never be the only consideration and it followed that protective sentences must be subject to a determinate limit. This is not to say that they need be inflexible and entail fixed terms of detention. It is already the case that only very short sentences in England are truly determinate. The prisoner is entitled to remission of one-third of the length of his sentence, so long as this would not reduce the period of his detention below thirty-one days, and so long as he does not forfeit it as the result of a disciplinary award. If the sentence exceeds 18 months he becomes eligible for parole after serving 12 months or one-third of his sentence, whichever is the longer: and about 60% of those applying for parole receive it sooner or later. A *long* sentence which specifies exactly the period for which a prisoner must be detained has not been a feature of the English sentencing system for over a hundred years. It is obviously inappropriate for protective purposes, since nobody can say with any confidence when release will become a justifiable risk. The court must determine the limit of the protection to be afforded to the public in each case and it is incumbent then on the executive to release the offender from detention as soon as it becomes clear that control without custody is practicable.

The protective sentence we propose may, therefore, be of any determinate length and, like an ordinary sentence, will obey the proportionality rule: the court will have regard to the gravity of the anticipated harm and the risk of its occurring. The sentence will represent the length of time beyond which the offender could not justly be detained even if he were still thought to be 'dangerous'. In practice it is likely that the changing disposition of the offender or the altered circumstances into which he would be released will, in many cases, dictate a much earlier release from prison and termination of licence than would be inferred from the sentence imposed by the court.

Two questions arise: should there be a statutorily prescribed upper limit to the length of a protective sentence? and should offenders under protective sentence be required to spend a minimum period in custody before consideration may be given to the possibility of releasing them on licence?

A statutory maximum?

The Advisory Council has been criticised for its recommendation that the length of special sentences outside the normal range should not be subject to a statutory maximum. However, we share the Council's view that it is both unnecessary and unwise to circumscribe judicial discretion in relation to the sentencing of a very heterogeneous group of exceptional offenders. Moreover, we were unable to see on what grounds we could rationally prefer one maximum length of protective sentence to another.

A minimum period in custody?

The question of imposing a minimum period of detention in custody arises because of the need to avoid the inequitable possibility that a prisoner under protective sentence might be released earlier than another serving a sentence within the normal range for a similar offence. We do not think it necessary to legislate against this possibility. We regard it as essential to avoid any arrangement that would impede the freedom of the executive to release on licence a prisoner serving a protective sentence as soon as it is practicable to do so. In particular, the date on which he becomes eligible for release on licence should not in our view depend upon any decision of the trial court. We therefore rejected a suggestion that the court, taking 'tariff' considerations into account, should stipulate a minimum period to be spent in custody; also another suggestion that the prisoner should be eligible for release on licence only at the end of a period equal to one-third of the maximum ordinary sentence for his offence (or whatever fraction for the time being governs eligibility for parole from an ordinary sentence); for this would enable the court to achieve the same effect by sentencing him for three times the minimum period it thought he should spend in custody. We think it important, as a matter of principle, that it should be possible in law for an offender who is given a protective sentence to be released from custody at any time during his sentence and that it should be left to the discretion of the executive to give appropriate weight to 'tariff' considerations. It seems unnecessary to require a review tribunal, with members of the judiciary among its membership, or the Home Secretary himself, to take them into account; they would do so in any case.

Abolition of other sentences

The existence of a single, semi-determinate protective sentence would imply that the courts should desist from the practice, disavowed by the Court of Appeal, of adding a covert protective element to the length of ordinary sentences of imprisonment; and that the existing extended sentence, insofar as it is meant to serve a protective function, would become redundant and should be abolished. We considered whether it would also imply that the life sentence should be abolished. To the extent that it serves as a protective sentence it would be superseded; but, of course, it has other functions. It is mandatory for murder and as a discretionary sentence for certain non-homicide offences it is variously regarded as a fitting punishment, a justifiable deterrent and until recently (because it allows for early release) a merciful sentence. It was not our task to consider it except as a protective sentence; and for this purpose we prefer the semi-determinate sentence we propose. However, there would be no case for providing alternative penalties for murder and manslaughter and for so long as the life sentence remains on the statute book for homicide we would propose that the new protective sentence should be restricted to non-homicidal offences.

Evidential and Procedural Requirements

A protective sentence, we took for granted, should never be mandatory. The mandatory life sentence for murder is under criticism; mandatory restrictions (for example, disqualification from driving) are a different matter because they are non-custodial. It would be impossible to define acceptable types of offence, offender or situation which would justify a mandatory custodial protective sentence. On the other hand, very few offenders are likely to be eligible for a protective sentence under our proposals, given the qualifying conditions we laid down; and fewer still will present a risk such as to call for a protective sentence – in other words, will be 'dangerous'. How shall the court reach a judgment?

We did not favour an attempt to prescribe statutory tests of 'dangerousness': for example, behavioural or medical criteria and probabilities of recidivism. It seemed to us that, given clear statutory indications of the interpretation to be placed on 'grave harm', the court must be left to judge from the nature of the offence and the offender's character, conduct and antecedents whether he presents an unacceptable risk of grave harm in the foreseeable future; providing only that there are evidential and procedural requirements which have the effect of ensuring that the judgment can be contested.

We considered three possible requirements of this kind:

1. a requirement that there must be good reason to believe that the offence of which the offender stands convicted and which has caused or risked causing grave harm within the meaning of the statute is not an isolated, out-of-character episode. We agreed that to be eligible for a protective sentence the offender must have been convicted (or 'found guilty' as a juvenile) of at least one other act of a similar nature. What other sorts of evidence are needed to meet this requirement: offences taken into consideration, cautions, statements from witnesses subject to cross-examination, statements in police antecedents reports or in reports by psychiatrists or probation officers?
2. a requirement that the court must have reports from social workers and/or psychiatrists. Must the reports *recommend* a protective sentence?
3. a requirement that the court must be of the opinion that no other form of sentence will provide adequate protection for others. How can this be made more than a mere formality? Should courts be required to state their reasons for this opinion?

We noted the recommendations of the Streatfeild Committee (Home Office 1961) concerning arrangements for providing the courts with information for sentencing. As regards persons eligible for preventive detention the Committee recommended that when a court is considering preventive detention it should normally have a general report from the prison authorities on the risk of continued recidivism on his part.

We ourselves would prefer, for the purposes of the protective sentence we propose, that the court should receive three independently prepared reports: from the police, a probation officer and a psychiatrist. Some overlap will be unavoidable and some degree of consultation between those responsible for preparing the reports is acceptable;

but it seems essential to us that differences between them should not be obscured and that the court should do its best to ensure that facts have been independently obtained and verified and opinions independently formulated.

Evidence from police records

We propose that the court should be statutorily obliged to obtain from the police and consider not merely a statement of antecedents but also a comprehensive report on the nature and pattern of the individual's offending. In most cases the court will be cognisant of the details of the present offence or offences from the trial. Where a guilty plea has been entered, it might be necessary for further evidence to be called and in that case the defendant must be given the opportunity to challenge it.

In either case, however, there are likely to be serious gaps in the court's knowledge of the offender's past criminal behaviour. The prosecuting counsel obtains from the police, and supplies to the court, a complete list of previous convictions; the name of the convicting court, the legal nature of the offence (theft, burglary, robbery, etc.) and the sentence received. But there is no systematic coverage of further details of past offending in social inquiry reports and psychiatric or medical reports; and the information included in such reports is usually dependent upon the offender's version of the facts, which may be highly inaccurate.

This is clearly unsatisfactory when the court is considering whether or not to impose a protective sentence; as much information as possible about previous patterns of offending should be made available to it. The court should know, for example: the precise nature of previous offences and the circumstances in which they were committed; the extent to which they were spontaneous or provoked; whether they were committed alone or in a group; and if in a group, its nature and the offender's role within it. It should also consider, in relation to both past and present offences, the offender's apparent intentions and motivations in committing them. Are his offences capable of rational explanation? If so, is the explanation related to circumstances which are likely or unlikely to be repeated? Were there disinhibiting factors at work, such as drugs, alcohol or fatigue? If so, are such factors likely to recur? To what extent was the offending compulsive or impulsive? Were the offences predictable or preceded by overt danger signals? To what extent were they easily detectable?

Under present arrangements there may sometimes be difficulty in assembling such information about an offender's record. Some aspects would be covered in reports by probation officers and others, but the primary responsibility for providing information about previous offences must lie with the police, who would rely for detail largely on the summary of the facts as contained in the statements of witnesses held in their records. These might not reflect the version of the facts which was accepted by the court, but the offender would still have the right to challenge any statement with which he disagreed and to call evidence in support of his version.

Statements about past acts, which might have amounted to offences but which did not result in convictions, present a special problem. It has been held that the prosecution can only include in the antecedent history facts which it is able to prove if called upon to do so. The need to produce evidence to prove an offence cannot be evaded by introducing it at the time of sentence. Nevertheless, on one argument it appears reasonable that cautions, at least, should be included in the police record and formally admitted at sentencing stage. On the other hand, without a revision of the present procedure for administering cautions, such a practice might lead to injustice. A person might well accept a caution at present, regardless of guilt, in order to avoid prosecution and it would be unfair that such a caution should unexpectedly be used against him in later proceedings. If certain safeguards were introduced, so that a caution could only be accepted after legal advice and after the implications of a caution in terms of future proceedings had been explained to the offender and he had signed a statement admitting the offence, then the formal admission of cautions might be more acceptable. Until such safeguards exist it seems preferable, on balance, not to interfere with the present practice of excluding from the offender's antecedents any cautions or evidence of other offences unless they can be proved.

Comments on past behaviour, whether or not it amounted to an offence or resulted in a caution, are commonly made in social inquiry reports and psychiatric reports, often with little or no substantiating evidence. More latitude is extended by the courts here than in respect of police reports, perhaps because the latter either are the prosecutors or are regarded as being on the side of the prosecution, whereas psychiatrists and probation officers are accorded an independent status which is thought to make them impartial. A social inquiry report may say, for example, that 'this man's wife lives in terror of his drunken violence', but the wife would rarely be produced to testify to the fact, and might in any case be too frightened to do so. There arises the problem of determining the reliability of this and other information which is not 'hard' (in the sense that age, sex and previous convictions are 'hard' information). The problem, of course, is not peculiar to the consideration of protective sentences. It simply becomes more acute because the consequences of accepting such evidence might be much more far-reaching. As the Scottish Council on Crime concluded, information of this nature is important and should not be excluded. The problem of weighing its credibility must be left to the courts to resolve, perhaps with the assistance of a practice direction from the Lord Chief Justice. The defence should and does have the opportunity to challenge such information, to produce evidence to rebut it, and to cross-examine probation officers, psychiatrists or others who include it in their reports. Contentious information should be proved wherever possible, and where no evidence at all can be given in support of facts which the defence disputes, such 'facts' should have minimal weight attached to them. Expressions of opinion and interpretation should always be seen to derive from factual information, and should be capable of being argued in a rational manner. Beyond that, the rules which should be incorporated in a practice direction would have to be determined by the Lord Chief Justice in the light of experience.

Social inquiry and psychiatric reports

We propose that the court should be required to obtain and consider two reports on the offender's character and circumstances: a probation officer's social inquiry report and a report from a psychiatrist. We think that these reports should go beyond their normal scope and be prepared in the knowledge that the court is considering imposing a protective sentence. The court should invite comment when necessary on particular aspects of the case under consideration.

It is not unusual for a social inquiry report to be required by law or in practice, before particular sentences are imposed. The long experience which the probation service has in writing such reports should be utilised in protective sentencing to provide much of the information which the court would require. However, we suggest that, when a protective sentence is under consideration, a *senior* probation officer or an officer with considerable experience of writing court reports should, if possible, be allocated the task. The report should, of course, contain comprehensive information on the offender's circumstances and history: for example, his occupation and work habits, his relationship with his wife, children or other dependents, if any, his childhood and adult history, and his response to other sentences which have been imposed on him in the past. It should also contain as much information as possible on the circumstances in which the offender might find himself if quickly released into the community, the extent to which he might be subject to pressure, provocation or temptation in his social and family circumstances to repeat his offence, and the problems and prospects of modifying these circumstances or removing him from them.

We have already referred at some length in chapter 2 to the controversy in the United States surrounding the participation of psychiatrists in the administration of criminal justice. Their role in this country is less debatable for a number of reasons and we were not at all persuaded of the extreme view that the courts should be denied the freedom to call them as expert witnesses in cases where it is concerned to assess an offender's 'dangerousness'; or that, if they are called, special safeguards are needed to prevent them from exceeding the limits of their competence. They should not be required to make recommendations, but nor should they be prevented from offering recommendations for consideration by the court.

There is no suggestion underlying the proposal that the court should be statutorily obliged to obtain and consider a report from a psychiatrist that all offenders under consideration for a protective sentence will show mental abnormality. The report should first establish that the offender is ineligible for a hospital order under the Mental Health Act and then inform the court if he is suffering from any discernible mental condition which might cause or influence him to inflict further grave harm. There can be little doubt that many of the offenders eligible for protective sentences under our proposals will show some degree of mental disturbance or personality disorder and it is essential that this should be recognised, its degree evaluated and its potential in terms of treatability and prognosis put before the court.

The psychiatrists who are appointed to prepare reports should be selected with great care to ensure that they are well qualified for the task. We rejected a suggestion that there should be an official register of suitable psychiatrists. It would be difficult to lay down requirements for inclusion in the register which would be independent of the standards laid down for the profession at large. Moreover, many able psychiatrists might be unwilling to be included in a register though not unwilling to assist the court from time to time by invitation. We hope that the courts might be encouraged by a practice direction of the Lord Chief Justice to exercise with care their power to appoint psychiatrists of their choice to prepare special reports where a protective sentence is being considered, so that the general quality of such reports may be maintained at a high level.

Notice to the defence and post-conviction adjournment

If the defendant is to be in a position to contest the appropriateness of a protective sentence, and if properly comprehensive reports are to be produced and examined by the defence, it follows that the court should be required to give notice of its intention to consider a protective sentence, adjourn, and remand the offender in custody for a suitable period to enable the necessary enquiries and studies to be made. We agree with the Streatfeild Committee that on balance the advantages of this course outweigh the disadvantages: 'The court has a most difficult decision to make and one with grave consequences for the offender, and if relevant information can be obtained only by a post-conviction adjournment, then such an adjournment must be accepted.' In any event, the offender will almost certainly receive a substantial sentence of imprisonment, and the time taken up by the adjournment should always count towards whatever sentence is imposed, whether an ordinary or a protective sentence.

A convicted offender should never be faced unexpectedly in court with reports or evidence upon which a protective sentence might be based. The giving of notice to the offender is not unprecedented. The statute which provides for extended sentences, for example, requires three days' notice to be given of the previous convictions and sentences of which evidence will be given, so that the offender can prepare to challenge them. Longer notice would be needed to give effect to our proposals. Moreover, in the case of the extended sentence, the required notice is usually given to the offender by the prosecution in advance of the court hearing. This has the advantage of obviating an adjournment. However, we would not expect, given our criteria, that the police or others would attempt to assess in advance whether a protective sentence might be considered.

Notice should be given as a safeguard in two respects. First, to secure adequate time for the prosecution and others to produce detailed antecedents and reports, and for the defence to collect information and reports pertinent to the appropriateness of a protective sentence. Secondly, to enable the defence to examine and rebut information which might be used by the court, whether presented by the prosecution or by probation officers, psychiatrists or others. It follows that the defence should be entitled to further adjournments if necessary for that purpose.

A reasoned sentence

A requirement that the court must be of the opinion that no other form of sentence will provide adequate protection for others (a requirement for the Danish sentence of *forvaring*) may sound a mere formality, since it is to be hoped that a court would not think of imposing it otherwise. But if the court is required to state its specific reasons for this opinion it would emphasise the special nature of a protective sentence, provide a further control over its use and make an appeal against the sentence easier to argue. We think the statute should include such a requirement.

Release from Custody

On the principle that a protective sentence should entail the minimum curtailment of the offender's liberty compatible with its purpose, he has the right, which we think should be given statutory expression, to be released from custody, assuming 'tariff' considerations have been satisfied, as soon as it ceases to be necessary for the protection of the public to continue to detain him.[2] Release on licence from a protective sentence is unlike parole from an ordinary sentence of imprisonment; it is not a privilege to be earned but a right to be claimed (Chapter 4). The arrangements for reviewing the case for continuing to detain a prisoner serving a protective sentence and for determining the conditions of his licence if it is decided to release him, must reflect this conceptual difference. We describe the necessary procedures in detail in Chapter 10; here it will suffice to say that the statute should provide for him to have access at frequent and regular intervals to an independent Review Tribunal of quasi-judicial composition and character. The decision to release him we propose should be left with the Home Secretary, subject to the requirement that before reaching his decision he should obtain and consider the advice of the Review Tribunal and an Advisory Board of different composition and character. The rationale of these proposals is also given in Chapter 10.

The right to prompt release from custody raises two undesirable possibilities: that the offender could be released sooner than if he had been serving an ordinary sentence for his offence, which would be inequitable; alternatively, that he could be kept in custody until very close to the time of his release at the end of his nominal sentence, allowing little or no time for him to adjust under supervision to life in the community, which would be unsatisfactory from all points of view.

As to the former possibility, we rejected as unnecessary the suggestion that the statute should impose a minimum period of detention in custody. We propose, however, to give some scope for avoiding the difficulty by making the date of first review discretionary. We propose that the Review Tribunal should be required to consider the case as soon as possible after the date of sentence and to fix the date of first review. In no case, however, should this be later than three years after the date of sentence, or such fraction of the length of the (protective) sentence as would determine his eligibility for parole from a non-protective sentence (at present, one-third), whichever be the less.

The latter possibility could be avoided by giving the Home Secretary discretion to extend the period of licence beyond the end of the nominal sentence imposed by the court. We propose that on the advice of the Review Tribunal or the Advisory Board the Home Secretary may require an offender to obey the conditions of a licence for a further period, not exceeding three years, after the sentence imposed by the court has expired, if he is of the opinion that this would be in the offender's interest or is necessary in the public interest.

Recall to custody

While on licence, the offender would be liable to recall to custody for a breach of its conditions or requirements; his licence would be revoked by a court and he would be subject to arrest on the ground that he was unlawfully at large with the balance of his sentence outstanding, to be served from the date on which he was returned to prison. We propose that there should also be provision for his immediate recall by the executive should his conduct give his supervising officer cause for anxiety. However, the power to recall in response to warning signs of further grave harm should be exercised sparingly and we propose that where a licensee is recalled to custody on the advice of his supervising officer the decision should be provisional until the case has been reconsidered by the Review Tribunal and the Advisory Board, to whom it should be referred promptly. Recall should not of itself preclude release on licence at some later date.

Notes

1. See the discussion on pp. 100–101.
2. We considered whether the maximum prescribed by the court should be shortened by remission. We took the view that, within the maximum, the only consideration which should be in the minds of those who would have to decide whether to release the offender from prison before the end of the sentence should be the nature and degree of risk involved and the presumption in favour of non-custodial control. Since the ability to avoid disciplinary forfeitures of remission may be a poor guide to a prisoner's likely conduct on release, there seems to be no case for conceding remission from a protective sentence. It would necessitate shifting the risk presented by the offender to other people at an earlier point than that specified by the court, and might encourage the courts in fixing the maximum to take the likelihood of remission into account. We consider this to be undesirable, as it would obscure the proper principles which should operate in determining the maximum.

On the other hand, there are practical difficulties in abolishing remission from a protective sentence. The possibility of forfeiting remission is believed to be an important element in the maintenance of reasonable behaviour by prisoners; and a custodial sentence which did not qualify for remission would undoubtedly provoke resentment. However, it is relevant to note that life-sentence prisoners do not earn remission, nor do mentally disordered offenders detained under hospital orders, yet they do not present insuperable problems for prison and hospital management. On balance, we are inclined to propose that the maximum length of a protective sentence should not be shortened by remission.

CHAPTER 9

Control without Custody

Licence Conditions

When parole licences were introduced the model used was a probation order from which the requirement to 'be of good behaviour and lead an industrious life' was directly copied. No such condition appeared on the much older life licence, nor does it appear today, the view being that 'lifers' are supervised fairly closely and any behaviour not thought to be satisfactory would be reported to the Home Office. The average length of the parole licence is about eight months and about 5000 are issued each year, as opposed to fewer than 100 life sentences. About 400 parolees are recalled each year, compared with a dozen or so 'lifers'. It is probably true to say that both because of the difference in numbers and because of the different conceptual view taken by the public and the probation service, 'lifers' receive much more 'personalised' treatment both from the Parole Board and from the probation service.

The Parole Board may insert any condition it thinks fit into licences of either kind. The standard requirements are that the licensee report to the supervising officer as instructed, notify him of any change of address and accept visits from him at his place of residence; but additional conditions are sometimes added to meet the special needs or failings of licensees. We think there would be scope for increased and more flexible use, with offenders serving protective sentences, of specific requirements and restrictions, aimed not only at resolving particular problems of vital importance to the offender, such as accommodation and employment, but also at providing a more effective means of surveillance and control. The development by the probation service in recent years of varying types of hostel accommodation, day centres and workshops allows for a wider use of such conditions and provides situations in which some degree of close support and monitoring of conduct is possible and already in evidence. We consider below the two main forms which specific prohibitions and restrictions could usefully take: viz., general restrictions on movement or residence and restrictions on employment.

When an offender serving a protective sentence is released from prison he will be on licence for the remainder of the sentence imposed by the court and possibly also for a further period, at the Home Secretary's discretion, of up to three years. The conditions of the licence (like the need for continued detention) will be frequently and regularly reviewed by a review tribunal and by the Home Secretary. They should, we think, be suspended after three years if the licensee's behaviour has given no cause for anxiety during that period. (The conditions of a 'lifer's' licence are frequently suspended after three years if he has behaved well and this is recommended by the probation service.)

Restrictions on Movement and Residence

A prohibition against certain activities or entry into particular localities could be an important means of control and prevention. This is likely to be appropriate in cases where the pattern of offending appears to be contingent upon specific situational factors which could be the subject of restriction: for example, if offences appear to arise from particular associations or are directed towards identifiable people. An offender who is thought likely to commit violent offences against his wife or family might be prevented from doing so if he is prohibited from having contact with them or from entering the area in which they live; or an offender who was previously involved in running a protection racket in a particular city might be prevented from living in or returning to that city during the period of licence. Such restrictions might be most suitable for the offender with an incentive not to reoffend and whose good intentions might stand a greater chance of success if he were kept away from temptation, pressure or provocation.

It could, of course, be difficult for the supervising officer to police such restrictions. For example, a prohibition on entering any establishment licensed to sell drink would be very difficult to enforce and might be expected to have little deterrent effect and little value as a protective device. Breaches of an order forbidding an offender from entering a particular area might have a better chance of being detected, particularly if the police in that area knew the offender by sight; but it would still be fairly easy for him to evade the restriction if he knew the area well. A prohibition against entry into a particular area or establishment might be more effective if it took the form of, or was accompanied by, a *requirement* that the offender reside and be under supervision in a locality sufficiently distant from the area in question to make it difficult for him to visit it.

Restrictions on Employment

Informal arrangements already exist in many professions to exclude corrupt, incompetent and otherwise undesirable practitioners or employees. Medical practitioners can be removed from the register, for example, and solicitors can be struck off the rolls. The Department of Education and Science and the Department of Health and Social Security have systems for blacklisting teachers, youth workers, social workers and others who have been convicted of a criminal offence or are guilty of other misconduct which makes them unsuitable employees; the systems incorporate their own internal appeal machinery. Restrictions on employment as a condition of licence would reinforce their arrangements. They could, for example, be used to prohibit child molesters from being employed in any capacity, and not merely as teachers, in schools or other institutions offering opportunities to commit offences against children. They could also be used to prevent offenders previously engaged in large-scale fraud from entering certain specified business occupations, or from setting up business on their own account. We have in mind the type of prohibition which can already be imposed by the Court under s. 188 of the Companies Act 1948, providing that where a person has been convicted on indictment of any offence in connection with the promotion, formation, or management of a company, or where it appears that he has been guilty of a fraudulent offence in connection with company business (whether convicted or not), he can be prohibited for up to five years from managing or taking a directorship in a company without leave of the court. Similarly, an employer who has a record of persistently endangering his employees by running an unsafe factory might be prohibited during the period of licence from managing a factory or being able to employ others.

Restrictions on employment in this context need not be confined to paid employment, but could extend when necessary to voluntary work. A child molester, for instance, might be prohibited from working in a voluntary capacity at youth clubs. It would again be the responsibility of the supervising officer to enforce such a restriction, perhaps by notifying all youth clubs in the area.

Supervision under Licence

A protective sentence should take a non-custodial form as soon as possible; yet it is evident that there are limitations upon the value of supervision and control in the community as a protective device. We devoted some time to an attempt to assess them realistically.

It is generally true that the results of research into the long-term effectiveness of probation and parole supervision in preventing recidivism have been overwhelmingly negative and taken as a whole they paint a discouraging picture (Brody 1976; Lipton et al. 1976). Nevertheless, there are grounds for believing that these results do not represent the true potentiality of supervision as a protective device.

First, the effectiveness of supervision has traditionally been gauged by its success in reducing reconviction rates after supervision has ceased.

This does not disprove its ability, while it lasts, to control and prevent crime. Indeed, there is some evidence that, while supervision has not affected recidivism in the long term, it does tend to postpone reconviction while it remains in force (Walker and McCabe 1973; Nuttall et al. 1977; McClintock 1977). It may therefore be rather more useful for protective than rehabilitative purposes. We can only guess at the cause of the postponement effect. It may be because the offender feels he is under surveillance; it may be the fact that he is more likely to be in a job or in stable accommodation while on supervision; or it may simply be that he is liable, while on parole, to recall or to a longer prison sentence if reconvicted of a new offence during the licence period. The length of time for which further offences are postponed is also unknown, as the effect has only been demonstrated in relation to fairly short-term supervision; and the use of supervision as a means of control in this sense has not been shown to apply to 'dangerous' offenders. Nevertheless, it is a positive feature of research results which has so far received too little attention.

Secondly, few investigators have attempted to differentiate types of offenders or offences in assessing the effectiveness of supervision. To the extent that they have, they have concentrated on probation and short-term parole cases. The value of supervision is bound to vary according to the circumstances of the offender and the types of offences he commits. Thus supervision might provide adequate protection against one type of offender while proving ineffective or even counterproductive when applied to another.

Thirdly, although existing methods of supervision may not be markedly successful, it should not be assumed that any form of supervision will be ineffective as a protective device. The traditional objective of the probation and after-care service in supervising offenders in the community has been to 'advise, assist and befriend' them. It is true that probation officers have always, in the main, accepted their role as agents of a system concerned to prevent criminal behaviour, and to that extent have accepted their special relationship with the courts and special responsibilities to society. In England and Wales, following the report of the Seebohm Committee (Committee on Local Authority and Allied Personal Social Services 1968) they firmly rejected any suggestion that they should be amalgamated with other personal social services and came down strongly in favour of retaining a separate status. Moreover, recent years have seen their increased involvement in settings with a more explicitly penal content than had hitherto been associated with probation. Parole, prison welfare work, community service orders and suspended sentence supervision orders are all examples of this trend. Probation officers have also shown themselves willing to exercise control in the supervision of parolees; of 394 recalls to prison in 1976, no less than half were for reasons other than a further offence.

These new tasks, however, have not been absorbed into the service without some questioning, and it remains true that all forms of supervision are primarily oriented towards the individual offender's welfare rather than stringent control and the protection of the public. For example, research by Davies (1972) and Morris et al. (1975) indicated that most probation officers did not perceive any difference between their role in the probation setting and in the parole setting, that their duty to exercise control over parolees was relegated to the background, and that parole supervision was usually neither frequent nor intense.

We believe that there may be more scope for the use of supervision as a protective measure following release from prison if increased emphasis is placed upon intensive control by supervision. If control within the community is to be a feasible proposition, then supervision must involve more innovative and resourceful intervention than at present. This is not to suggest that traditional counselling, practical help with finding accommodation or employment, the provision of material support, and referral to other social services and welfare agencies, are not all worthwhile enterprises and forms of control in themselves. However, the type of control we have in mind is closer to the technique that Studt (1972) has termed surveillance – frequent contact, surprise visits and involvement with the offender in as many different social situations and roles as possible. It requires a more suspicious and critical attitude on the part of the supervising officer, and the focusing of more attention on undesirable behaviour and events. Such a stance, designed to detect signs of deterioration in the licensee's situation, is likely to conflict at times with the 'casework' relationship upon which traditional supervision is supposed to be based, and might require violation of the trust and confidentiality of the relationship for the purposes of detection and control. As part of a protective sentence, however, it is a more appropriate approach, and in that context should be accepted as part of the supervisory process. It might require, for example, that an officer supervising a sexual offender should warn third persons of his proclivities if the officer has reason to believe that he may otherwise be tempted to reoffend; or it might need an active and direct involvement in the offender's leisure time and the prohibition of activities or associations which could encourage reoffending.

There is little empirical evidence to support or contradict our contention that this approach could be more effective than present methods of supervision. It has rarely been attempted in this country, and there is therefore little research on which to draw. Several attempts have been made in the United States, but it is difficult to evaluate their success or the precise basis upon which they operated. Studt, in a study in California (1972), compared the work of control-oriented officers with that of help-oriented officers. She suggested that the combination of the two techniques tended to reduce the effectiveness of both, and that the officers who emphasised surveillance spent more time on average on each case, whilst doing little to protect the community from criminal acts and making the parolees feel insecure in their efforts to survive in society. However, there are some grounds for believing that this may have been the result of a lack of clarification of the officer's role, and a misrepresentation of the nature of the relationship. Parolees who were recalled, for example, felt bitter about what they saw as the officer's violation of their relationship with him. It is important, therefore, that the offender be made aware of the nature of supervision upon his release, the degree of control involved and the consequences of misbehaviour. Although this might result in a more superficial relationship and encourage some deception on the offender's part, this would be outweighed by the benefits of the more specific and concentrated surveillance which supervision would entail.

Moreover, supervision can be effective in protecting the public merely by detecting danger signals which might indicate an immediate likelihood of reoffending, and as a means of enforcing requirements or restrictions inserted as conditions of licence. Recall for breach of licence need not therefore be regarded as evidence of the failure of supervision; it may rather indicate that it has been a success in terms of protection.

There are still, of course, inherent limitations upon what can be achieved by way of supervision on licence. A supervising officer cannot be with the offender for 24 hours a day, and it is naturally often difficult for him to perceive an offender's relapse, as he may have no reason to doubt what the offender tells him in interview and no way to check its veracity. Nor can the supervisor realistically be expected to prevent his client from associating with other criminals or from engaging in criminal activities, simply by virtue of the fact that he sees him in his office or elsewhere at regular intervals. The circumstances, therefore, in which release on licence under a protective sentence might be appropriate would need careful selection in relation both to the offender's situation and to the types of offences he was thought likely to commit. For example, a married man might be more suitable than a single itinerant offender for supervision, as there would be an opportunity to check with his wife on his progress; or violence in the family might be more easily prevented than sexual offences against children unknown to the offender, as the supervisor could check for signs of deterioration in the domestic situation. In other words, success is more likely to be achieved with those offenders whose offending results from a known precipitating factor or factors, or where there are likely to be signs of breakdown before reoffending actually occurs.

At present nearly all supervisory functions after sentence are undertaken by the Probation and After-Care Service. But since we are advocating that supervision in the community under a protective sentence requires a change in emphasis towards stricter control and surveillance, it should not be assumed that the probation service is necessarily the appropriate organisation to do it. However, although in principle it might be desirable to involve another service or create a new one for the purpose, this would appear to be impracticable.

Other existing penal agencies are at present not equipped to undertake the task. Although prison officers in certain prisons sometimes maintain contact with offenders after release on an informal basis, the prison service is ill-suited to undertake a task of this nature. Additional training would be needed and limitations in manpower would be even more severe than those affecting the probation service. Furthermore, without full-time secondment of officers for the purpose of doing this work, it would inevitably interfere with shift work and hamper the smooth administration of prisons. Finally, prisons are often geographically situated in a location away from areas where this type of supervision would need to be given, and if it were envisaged that this would be an ongoing process after a custodial term, prisoners would usually be residing in a different area from that in which the prison was located. We have also considered the police, but although they have on occasions become involved in administering sentences (e.g. attendance centres), an extension of their role in this way would not be desirable or welcomed.

In principle, an entirely new agency created for the purpose might be an advantage. However, the number of offenders requiring this type of supervision is bound to be small, and a new service, when spread over all areas, would be underused and could not be justified. In any case, a multiplication of penal agencies should, if possible, be avoided. In our view, therefore, the probation service is the only agency with the requisite training and experience to deal with high-risk serious offenders within the community.

There may be opposition by some within the probation service to this extension of their role. First, it will be argued that the resources of the service are already overstretched, and that any expansion in its tasks would inevitably have an adverse effect upon existing supervisory and report-writing functions. We do not underestimate the additional demands which supervision under the terms of a protective sentence would make upon individual probation officers; but the number of offenders involved would be small and would not, in any case, represent an addition to the case-load of the service as a whole. It may be that some expansion would be called for, in which case, since it would have the effect of reducing the time during which offenders needed to be kept in custody, it might be reasonable to charge the cost in full to central government. There is some precedent for this; it was done, for example, during the experimental period of community service schemes from 1973 to 1975.

Another objection which might be levelled at our proposal for more stringent supervision of this group of offenders by probation officers is that it is incompatible with the helping and caring ethos upon which the probation service is based and also contrary to recent trends in the Probation Service towards a reduction in the length of supervision: for example, the shortening of borstal licence from two years to one year by Schedule 12 of the Criminal Justice Act 1977; and the rise in the absolute and proportionate number of short and medium term probation orders and the decline in the use of three-year orders (Home Office Criminal Statistics 1976: para. 5:37). However, while the supervision at present provided by the probation service may be more likely to be effective within the context of a short-term relationship for the achievement of specific goals, this is not the case when the primary objectives are surveillance and protection of the public.

Whatever the effectiveness or otherwise of stricter control within the community, some probation officers will object that their task is not to be agents of social control. This objection is misconceived. The dichotomy between control on the one hand and care or support on the other obscures the extent to which they overlap and merge. Traditional casework methods, to the extent that they are designed to induce the offender to conform to socially acceptable modes of behaviour, can be seen as a form of social control. Conversely, overt coercion can be for the benefit of the individual offender to the extent, for example, that it prevents him from serving a further term of imprisonment. The real issue is not, 'Should probation officers control?', but rather 'By what means should they control?' Surveillance, detection and the welfare of society do not rule out the provision of casework help and support; they are an alternative and no less valid approach to the same problem. Probation officers plead for a curtailment in the use of imprisonment and the greater use of resources within the community. However, the early release from detention of serious offenders who present a risk of reoffending can and should only be achieved if measures offering a reasonable level of protection to the community are available. Those who want less use of prison for protective purposes must be prepared to pay the price, which is more control in the community.

Lastly, it may be objected that in practice the need to exercise stricter control and surveillance would unduly interfere with existing objectives and techniques within the probation service; that is, that control and treatment are only minimally reconcilable within the same agency, and that any shift in the precarious balance between the two would inevitably reduce the effectiveness of both. This was, for example, a common response by probation officers to the proposals of the Younger Report (Advisory Council on the Penal System 1974) for more intensive and coercive supervision. This difficulty can easily be overstated. We do not see any reason why probation officers should not be able to adapt to the type of offender with which they are dealing by changing their approach. However, we do propose that the supervision of offenders released on licence under a protective sentence should be delegated in each area to an individual officer or officers for whom this work would be a special responsibility. It is essential that the specialised nature of this work be emphasised and its different approach given recognition. This might, of course, only be a short-term assignment in the probation officer's career, like community service or prison welfare work. There is some evidence that older and more experienced officers are more prepared to exercise control and more confident of the circumstances in which breach proceedings should be instituted (Lawson 1977). It might be more appropriate, then, if this work were undertaken by Senior Probation Officers or officers with several years experience in the service.

CHAPTER 10

Reviewing Protective Sentences

Points of principle in the review of protective sentences are discussed in Chapter 4. The presumption underlying our proposals is that the present arrangements for granting parole to prisoners serving determinate sentences and release on licence to those serving life sentences would need recasting under new legislation to make them suitable for cases of protective sentencing; and that neither wholly discretionary nor wholly judicial procedures would be appropriate for this purpose. The former would provide inadequate protection of the rights of prisoners and the latter would risk doing less than justice to the public interest.

It can be argued that justice does not require that non-protective sentences be kept under review and that the concept of parole as a privilege is not unjust when the purpose of the sentence is punishment.[1] Fairness to dangerous offenders, however, whether they be serving a protective sentence in prison or detained in a secure mental hospital, requires that the case for their continued detention be independently examined under procedural rules apt for their special circumstances, and in this chapter we consider what these might be for prisoners under protective sentence.

On the view that anyone who is deprived of his liberty should have the right to challenge his detention in a court of law, as provided by the European Convention on Human Rights (Article 5, para. 4) of which the United Kingdom is a signatory, review procedures for offenders sentenced to be detained for an indefinite period should incorporate such a right. If, however, they are sentenced for a finite period, this judicial control would not be called for. Since we propose that protective sentences should be of determinate length, we have omitted it from the procedures we recommend in this chapter.

We believe that the decision to detain or release a prisoner under protective sentence should rest with the Home Secretary for the duration of the sentence imposed by the court; that the prisoner should be given a right of access at prescribed intervals to an independent review tribunal of quasi-judicial composition and character; and that before reaching a decision to detain or release him the Home Secretary should refer his case to an Advisory Board of professional and lay persons which would sit in private as a case-conference with access to all available evidence, including the report and advice of the Review Tribunal.

The Mental Health Review Tribunals to which the Home Secretary refers the cases of 'restricted' offender-patients for advice may fairly be described as quasi-judicial bodies, but the description does not fit the Parole Board to which he refers the cases of life-sentence prisoners. Their composition and powers are not dissimilar, however. A legally qualified member always sits as President of a Mental Health Review Tribunal, whilst the cases of life-sentence prisoners are considered by a panel of members of the Parole Board which always includes a High Court Judge. Both bodies have the duty to advise the Home Secretary on the cases he refers to them and neither may order the release or discharge of these offenders from detention. The Home Secretary may release a life-sentence prisoner on licence only if he is recommended to do so by the Parole Board and after he has consulted the Lord Chief Justice and, if he is available, the trial judge. His discretion is unfettered in relation to 'restricted' offender-patients in secure hospitals; but before consenting to the discharge of such a patient he will, in practice, seek the advice of the Advisory Board on Restricted Patients and will feel bound by a recommendation not to release.

The similarities in their composition and powers conceal an important difference of function which is reflected in the contrasting procedures of the Mental Health Review Tribunals and the Parole Board respectively. The Tribunals are governed by procedural Rules whilst the Parole Board works informally, and this difference is crucial alike for the rights of offenders and the quality of decision-making. The prisoner's rights are best safeguarded by giving him the right to contest the case for continuing to detain him before an independent tribunal of quasi-judicial composition and character. An objective assessment of the risk he presents is best given by an advisory panel or board of professional and lay persons sitting privately in case-conference.

It can be argued that the functions of the two bodies are not sufficiently different to justify giving them separate existence and that they would in effect have the same function, to recommend whether the offender shall continue to be detained, though they would have to exercise it by different procedures and on the basis of different information (the tribunal would have to reach a view of the case with the handicap of a procedure which could and often would exclude from its cognisance much relevant information about it) and this would breed the likelihood of their reaching conflicting conclusions. The Home Secretary would be almost bound to prefer the recommendation based on a wider range of evidence. Would this not make the tribunal rather an unreal safeguard?

We felt the force of this argument but we did not think it would be right to abandon the proposal for an independent tribunal. The prisoner must be able to contest the case for continuing to detain him just as we have argued that he must be able to contest the sentence when it is imposed by the court. He cannot contest the decision to detain him which is reserved for the duration of his sentence to the Home Secretary; and it is true that the Home Secretary is almost certain to prefer the recommendation of the board to that of the tribunal. However, the board ought not to make its recommendation without hearing the prisoner's case; and that case is best presented by means of a formal hearing before an independent tribunal of quasi-judicial composition and character.

It is true that such arrangements would be much more time-consuming and expensive than the present arrangements for the review of life sentences by the Parole Board; but they would not be more so than the present arrangements for reviewing the cases of 'restricted' offender-patients in secure hospitals and there seems to be no logical reason why concern for the rights of the dangerous offender should not be the same, whether he be detained in a hospital or in a prison; nor why the review-process as a whole should not be substantially the same in either case.

A Quasi-judicial Review Tribunal

In formulating our proposals we have drawn heavily on the Discussion Paper issued in 1978 by the Committee on Mental Health Review Tribunal Procedures.[2] Mental Health Review Tribunals work to procedural Rules made by the Lord Chancellor under section 124 of the Mental Health Act 1959. The Committee was formed in 1977 to undertake the first thorough review of the Rules since the Tribunals were established 18 years ago.[3] The Review Committee proposes, in the Discussion Paper, that most of the Rules which do not at present apply to the cases of patients subject to special restrictions should be extended to cover the cases of these mentally disordered dangerous offenders. We see no reason why such Rules should not, with few modifications, apply also to review tribunals charged with reporting and advising on the cases of dangerous offenders not deemed to be mentally disordered, serving protective sentences in prison.

The quasi-judicial procedures of the Mental Health Review Tribunals, though they depart to some degree from the comprehensive standards of a fully judicial procedure, embody the standards of natural justice. They secure the rights of the parties to be heard, to obtain and present evidence of their own and to challenge the evidence provided by other parties, and to know the reasons for a decision. We have taken them as a point of reference in formulating our own view of the procedures which should govern the work of the independent review tribunal to which we propose that prisoners serving protective sentences should be given right of access. We have not attempted to decide the scope and formulation of a complete set of procedural rules for this purpose[4] but have confined ourselves to what seemed to be the crucial matters requiring to be regulated, and which generate most controversy: representation of the parties; disclosure of information; and the giving of reasons for decisions.

We begin with *representation of the parties* and consider first the prisoner. Under present arrangements for the review of a life sentence the prisoner is given certain rights which are embodied in the rules, made under statute by the Secretary of State, for the local review committee which first considers his suitability for release. A prisoner must be informed of his right to make written representations and any such representations must be considered by the committee. He is entitled to consent, or to refuse, to be interviewed by a member of the committee (who must not be a prison officer) and to make any representations he wishes to be considered by the committee; the interviewing member must make a report, a copy of which must be sent to the Secretary of State and must be considered by the committee. In due course, his case is considered by a panel of members of the Parole Board, with benefit of all the papers from the local committee, but without recourse to further submissions from him and he does not appear in person before either the Committee or the Parole Board.

The position of a mentally disordered offender-patient is quite different. The Rules for the Mental Health Review Tribunals provide for him to be represented before the Tribunal hearing his case; and the Committee reviewing the Rules propose in their Discussion Paper that this provision should apply equally to 'restricted' (i.e. dangerous) offender-patients whose cases are referred to the Tribunal by the Home Secretary. There seems to be no reason why prisoners under protective sentences should not be given the same right of representation before a reviewing body.

The Committee point out that a capable and experienced representative can help a person whose case is before a tribunal to marshall his evidence and, at the hearing, to present the argument to the Tribunal more quickly and effectively than he could do on his own. They suggest, moreover, that should the Tribunal exercise its discretion to withhold evidence from an offender-patient, or if he is asked to leave the hearing whilst certain evidence is being given, there should be someone present to question and comment on such evidence on his behalf. Accordingly, they propose that the representative be given a right, not shared with others, to see and hear all the evidence put to the Tribunal.

Admittedly, as the Committee acknowledge, this would place the representative in a very privileged position. Members of the Tribunal, and anyone who is permitted to present his evidence in private, would need to feel complete trust that the representative would not communicate anything he heard without leave of the Tribunal. On the assumption that members of the legal profession could be relied upon not to betray such confidence, not only by custom but also because they are bound by the disciplinary code of their profession, the Committee propose that barristers and solicitors should be allowed to act as representatives. They also propose that the Tribunal be empowered to authorise other suitable persons to act *ad hoc*; for example, those with a relevant professional background or experience, who regularly undertake tribunal work and who may have undergone a suitable training course.

We turn now to the authority seeking to show good cause why the prisoner should not be released on licence. In the case of a mentally disordered offender the 'responsible authority' is defined under the Tribunal Rules as the managers of the hospital in which he is detained; in the case of a prisoner the responsible authority would presumably be the governor of the prison in which he is detained. It may be questioned whether the governor is likely to be well-qualified for this task. It should be made clear that he would assume formal responsibility for the statement of the case for continuing to detain the prisoner, prepared with the assistance of others, just as the managers of the offender-patient's hospital (who are not psychiatrists) assume formal responsibility for the statement, prepared by professional members of the hospital staff, which is presented to the Mental Health Review Tribunal.

It is a noteworthy proposal of the Committee reviewing the procedures of the Mental Health Review Tribunals that the Rules should recognise the different needs for representation of the offender-patient on the one hand and the responsible authority on the other, and provide separately for each. The Committee did not think that a representative of the responsible authority, or of any other body or individual attending the tribunal need have an unqualified right to remain throughout the hearing and see any evidence, as they suggest for the offender-patient's representative. They point out that the offender-patient may, for example, wish to give evidence in the absence of any person from the health authority, including his medical officer, and they suggest that it should be open to the tribunal to agree to such a request, just as it would be open to it to exclude the offender-patient at the request of the medical officer. Accordingly, they propose that both parties, the responsible authority and the offender-patient, should be represented by a person who could act on their behalf.

We think these arguments apply *mutatis mutandis* to the prisoner whose protective sentence is under review and that the same provision should be made for the separate representation of the responsible authority before the review tribunal considering his case.

Mental Health Review Tribunals are required to provide for the *appearance of the parties*, that is to say, for them or their representative to address the tribunal, to give evidence, to call witnesses and to cross-examine. We see no reason why these arrangements should not be a feature of the hearing procedure of a tribunal dealing with the cases of prisoners under protective sentence.

It is obviously of great importance to provide for the *disclosure of information*. Anyone whose case is under consideration by a review tribunal must be able to prepare to meet the major objections which the authority is making to his discharge or release from detention and to correct errors of fact that may be contained in statements provided for the tribunal. Mental Health Review Tribunals are required to disclose all relevant evidence put to them including, in particular, the authority's statement of the case against discharge, except in so far as they consider it undesirable to do so in the interests of the offender-patient or for other special reasons.

There may be good reasons for withholding certain evidence from an offender–patient (for example, his medical report). But the Committee expressed their view in the Discussion Paper 'that authorities must guard against asking for any part of the [authority's] statement to be withheld without strong reasons, and that Tribunals should be ready to disregard such requests where they are not satisfied with those reasons'. In any case, they pointed out, the patient's representative should always receive all relevant evidence.

We think these proposals for the disclosure of information under safeguard of the tribunal's discretion to withhold, are equally appropriate to the needs of tribunals concerned with prisoners under protective sentence. It is often pointed out that it could have serious repercussions on the management of prisons if reporting officers had to give evidence in front of the prisoners on whom they were reporting, or if their written reports were made available to them. We accept that this could be a real problem and that the Tribunal might often feel it necessary to grant a request for evidence to be withheld from the offender (though not from his representative). However, we share the Committee's view of the need for authorities to exercise restraint in asking for evidence to be withheld and for tribunals to be prepared to refuse a request when they are not satisfied that it is well-founded.

The Committee drew attention in the Discussion Paper to differences of view, which were also present among us, on *hearing procedure*, which is to say, whether tribunal hearings should be governed by fairly loose rules of procedure which could be adapted according to the circumstances of the case, or by more structured rules whereby the pattern of the hearing would be known in advance. The more structured approach would entail spelling out the rights of the parties to obtain and present evidence of their own and to challenge the evidence provided for other parties. Procedural rules would need to provide specifically for contingencies: for example, that if there is any material challenge to the accuracy of the report of a social worker on the offender's circumstances, the social worker should be called as a witness and be subject to examination; or that if the tribunal adjourns to obtain additional information, this should be disclosed to the parties (subject to the usual safeguards of withholding information in proper circumstances) and the tribunal should reconvene at the request of any of them.

We are inclined, on balance, to favour a less structured approach to the problem of securing a fair hearing for the prisoner under protective sentence. Review tribunals should be given as much flexibility as is compatible with ensuring that all parties are given adequate opportunity to give evidence and question that of others.

The requirement of natural justice that a tribunal shall *give reasons for its decisions* is less easy to meet in respect of the cases of dangerous offenders, whether or not they are mentally disordered. In the cases of offender-patients not subject to special restrictions, Mental Health Review Tribunals are required to communicate their decision to all the parties who may then, within three weeks of receiving notice of the decision, request the Tribunal to give their reasons. The Tribunal must comply with any such request, except when they consider that it would be undesirable to do so in the interests of the patient or for other special reasons.

It is pointed out in the reviewing committee's Discussion Paper that this Rule could not apply as it stands to the cases of restricted patients, if for no other reason than that the Tribunal has no power to order discharge and merely offers information and advice to the Home Secretary:

> The advice which the tribunal offers to the Home Secretary, following the case of a restricted patient, is different in kind from the tribunal's decision and accompanying reasons produced after considering an application from an unrestricted patient. In addition to the specific recommendations which may suggest a number of alternative or complementary courses, the tribunal generally includes information about the patient and the conclusions which the tribunal has reached about his progress in hospital and his possible future prospects on discharge. The tribunal's purpose is to provide background information and advice which will enable the Home Secretary himself to reach a decision on the case. It is clearly important that his decision should be based on the fullest possible information. Were tribunals to know that this document were to be seen by the patient, the advice might not be as full and frank as it is now; the quality of tribunal advice would suffer and with it the decisions of Ministers. For this reason it is suggested that the tribunal's letter of advice should, as now, remain confidential to the Home Secretary.

The Committee nevertheless suggest that as soon as the Home Secretary's decision on his case is known, and in any case not more than three months after the hearing, the Home Office should write to the restricted patient setting out the principal recommendations forwarded by the Tribunal to the Home Secretary and giving the Home Secretary's decisions on each. They go on to say, 'The Committee thinks that the Home Secretary ought not to be inhibited, in taking a decision for which he is solely responsible, by the knowledge that the tribunal's recommendation to him might be made public.' They recognise possible drawbacks; for example, a patient might, having had a tribunal's advice for his discharge rejected, believe that any further tribunal hearing would be worthless and might, correctly or not, suppose that a Ministerial rejection of a tribunal recommendation resulted from counter-advice given by his medical officer. But they considered these possible difficulties to be outweighed by the advantages.

We noted that though parole for prisoners was and had always been a privilege, the Parole Board together with the Home Office had, nevertheless, given thought to seeing whether reasons for refusing parole could be given. In the Parole Board report for 1975 the matter is referred to and the arguments for and against giving reasons for the refusal of parole are set out. The Board reported that they had not so far been able to devise any way of meeting the pressure for the giving of reasons, but that they had not abandoned the search for a solution. The Board's concern with the problem was reiterated in the reports for 1977 and 1978, but the latter concluded: 'The Board still feels that the giving of reasons is incompatible with the present administrative system of parole and that it would be wrong to alter the system except by recasting it under new legislation.'

The Home Office, meantime, carried out a number of experiments to see if a satisfactory list of causes for concern could be devised so that the individual prisoner could be advised of the particular causes of concern in his case. However, in their Report for 1979 the Board argues that the so-called 'Reasons' experiment should be abandoned, 'except in so far as it may be a useful tool for the Board in making a decision', reiterating the fundamental objection that to give reasons for adverse decisions 'would be to substitute for a system under which Parole is a privilege to be earned a system under which it would be a right to be claimed, thus leading almost inevitably to a change in the system without Parliamentary intervention'.

We take the view that for prisoners serving protective sentences, release on licence cannot be conceived as a privilege to be earned; it must be a right to be claimed. We acknowledge the difficulties, however. In a few cases disclosure of reasons would be to the serious detriment of the prisoner; as, for example, when medical reports show him to be a potential danger, perhaps to children, and there is no treatment possible. In a larger number of cases there are ethical problems about disclosing reasons, in particular, arising out of information given in confidence, for instance by doctors and probation officers. A full statement of reasons would inevitably reveal at least the main features of the reports made by members of the prison staff and the Probation and After-Care Service. This would make them reluctant to provide frank and helpful reports and could cause particular difficulties for medical officers. Furthermore, there could be adverse psychological effects from giving reasons in some cases, particularly to those who are mentally and socially inadequate.

Nevertheless, we are inclined to favour giving to prisoners under protective sentence, as to restricted patients in secure hospitals, a statement of the principal recommendations forwarded by the review tribunal to the Home Secretary. We regret the abandonment of the 'Reasons' experiment which we note was confined to the formulation of reasons for the decisions of the Parole Board and local review committees and was not directed to the problem of communicating them to prisoners.

The difficulty experienced by the Parole Board and local review committees in formulating agreed reasons for refusing parole in certain cases is relevant, not only to the destructive effect of uncertainty on the morale of prisoners, but also to the problem of developing consistency in the exercise of administrative discretion. We noted with interest that in the United States guidelines have been formulated to produce consistency in the exercise of discretion by Parole Boards; and this development has also made it possible for decisions to be challenged and defended (Kress and Wilkins 1976). However, this attempt to introduce a formal system of administrative case law cannot be made to cover the cases which concern us. The most serious offences, which in our view should alone put an offender at risk of a protective sentence, defy analysis for this purpose. Such offences were reported as being too few in number and too diverse in character and degree of seriousness to permit the extraction of norms and the formulation of guidelines.

The advice of the review tribunal in the cases of dangerous offenders, like the decisions of the Home Secretary, is bound to be wholly individualised. The hope must be that any communicating of recommendations to the offenders concerned can be done without lapsing into uninformative and unconvincing stereotypes and that enough can be said without detriment to the prisoner to enable him to know the case he has to meet on the occasion of the next review.

It is sometimes argued that if a prisoner's rights must be secured by allowing him access, as of right, to an independent review tribunal, it must follow that the public interest should be acknowledged by requiring the tribunal normally to sit in public and permitting the media normally to give publicity to the proceedings.

The case for *open hearings and publicity* seems to be stronger in respect of legally sane than for mentally disordered offenders, whose rights as patients must include the right to be protected against the adverse effects of publicity. Mental Health Tribunals sit in private, unless a hearing in public is requested by or on behalf of an offender-patient and 'the Tribunal are satisfied that a hearing in public would not be detrimental to the interests of the patient and would not for any other reason be undesirable'. There is also a Rule prohibiting any publicity concerning the hearing without the express consent of the Tribunal. However, the Committee on the Review of Tribunal Procedure make this comment:

> this is thought to be unnecessarily restrictive, and that it would be sufficient to reverse the emphasis, permitting publicity except where the tribunal directed otherwise in the interests of the patient's mental health. It is recognised that publicity might, of course, be harmful in other directions, for example, in hindering the patient's chances of rehabilitation, and in limiting the Rule in this way a heavy reliance would need to be placed on the discretion of those attending.

We accept the desirability, in principle, of open hearings when the cases of prisoners serving protective sentences are before a review tribunal; but not in the spirit of seeking to secure for the public its 'day in court' (Arthur and Karsh 1976). The public interest, in our view, is best secured by giving to the Home Secretary the decision to release for the duration of the sentence imposed by the court. The review by tribunal is intended primarily to protect the prisoner's right to contest a decision to keep him in custody. It will also serve to air the case against releasing him. However, it must not be allowed to prejudice his chances of rehabilitation in the event of his being released notwithstanding opposition from the public; and the tribunal will often have good reasons for prohibiting publicity.

An Advisory Board for Special Offenders

We do not think the Home Secretary should reach a decision in the case of a prisoner under protective sentence without the further advice of a specially constituted Advisory Board. In our view, such a requirement is in the interest of both the prisoner and the public. The Home Secretary ought not to reject the advice of an Independent Review Tribunal to release on licence a prisoner under protective sentence, without a very careful assessment of his case by a panel of professional and other persons qualified to examine and evaluate the widest range of information about him. Nor ought the Home Secretary to order the release of such a prisoner on licence without the safeguard of a further thorough scrutiny of his case by an Advisory Board which is likely, by virtue of its composition and working methods, to produce as reliable an assessment as possible of the risk he presents.

To have two distinct bodies, one to safeguard the interests of the prisoner and one to safeguard the interests of the public, is on the face of it a cumbersome arrangement. Surely, it will be said, the right thing is to have one body whose duty is to strike a balance between the two interests and offer advice on that basis to the Home Secretary? The present arrangement for offender-patients is not an ideal precedent; it is clumsy and came into being only when further safeguards were thought necessary following the case of Graham Young and it did not seem practicable to cast the Mental Health Review Tribunals, whose main responsibilities relate to non-offenders, in that role.

The argument is persuasive only on one of two assumptions: either that the prisoner's right to contest a decision to keep him in custody need not be secured by the rule-governed procedures of a quasi-judicial Review Tribunal; or that such a Tribunal would be as likely as a committee of the Parole Board sitting in case-conference to produce a soundly-based answer to the question whether the prisoner may be released without unacceptable risk to the public. Since we were unable to accept either assumption, we opted reluctantly for the complications of the dual system.

We think that the Parole Board, which has some 45 members appointed by the Home Secretary, comprising members of the judiciary, senior ranking probation officers, psychiatrists, criminologists and laymen, might well be the appropriate source for an advisory Board of the kind we have in mind, just as, under the present arrangements, it provides a panel of five members to which the cases of life-sentence prisoners are referred.

Careful minuting of the Board's proceedings and periodic reviews of the advice tendered to the Home Secretary would help to achieve a measure of reliability and validity in its judgments. There will, of course, be no way of evaluating the Home Secretary's decisions, except in so far as they are decisions to release on licence.

Notes

1. See the judgment in *Payne* v. *Petch*, 30 vii 1979, Court of Appeal (Criminal Division). Unreported.
2. Issued by the Chairman from the Lord Chancellor's Office 1 August 1978.
3. Chaired by the Lord Chancellor's Office, its membership includes the Chairman of the Trent and the South-East and South-West Thames Mental Health Review Tribunals, the Clerk of the Merseyside MHRT Office, the Secretary of the Council on Tribunals and representatives of the DHSS, the Home Office and the Welsh Office. The Committee was established in the context of the general review of the powers and functions of these tribunals, as distinct from their procedures, which is already being undertaken by the Inter-Departmental Committee on the Review of the Mental Health Act, 1959.
4. The Rules for Mental Health Review Tribunals are reproduced in the Discussion Paper issued by the Committee on Mental Health Review Tribunal Procedures, 1978. They number 31.

Principal Proposals

1. The sentencing of 'dangerous' offenders should be the subject of legislation. It is desirable that the distinction implicit in the present sentencing practice of the courts, between the ordinary and the exceptional, 'dangerous' offender, should be formalised so as to facilitate a substantial reduction in the length of sentences of imprisonment for ordinary offenders (not excluding those whose offences are the worst of their kind) whilst continuing to provide a necessary measure of protection for the public against the exceptional, high risk, serious ('dangerous') offender.

2. The wholly indeterminate life-sentence of imprisonment should cease to be available for non-homicidal offences and the use of determinate sentences of imprisonment for the protection of the public should be statutorily controlled.

3. No protective sentence of imprisonment (i.e. no sentence of imprisonment which, in order to protect the public against a risk of future harm, is made longer than would be justified on other grounds alone) should be imposed on an offender unless the following conditions, to be provided by law, are satisfied.

4. The law should provide that:

Grave Harm
(i) the public should be entitled to the protection of a special sentence only against grave harm: *grave harm* should be interpreted in this context as comprising the following categories: death; serious bodily injury; serious sexual assaults; severe or prolonged pain or mental stress; loss of or damage to property which causes severe personal hardship; damage to the environment which has a severely adverse effect on public health or safety; serious damage to the security of the State;

A Protective Sentence
(ii) subject to the restrictions in (iii)–(vi) and the safeguards in (vii)–(ix) below, the Crown Court should

be empowered, for the protection of others against grave harm by an offender, to sentence him to imprisonment for a specified period greater than that which would ordinarily be specified, but proportional to the gravity of the anticipated harm and the court's estimate of the duration of the risk: such a sentence should be called a protective sentence;

(iii) a protective sentence should not be imposed unless the court is satisfied that by reason of the nature of his offence and his character, conduct and antecedents the offender is more likely to do further grave harm than other grave offenders of similar age and sex and that there is no other permissible way of dealing with him which offers the necessary degree of protection for the public;

Restricted Eligibility

(iv) an offender should be eligible for a protective sentence only if he has done, attempted, risked, threatened or conspired to do *grave harm* as defined in (i) above *and* has committed an act of a similar kind on a separate occasion from the instant offence;

(v) a protective sentence should not be imposable for murder or manslaughter so long as the life sentence is available for these offences: but the life sentence should not be available for any other offence;

(vi) a protective sentence should not be imposed on an offender who is below the age of 17 at the time of sentence; nor on one who is eligible, by reason of his mental condition, for a hospital order under the Mental Health Act 1959; unless, though eligible, he cannot be placed in a suitable hospital;

Procedural Safeguards

(vii) a protective sentence should not be imposed without giving the offender prior indication that the judge has this in mind, so that he may prepare his arguments against such a sentence;

(viii) before imposing a protective sentence on the offender the court should receive full reports from the following: a psychiatrist, on his mental condition, with particular reference to the possibility that he may be eligible for a hospital order under the Mental Health Act 1959; the police, on the nature and circumstances of his offence and record of past behaviour; and a probation officer, on his background and circumstances. These reports should be prepared in the knowledge that the court is considering a protective sentence;

(ix) should the court decide that a protective sentence is necessary for the protection of the public, it should state its reasons for so deciding;

The Right of Appeal

(x) the cases of offenders so sentenced should be reviewed by the Court of Appeal (Criminal Division): they should be referred to the Court at once, without the procedure of making an initial appeal to the single judge for leave to appeal; the offender should be entitled to legal aid for an application for leave to appeal, with the effect that his application can be heard direct by the full court before whom he will be legally represented;

Release on Licence

(xi) a protective sentence should entail the minimum curtailment of the offender's liberty compatible with its purpose: such a sentence will be initially served in custody but the offender should be released on licence at the earliest opportunity. The conditions of licence should favour specific rather than general curtailments of liberty;

(xii) the decision to release an offender on licence and to modify or terminate the conditions of the licence should rest with the Home Secretary for the duration of the sentence imposed by the court, subject to his receiving the recommendations of an independent Review Tribunal of quasi-judicial composition and character to which the prisoner should have right of access, and the further advice of an Advisory Board charged to consider his suitability for release or changed conditions of licence, with special reference to the public interest in his continued detention;

(xiii) a prisoner released from custody in the course of a protective sentence should be subject to licence involving supervision by the probation and after-care service and the possibility of recall to prison until the sentence imposed by the Court has expired. On the recommendation of the Advisory Board the Home Secretary should be empowered to require an offender to obey the conditions of a licence for a further period, not exceeding three years, after the sentence imposed by the Court has expired, if he is of the opinion that this is desirable in the offender's interest or necessary in the public interest;

(xiv) the Review Tribunal should consider the case of an offender as soon as practicable after a protective sentence has been passed and should fix the date for first review: in no case should this be later than that on which the prisoner will have served one-third* of the sentence imposed by the court or three years, whichever shall be less. The Tribunal should thereafter review his case at intervals of not more than two years.

*or whatever fraction (at present one-third) as would determine his eligibility for parole from a non-protective sentence.

The Consultative Document and List of Respondents

A CONSULTATIVE DOCUMENT*

March 1977

*This is a consultative document, not an Interim report. After a brief account of the full range of questions that seem to us to be raised by our terms of reference, we indicate the direction of our thinking on a selection of questions to which we have so far specifically addressed ourselves and upon which we invite comment.

CONTENTS

INTRODUCTION

We agreed at the outset that we could not take the idea of 'dangerousness' itself for granted. It is often defined so as to be unhelpfully imprecise, circular, misguided or irrelevant for practical penological purposes. Moreover, it raises anxiety and is therefore particularly open to abuse. Leading critics have suggested a moratorium on the use of the term. This is tempting; but it would not achieve a moratorium on the gravely harmful behaviour which gives the term life.

We made it our first task to re-examine the idea of 'dangerousness'. We have tried to put it into better perspective and, by recognising the variety of ways in which in modern industrial societies the general public is at risk of suffering grave harm, to rid the concept of the irrational element in the anxiety it evokes when it is associated exclusively with violent sexual and other assaults against the person.

We have also taken account of the important point (made among others by the Butler Committee in the course of their discussion of dangerously violent behaviour) that the 'dangerousness' of a potential offender in the majority of cases is dependent on the circumstances in which he finds himself as well as on his personality. Moreover, we have considered and recognise the force of the argument that no significant impact can be made on the social phenomenon of gravely harmful behaviour by measures directed solely against individual offenders, and that what are needed (difficult though it may be to devise them) are more broadly conceived social policies directed against such social practices or other features of social life as can be shown to make such behaviour more likely to occur.

We have in no sense defined away the problem of 'dangerousness', but we have come to see it as a larger and more complex social problem than that implicit in conventional definitions and approaches. By the same token, we have come to see the problem of protecting the public from the risk of grave harm in wider perspective; if there are many ways of placing the public at risk of grave harm, it follows that we cannot view the problem of protection solely in terms of incarceration.

We have spent much time in considering the merits and drawbacks of protective penological measures directed towards offenders judged 'dangerous', because this represents the hard core of our brief. The questions raised in this consultative document are concerned exclusively with the definition of the risk of grave harm which an offender may present; and with the problem of making the difficult move from the definition of gravely harmful behaviour to the identification of those likely to cause it and the formulation of protective penological measures to restrain them. We are conscious, however, that there are social costs as well as benefits attaching to the policy of attempting to contain gravely harmful behaviour simply by restraining potential offenders and that, to identify and take protective measures against individuals in the expectation that they will cause grave harm is an enterprise which is not only fraught with the scientific and technical, the ethical and procedural difficulties we have been exploring, but is likely, after all, to touch only part — and possibly only a small part — of the problem of 'dangerousness' as a feature of life in modern societies.

We are of course aware that there are serious objections to the introduction of a category of 'dangerous offender' into the criminal law both as a matter of principle and on practical grounds. For example, it is argued that the potentially dangerous offender is too narrowly defined as the persistently violent offender; that the qualitative and quantitative significance in our society of this type of offender is greatly exaggerated and that the mass media contribute to the exaggeration; that the processes of law enforcement work selectively and inequitably in respect of all offenders, including those regarded as dangerous; that the theory and practice of the 'treatment' of offenders are both suspect; and that imprisonment manufactures as much harmful behaviour as it restrains.

We shall give full consideration to these and related views in our final report.

We shall welcome comment on any aspect of our problem; but our aim at this juncture is to elicit views on the particular questions set out below. We are seeking comment from laymen as well as from persons professionally concerned in the matters that interest us. Since we are at this stage seeking comments for their own merit, and not as being representative of the views of professional or other interest groups, we are not inviting organisations to submit their collective views in the form of official memoranda; we hope that their officers will give us the benefit of their opinions as individuals and will indicate, if they can, the extent to which these are likely to be representative of those held by members of the organisations they serve. In this way we hope to obtain comments of greater force and variety than are likely to be forthcoming from organisations as such and also to shorten the period of consultation.

We shall be grateful for your reply to any or all of the questions which follow as soon as you can conveniently let us have them. They will be of greatest use to us if they reach the secretary at the *Institute of Criminology, 7 West Road, Cambridge CB3 9DT*, by *Monday 16 May 1977.*
(Please make clear to which particular question your comments are addressed.)

I
WHAT IS GRAVE HARM?

It is much harder than most people think to identify 'dangerous' offenders and to justify taking steps to protect the public against them which involve in one way or another restricting their freedom. When we describe an offender as 'dangerous' in everyday speech, we usually mean that there is a substantial probability of his committing a further offence involving grave harm to another person or persons and we take it for granted that it is justifiable to protect the public against this risk. But if we are to identify offenders to whom the label 'dangerous' can properly be applied, we must be able to say exactly what we mean by 'grave harm' and 'substantial probability', and we must be able to justify taking special measures against potential, as well as actual, offenders.

The commonsense meaning of 'grave' harm is uncertain. Some people think of it only as serious physical injury, while for others psychological harm or the loss of or damage to property would also constitute grave harm. For our purpose in defining 'dangerous' however, no kind of harm is grave harm unless protection against the risk of its being perpetrated is more important than the freedom of a potential offender, however hard it may be to identify him. More precisely, any kind of harm is grave harm if it is demonstrably serious enough to justify protecting the public from anyone who can be shown to be likely to cause it, by imprisoning him or otherwise restricting his freedom for longer periods than can be justified on other grounds — for example, to punish him for some actual offence, to deter others from offending in the same way, to declare society's disapproval of what he has done, or even to treat or rehabilitate him.

A start can be made with the problem of defining grave harm in this sense by taking the categories of offence known to the criminal law. Of course these have been devised for the purpose of attributing criminal responsibility in terms of the acts and intentions of individuals, and not as a means of defining types and degrees of harm which result from their behaviour. Nevertheless, they offer a convenient starting-point;

we have therefore provided in the Appendix a list of these offence categories, each of which covers actions which might be thought to involve
harm against which the public needs special protection. They range
from those that everyone is agreed cause grave harm in all or most cases
to those about which some would say that they rarely or perhaps never
cause grave harm. Certainly the list goes beyond our own view of what
it should include.

WHAT IS YOUR VIEW OF THIS LIST AS A LIST OF OFFENCES RESULTING IN GRAVE HARM?

*Please cite the list-number of any offence in the Appendix which
you think causes grave harm, listing separately those which do so
in all or most cases and those which do so less frequently but
often enough to justify in your view special protective measures
against potential offenders. Please mark with an asterisk any
offence in either category for which you think protective custody
would not be justified, though non-custodial measures, if suitable
ones could be devised, would be justified.*

*If there are other offences, not included in the Appendix, which you
think cause grave harm, please specify them and say in each case
whether they would justify custodial or non-custodial measures
of protection.*

It is sometimes suggested that the criminal law as it now stands fails
to declare as offences some actions which result in grave harm (e.g., in
the field of environmental pollution).

Can you suggest any such actions?

Grave harm arises from many different kinds of behaviour in different circumstances, so that even if it is covered by the criminal law, the
various kinds of behaviour that cause it may not correspond to the legal
classification of offences. Grave harm may not be readily defined and
classified in these terms, and some people find this disturbing. For
example, widespread 'mugging' resulting in minor personal injuries may
cause greater public anxiety than domestic violence resulting in grievous
bodily harm; some might argue that burglary in a dwelling is more
serious than burglary in a warehouse; and others might say that it is
more important to protect the public against corrupt practices in the
public service than in the private sector.

*Can you suggest ways of redefining any of the offences in the
Appendix so as to provide a more precise account of the grave
harm you think they cause? For example, could they be sub-
divided according to their social context, the circumstances in
which they are committed, or their consequences?*

II
CAN PROTECTIVE MEASURES BE JUSTIFIED?

A serious offence does not make a dangerous offender unless there is a likelihood that it will be repeated despite the usual precautions provided by the law and the agencies of law enforcement.

But special precautions applied to a potential offender restrict in a greater or lesser degree his freedom and some people take the view that it is never just to do this in the expectation that he will do harm. They argue that if a person is being declared dangerous and deprived of his freedom, we should never depart from the principle of justice, enshrined in the common law rule for criminal trials, that a person's guilt must be proved beyond reasonable doubt before he may be convicted and punished; but that it is impossible to be certain of a person's future actions. However, most people are prepared to grant that there are exceptions or qualifications to this principle, and that, providing that the guilt of an offender in respect of at least one past offence has been established, protection of the public can, in certain stringently defined circumstances, be a sufficient ground by itself for restricting his freedom. Even so, there are radical differences of opinion as to how protecting the public is related to other penological objectives; as to how serious the first offence must be for prediction of further offences to be taken into account; and as to whether the offence which the offender is judged likely to commit must be the same sort of offence as the offence of which he has already been convicted.

We consider different aspects of these questions at various points in the rest of this document.

III
PROBLEMS OF PREDICTING CRIMINAL BEHAVIOUR
AND ASSESSING DANGEROUSNESS

If preventive measures are justified, then it is impossible to evade the notoriously difficult problem of prediction; and these we have considered at length. If it is impossible to have proof beyond reasonable doubt, how great must the likelihood be that an offender will cause serious harm if not detained or otherwise restrained? By what method is this likelihood to be judged?

Two sorts of mistake are possible in deciding whether or not an offender should be considered dangerous. On the one hand, an offender who, if released, would no do further serious harm, and may be unnecessarily detained for a long period, while on the other hand an offender may be released who in the event does cause further serious harm.

It is sometimes assumed that the two sorts of mistake are equally undesirable.

But may it not be unjust to risk mistaken detentions for the sake of avoiding mistaken release?

On the other hand, may it not sometimes be more important to avoid a mistaken release, with its grave consequences for others, than a mistaken detention?

If so, for which of the offences listed in the Appendix, and in what circumstances, would you consider this acceptable?

Prediction is of two kinds: the forecasting of criminal behaviour in classes of offenders by statistical (i.e., actuarial) methods, and the assessment of dangerousness in individual cases.

Actuarial Prediction

It is virtually impossible, at present, to make useful statistical predictions of further criminal behaviour in groups of serious offenders classed according to characteristics they hold in common. We have reviewed attempts to relate the probability of a repetition of the offence to the kind of offence in question. We conclude that, in the present state of knowledge, offenders cannot be satisfactorily screened by actuarial formulae. For example, from a strictly actuarial point of view, a man who commits a serious violent or sexual offence cannot be assigned to a class the members of which are more likely than not to commit a further serious offence. Any such classification of offenders on the basis of criteria available at present would be wrong in more cases than it would be right.

The inference is clear: an offender should not be treated as dangerous only on account of the rate of repetition of serious offences among a class to which he belongs.

Prediction in Individual Cases

Even if an acceptable and useful actuarial formula could be devised, for assigning an individual offender to a class the members of which have in general a high probability of repeating a serious offence, this would establish no more than a *prima facie* case for applying preventive measures to him. *We are considering what rules and principles could be devised to help in deciding when to apply protective measures in individual cases.*

The notion of an individual propensity to offend raises difficulties. It may or may not be a wilful propensity, and it may or may not be caused by or associated with a mental disorder which could of itself

make an offender less responsive to normal measures of social control.
We are excluding from consideration mentally disordered offenders
who are dealt with within the hospital system, since the problems they
raise have recently been fully examined by the Butler Committee.
*We are concerned with offenders who are 'normal' in the sense that
the courts have not dealt with them under the Mental Health Act,
1959,* or its equivalent in other parts of the United Kingdom* (though
they may indeed be characterised by psychological abnormalities
and handicaps).

Completely accurate assessments of dangerousness in individual
cases are of course impossible, and there is the difficulty of principle,
that an offender's dangerous propensities cannot be assessed, nor his
behaviour predicted, in abstraction from the circumstances in which
one supposes him to be placed. Nevertheless, in practice the courts in
passing sentence, and the parole authorities and the Home Secretary
and his officials in the Home Office in considering release do treat some
'normal' offenders as dangerous. *We are considering whether this existing practice should be formalised, whether the procedure should be
more clearly defined, and whether its application should be limited
or extended.*

There are a great many grounds on which a sentence may be initially awarded, and a great many grounds on which it may be subsequently reconsidered. But for any sentence, whether determinate
or indeterminate, which is partly or wholly designed as a protection
for others, it is particularly necessary to have regular review, to consider whether the need to protect others still requires the offender
to be detained.

The English and Scottish parole systems in effect guarantee that,
unless the prisoner refuses to apply for parole, any determinate sentence
will be reviewed in time for him to be released after one-third of his
sentence (or one year, if that is longer), and thereafter at such intervals
as may be determined. For the review of life sentences the arrangements
are discretionary and more complicated, but broadly speaking each case
is considered in the Home Office soon after sentence, and again by a
joint committee of representatives of the Home Office and the Parole
Board at about the three-year stage, when the time is fixed for the first
formal review. From then on all life-sentence cases are reviewed at
fairly frequent intervals.

However, it is not fixed by law either what considerations shall
guide a court in pronouncing sentence or what considerations are to be

*Offenders may be judged to be mentally disordered and dealt with under the
Mental Health Act if they are found to be suffering from mental illness, subnormality, severe subnormality, or psychopathic disorder. But as most so-called
psychopaths are at present dealt with under the penal system rather than the
hospital system, we have paid some attention to the problems they present.

taken into account when either a fixed or life sentence is reviewed. *We are considering how assessments of dangerousness in relation to any form of protective sentence can best be made, so as to ensure that sentences of imprisonment intended to protect the public shall be used as sparingly as possible, and shall be imposed and administered in conformity with the highest standards of justice.* We think that there is a form which might be adhered to both by the court initially, and by the reviewing body subsequently, in arriving at a judgment of the offender's dangerousness.

First, we think that there should be qualifying conditions about which the court or reviewing body would have to be satisfied before considering any offender dangerous. We should then like there to be guidelines to assist those responsible for assessing dangerousness to develop a consciously consistent practice over many cases. Though we acknowledge the impossibility of standardising assessments which can only be based on the intuitive evaluation of diverse opinions and various amounts of available information, we nevertheless think that it would make for a more controlled and informed use of intuition if assessors were provided with a standard range of considerations essential to a fair and balanced judgment.

We should value your comments on the following two lists of questions, to be considered by a court or by a reviewing body: the first indicating the qualifying conditions which would always have to be met; the second acting as a guide to the principles of individual assessment.

Do you consider it desirable to have standard lists of questions like these?

Do you consider that the lists we have suggested contain unsuitable or useless questions?

Are there any other questions which either list ought to include?

If you have experience of relevant reports or records (e.g., social inquiry reports or prison records) could you estimate the chances of regularly assembling, for every offender under consideration, a full set of answers?

Do you consider the same pair of lists to be suitable for both a court in deciding on a protective sentence, and for a reviewing body considering release?

LIST ONE

1. Has the offender committed one or more offences on a list of qualifying offences?
2. Has his offence caused, or was it likely to cause, harm of a certain kind and degree?
3. Is there evidence, in the form of previous convictions of a similar kind, that the offender is more likely than most such offenders to repeat his behaviour?
4. Is the offender not a case for psychiatric disposal?

LIST TWO

1. What were the circumstances of the offence? (e.g., Was it committed alone or in a group? Was it spontaneous or provoked? What degree and quality of violence was involved? Were there disinhibiting factors at work, such as drugs or alcohol, companions or fatigue?)
2. What are the offender's circumstances and history? (e.g., age, sex, occupation, marital status, dependants, childhood history and adult record, including conduct in custody).
3. Is the offence susceptible of rational explanation? (e.g., in terms of the choice of victim or the offender's personal circumstances and history).
4. What are the offender's intentions? Does he evidently, or avowedly, intend to repeat the offence?
5. What is known of the offender's character? (e.g., Is he known to have a capacity for sympathy with others or for learning from experience?)
6. What circumstances will the offender find himself in when released? If he intends to repeat his offence, will his circumstances frustrate or modify his intentions? If he does not intend to repeat his offence, will he nonetheless be subject to temptation and pressures to do so, in his social and family circumstances?
7. How far can the offender's circumstances on release be controlled, for example by imposing adequate measures of supervision, to ensure that he is not a danger to others?

What standards of evidence and proof should be met, in deciding to impose or to continue a protective sentence?

What weight should a body assessing dangerousness in a normal offender attach to the views of psychiatrists, psychologists, prison officers, prison welfare workers, prison chaplains, prison visitors, police officers, probation officers, social workers? Please say if and why you think any of these persons have more or less than the others to contribute to the assessment of dangerousness. Are there any others whose opinion should be consulted?

To what extent should the assessing body accept the word of those consulted?

How can the offender be given the opportunity to challenge it effectively?

What standards can the assessing body impose on information which concerns matters of opinion or interpretation?

What standards can it impose on evidence as to facts about the offender's circumstances and history? Should the standards be equal to those required in court?

Should an assessing body be required to say why it considers that no measure short of detention will provide adequate protection for the public?

What sort of reasons should be acceptable? Should they be advanced in detail and supported by evidence?

Under present arrangements, in so far as explicit assessments of dangerousness are made, they are made by the Parole Board. *We are considering whether the Parole Board is the body best suited to this task, if there is a need for some degree of formalisation in the administration of protective sentences.*

If you are in a position to comment, we should like to know how you think Mental Health Review Tribunals compare with the Parole Board, in respect of their composition, powers, and modes of operation, for the purpose of assessing dangerousness.

IV
SENTENCES – ALTERNATIVE FORMS
AND PROCEDURES

Determinate Sentences

The English sentencing system does not cater explicitly for dangerousness.* The great majority of offenders who are considered by the courts to be dangerous, in the sense of being likely to commit or repeat a

---

*The Powers of the Criminal Courts Act, 1973, provides for an extended sentence (i.e., a prison sentence longer than would be considered appropriate for the actual offence): but the rubric to the statute makes it clear that this is intended for 'persistent offenders'. Moreover, although the definition of the sort of offender who is eligible for the extended sentence is restrictive and complex, it is possible to qualify for it by a series of imprisonable offences which involve no great loss or harm.

serious offence, are given sentences of determinate length within the normal range for the offence of which they have been convicted; but the sentences may be longer than they would otherwise have been because of the court's estimate of the likelihood that the offender will commit or repeat a serious offence, and in order to protect the public. Neither the extent nor the rationale of this protective element in normal-range sentences is known, since it is seldom made explicit by the court. Such an element may even be present in sentences for offences which, by common agreement, would not entail grave harm, even though there may be a high probability of repetition. In many cases the protective element in sentences may be inequitably (because inconsistently or irrationally) determined. *We are considering whether it would be feasible to rationalise the administration of a protective element in sentencing by confining its use to specified offences generally agreed to entail grave harm, and to offenders selected by reference to specified criteria.*

> *Should the courts then be required, when pronouncing ordinary sentences, to discount any estimate of the likelihood that the offender will commit a future offence; or should they merely be required to make explicit any protective element in an ordinary sentence.*

> *For which, if any, of the offences listed in the Appendix and under what circumstances, do you consider a protective element in determinate sentences to be appropriate?*

> *Should it take the form of an addition to the length of the sentence, or might it take the form of withholding the right to remission or the possibility of parole?*

> *Should the length of a protective extension be fixed by statute, or by the judge in individual cases?*

> *Should it be possible for the protective extension to bring the total sentence beyond the normal range for the offence in question? What sort of length of extension would you consider appropriate?*

The Life Sentence

The most explicit recognition of 'dangerousness' in English sentencing practice is found in the use of the *life sentence*. This must be imposed for murder, and may be imposed for a number of other offences (e.g., aggravated burglary, rape, arson, manslaughter). When the sentence is not mandatory it seems to emerge from judicial practice that the offender must either be suffering from a mental disorder or be in some other way of unstable character, and that there must be a likelihood of his committing further grave offences. He must have committed a grave offence already, but its gravity is not the first consideration; if the risk of a future grave offence is substantial, a life sentence may be imposed even though the current offence would not justify a long fixed term.

We have considered the advantages and disadvantages of the life sentence, as it is used and administered at present, as a protective measure for dealing with 'dangerous' offenders. We think that the most important question regarding the life sentence, apart from the question of indeterminacy, concerns the method of review and release. In particular we have noted:

1. That in the present system for reviewing life sentences the decision whether to release is finally a matter of executive discretion, resting with the Home Secretary, subject only to the advice and the veto of the Parole Board.
2. That a different procedure is provided for offenders detained under s. 60 of the Mental Health Act. This allows for the offender to appeal to the Mental Health Review Tribunal against the decision of a doctor. It gives the offender the right of representation at the sitting of the Tribunal, and it requires reasons to be given for the decision it makes.

Could the review of life sentences be improved by making it more like the procedure under the Mental Health Act, or in some other way?

Even if the review of life sentences remains with the executive, various procedures might be favoured for the giving of advice by an independent body, like the Parole Board, or like the Mental Health Review Tribunal.

Would the decisions of individual cases necessarily be improved by adopting a more judicial procedure?

Should there be representation of the offender, judicial standards of evidence, the giving of reasons for the decision, and the right of appeal?

Should the procedure be more radically changed, to place the decision entirely in the hands of a judicial or quasi-judicial body?

Alternative Forms of Indeterminate Sentence

Would you like the life sentence to remain in its present form?

If not, what other forms of sentence would you favour?

In devising a form of sentence appropriate for dealing with dangerous offenders, a number of factors need to be considered:

1. *Indeterminacy*
   (a) Wholly indeterminate sentences.

Are you opposed to these in principle?

(b) A semi-determinate sentence, i.e., with a minimum or a maximum, or both, fixed by statute, or fixed by the court within statutory limits, leaving the actual date of release to be determined by another body.

(c) A renewable sentence, i.e., a sentence of a length fixed by the court, with the express proviso that before its termination an application could be made to the court to extend it for a further fixed period.

2. *Regularity of review*
   A sentence might be subject to statutory review at intervals fixed by statute, or fixed by the reviewing body.

   Should the prisoner have a right to review?

3. *Decision to release*
   (a) By the executive.
   (b) By the court.
   (c) By some form of independent body set up for the purpose.

4. *Conduct of review*
   (a) A case conference study of the individual offender.
   (b) A review judicial in form, and determined by the balance of arguments.
   (c) A review judicial in form, and with the onus lying on those who hold that the prisoner should be detained longer to show why this is so.

5. *Position of the offender after release*
   Should there be supervision of the offender after his release, and power on the part of the reviewing body to recall him —
   (a) for the remaining period of his original sentence, or a fixed proportion of it;
   (b) for a further period fixed by the court, within statutory limits, when pronouncing the original sentence;
   (c) for a period fixed by the reviewing body, within statutory limits, at the time of release?

Many combinations of these features in a single form of sentence are possible. For example, an indeterminate sentence, subject to regular quasi-judicial review before release, with the possibility of recall by the same procedure during a fixed period of supervision after release; a sentence fixed only as to the minimum, after which the offender has the right to be released unless it can be shown before a quasi-judicial body that his continued detention for a further fixed period is justified; a sentence with a maximum period at any time before which it is possible for a reviewing body to release him, with supervision and the power of recall until the end of the maximum period.

Can you suggest other forms of sentence framed in this way, or other features which might be incorporated in the form of a sentence?

For any proposed form of sentence, further questions arise:

For which offences or offenders would such a sentence be available?

Should a new form of sentence be considered only for those offences which are already subject to a life sentence, or should it be extended to other offenders?

Should a new form of sentence ever be mandatory, as the life sentence at present is for murder?

Should more than one new form of sentence be introduced, for the same or different offences?

Should the life sentence in its present or a modified form be preserved alongside whatever new proposal is adopted?

Protection without Custody

Imprisonment, while it lasts, incapacitates a potential offender and in that sense offers the maximum protection against the risk of his causing grave harm in the futute. But imprisoning potential offenders is a repugnant as well as a costly protective measure, and is only acceptable, if ever, as a last resort. Control in the community is a less drastic curtailment of freedom and is to that extent less repugnant. It is certainly less costly than imprisonment; but is it practicable and can it ever be effective as a protective measure? *We are considering whether, in cases where it is agreed that there is need for protection, more use could or should be made of control without custody, either as a direct sentence of the court or as a period of licence following release from detention.*

At present, if parole is granted to an offender serving a determinate sentence the licence remains in force only until the normal remission date (i.e., at the expiry of two-thirds of the sentence), with the exception of licences following extended sentences and young prisoner sentences of 18 months or more which remain in force for the whole of the length of the sentence. When a prisoner serving a life sentence is released, he remains subject to recall for life; but specific requirements and restrictions are usually lifted after some years.

A supervising officer cannot be with a licensee for twenty-four hours a day and cannot hope to control or even oversee more than a few aspects of his life. There are undoubtedly limitations on the possibility of generalised supervision of an offender's life in the community.

But are those limitations as severe as is sometimes supposed?

Of the limitations which do exist, to what extent do you think they are due to scarcity or poor deployment of resources of money and/or manpower, and to what extent are they due to difficulties of principle (e.g., the definition of the supervising officer's role)?

If you think that 'dangerousness' can in some cases be effectively dealt with by measures directed against individuals but short of custody, please specify both the harmful behaviour and the kind of arrangements for control without custody you have in mind.

Should the court or a reviewing body have the power to restrict a potential offender's freedom of movement, choice of occupation, or right to engage in specified activities?

If so, for what kinds of behaviour would such powers be appropriate?

Should it be possible to provide for a licence period which would continue beyond the two-thirds remission date for determinate sentences of imprisonment awarded on protective grounds (as the extended sentence and the young prisoner sentence now provide) or even beyond the end of the sentence itself?

Should it be possible to provide for release on licence (either at the time of sentencing or after a period of detention), conditional upon frequent review for reassessment of the offender's capacity for grave harm?

If so, how frequently is it realistic or desirable to undertake such reassessments (bearing in mind the great uncertainty of long-term predictions of an individual's behaviour)?

Is it realistic to suppose that such a review could be designed not only to consider the question of detaining an offender or recalling him to detention but also to consider ways of steering him away from a situation or mode of behaviour thought likely to increase the risk of his causing harm?

APPENDIX

Offences against the Person

Common law offences:
1. Murder or attempts thereat
2. Manslaughter
3. Causing an affray
4. Kidnapping

Offences against the Person Act 1861:
5. Wounding with intent to do grievous bodily harm (s. 18)

6. Unlawful wounding or inflicting of grievous bodily harm, with or without any weapon or instrument (s.20)
7. Conspiracy or incitement to murder (s.4)
8. Attempting to choke, etc., or using chloroform, etc., with intent to commit an indictable offence (ss.21—22)
9. Administering poison, etc., so as to endanger life or with intent to injure (s.23)
10. Causing bodily injury by explosives or causing explosions, etc. (ss.28—29)
11. Setting man-traps, etc., with intent (s.31)
12. Doing certain things with intent to endanger railway passengers (ss.32—33)
13. Attempts to procure abortion (ss.58—59)
14. Abandoning or exposing children under 2 years (s.27)
15. Assault occasioning actual bodily harm (s.47)

Explosive Substances Act 1883:
16. Causing explosions likely to endanger life but not necessarily with intent to do so (s.2)
17. Making or keeping explosives with intent (s.3)
18. Making or possessing explosives under suspicious circumstances (s.4)

Hijacking Act 1971:
19. Hijacking aircraft (s.1)

Protection of Aircraft Act 1973:
20. Destroying, damaging or endangering aircraft (ss.1—3)

Firearms Act 1968:
21. Use of firearms to resist arrest (s.17)
22. Carrying firearms with criminal intent (s.18)
23. Trespassing with a firearm (s.20)

Infant Life (Preservation) Act 1929:
24. Child destruction, i.e., destruction of a foetus capable of being born alive (s.1)

Infanticide Act 1938:
25. Infanticide (s.1)

Children and Young Persons Act 1933:
26. Child cruelty, neglect, etc. (s.1)

Theft Act 1968:
27. Robbery (s.8)

28. Blackmail (s.21)

Criminal Damage Act 1971:
29. Arson (s.1)
30. Criminal damage with intent to endanger life (s.1)

Sexual Offences

Sexual Offences Acts 1956 and 1967:
31. Rape (s.1)
32. Incest (s.10)
33. Buggery with a boy under the age of 16 years or with animal (s.12)
34. Buggery under other circumstances without consent (s.12)
35. Buggery under other circumstances with consent (s.12)
36. Sexual intercourse with a girl under 13 (s.5)
37. Sexual intercourse with a girl under 16 (s.16)
38. Indecent assault on female (s.14)
39. Indecent assault on male (ss. 15—16)
40. Man living on earnings of prostitute (s.30)
41. Woman controlling prostitutes (s.31)

Indecency with Children Act 1960:
42. Gross indecency towards a child under 14 years (s.1)

Property Offences

Common law:
43. False statements relating to income tax

Theft Act 1968:
44. Aggravated burglary (s.10)
45. Burglary (s.9)
46. Theft (s.7)
47. Obtaining by deception (ss 15—16)
48. Falsifying accounts (s.17)
49. Handling or receiving stolen goods (s.8)
50. Removal of articles (e.g., works of art) from public places without authority (s.11)
51. False statements by company officers to deceive members or creditors (s.19)
52. Destruction or concealment of certain documents for gain (s.20)

Forgery Act 1913:
53. Forgery or uttering forged document (ss.2, 3, 6)
54. Demanding property on forged document (s.7)

Criminal Damage Act 1971:
55. Destroying or damaging property (s.1)
56. Threats to destroy or damage property, e.g., bomb hoax (s.2)

Malicious Damage Act 1971:
57. Exhibiting false signals to ships with intent (s.47)
58. Obstructing, etc., railway with intent to obstruct, etc., anything using the railway (s.35)
59. Unlawfully obstructing railway (s.36)

Prevention of Fraud (Investment) Act 1958:
60. False or misleading statement to induce investment (s.13)

Protection of Depositors Act 1963:
61. False or misleading statement to induce deposits (s.1)

Customs and Excise Act 1952:
62. Improper importation of goods (s.45)
63. Improper exportation of goods (s.47)
64. Untrue declarations to customs (s.301)

Coinage Offences Act 1936:
65. Counterfeiting coins (s.1)
66. Uttering, etc., counterfeit coin (s.5)

Drugs Offences

Misuse of Drugs Act 1971:
67. Importation or exportation of controlled drugs (s.3)
68. Production or supply of controlled drugs (s.4)

Driving Offences

Road Traffic Act 1972:
69. Causing death by reckless or dangerous driving (s.1)
70. Reckless and dangerous driving (s.2)
71. Driving when unfit through drink or drugs (s.5)

Miscellaneous Offences

Common law offences:
72. Fabrication of false evidence with intent to deceive a judicial tribunal
73. Effecting a public mischief or conspiracy to do so (e.g., disseminating false information with intent to cause alarm)

Criminal Law Act 1967:
74. False report to police tending to show that an offence has been
    committed or giving rise to apprehension for the safety of per-
    sons or property (s.5)

Perjury Act 1911:
75. Perjury (s.1)
76. False declarations and statements in other than judicial proceedings
    (ss.2—6)

RESPONDENTS TO THE CONSULTATIVE DOCUMENT

Representatives of Official Bodies

Conference of Chief Probation Officers
Department of Health and Social Security
Home Office
National Association of Probation Officers (Merseyside Branch)
National Association of Probation Officers (West Yorkshire Branch)
Police Federation
Scottish Association for the Care and Resettlement of Offenders
Scottish Association for the Study of Delinquency
Scottish Home and Health Department

Individuals

Dr D. Anton-Stephens (Psychiatrist and Parole Board member)
Mrs Alan Bainton
Miss E.E. Barnard (Lecturer in Criminology, Sheffield)
Mr Phillip Barrie (Chairman, Scottish Parole Board)
Dr A.E. Bottoms (Professor of Criminology, Sheffield)
Mr W.G. Carson (Lecturer in Criminology, Edinburgh)
Mr P. Cavadine (Information Officer, N.A.C.R.O.)
John Conrad (Academy for Contemporary Problems, Columbus, Ohio)
Dr B.D. Cooper (Senior Medical Officer, H.M.P. Parkhurst)
His Honour Judge David QC., DL
Mr G.S. Ecclestone (Secretary, Board for Social Responsibility of the
    General Synod of the Church of England)
Mr P. Faulkner
Mrs M.A. Fearnley
Mrs Roderic Floud (Magistrate and Social Worker)
Mr R.G. Gregory
Lord Hunt

The Hon. Mr Justice Lawson
Dr M.J. MacCulloch (Principal Medical Officer, D.H.S.S.)
Mr Hugh Marriage (Principal Psychologist, Home Office Prison Department, South East Region)
Dr Geoffrey Marshall (The Queen's College, Oxford)
Detective Chief Superintendent S.J. Moore (New Scotland Yard)
Sir Louis Petch (Chairman, Parole Board of England and Wales)
The Hon. Mr Justice Phillips
Mr Herschel Prins (School of Social Work, University of Leicester)
Dr Bruce Ritson
Dr P.D. Scott
Mr A.V. Sheehan, (Deputy Crown Agent, Scotland)
Mr Leslie Smith (Department of General Education, Loughborough Technical College)
The Rt. Hon. Lord Justice Waller
Dr W.A. Weston
Mr Leslie T. Wilkins (Professor of Criminal Justice, University of Albany)
The Hon. Mr Gordon Wilson, M.P.

List of Institutions Visited

Members of the Working Party visited the following institutions during 1976 and 1977. Discussions were held with members of the staff and, in the case of the prisons, with selected groups of prisoners.

H.M.P. Albany
H.M.P. Kingston
H.M.P. Leyhill
H.M.P. Parkhurst
Special Unit, H.M.P. Barlinnie
H.M.P. Wakefield
Broadmoor Special Hospital
Rampton Special Hospital

Determining 'Dangerousness': Methodological Problems and Empirical Findings

Predictive judgments of future behaviour are statements of probability. They have the same logical form regardless of the method used to arrive at them and the relative precision of the formulation. Whether an offender is simply labelled a 'good' or a 'bad' risk, or whether the risk of his causing further harm is roughly expressed in words such as 'not very likely', 'more likely than not' or 'virtually certain' to cause further harm, or is given a numerical value such as 25, 55 or 90%, he is, in effect, being classified; he is being directly or indirectly assigned to a class of which, if it were large enough, we could expect the more or less precisely indicated fraction to cause further harm. It is logically irrelevant how the classification is arrived at — whether by means of case-studies of individuals in isolation (the so-called 'clinical' method) or by means of a statistical exercise (the so-called 'actuarial' method).

The central question in the controversy over the use of the concept of dangerousness in criminal justice is the rationality of the classification and differential treatment of serious offenders. The justification for any departure from equal treatment of serious offenders for the protection of the public depends, first and foremost, on the possibility of making a rational classification of these offenders for this purpose: those to be treated as 'dangerous' must be shown to constitute a distinctive sub-class, definable as relatively and absolutely high-risk serious offenders. Critics of protective sentencing have focused attention on the theoretical and practical difficulties — some would say, the impossibility — of identifying such a sub-class and cite the findings of a number of empirical attempts to do so.

The prime obstacle to the attempt to distinguish high-risk from other serious offenders is the infrequency with which serious offenders in general repeat their serious offences. If the chance or random probability of their doing so is less than 50%, assessors are statistically more likely to be wrong than right in their judgments of individual offenders as *dangerous*, no matter what method is used or how skilfully. Fewer mistakes would result from treating the whole group alike, as good risks. A classification which yields a higher than random probability of falsified judgments must be suspect; but the point is often overlooked in designing and evaluating attempts to predict the future behaviour of offenders.

The work of Glueck (1960), which is often cited as a successful attempt at prediction, provides a simple illustration of the problem. Glueck devised a Delinquency Prediction Table and applied it in 1953 to a sample of 223 boys entering New York schools at about age 6. Of these boys, 37 were classed with the use of the table as potential delinquents and 186 as potential non-delinquents. However, seven years later, in 1960, only 23 were reported as having been 'adjudicated delinquent' and 200 had stayed clear of the law. The random probability of becoming delinquent within seven years for this group of boys was, therefore, 11%; but the use of the prediction table had yielded a probability of 15%. Had all the boys been classed as potential non-delinquents without the use of the table, the number of falsified judgments would have been 23 instead of 34. Though clinicians may argue that the discrepancy would have been smaller had the classification been based on case-studies instead of a prediction table, it certainly could not have been eliminated. The most subtle predictive devices will fail to uncover high-risk sub-groups of offenders if the sample populations to which they are applied are, so to say, not very recidivist to start with, as indicated by a low rate of further offending. Glueck could not go far wrong in classifying boys in his sample as potential non-delinquents and the proportion of *false negative* judgments was only 5.4%; but the chances of his mis-classifying boys as delinquent were high and the proportion of *false positive* judgments was 64.8%.

The remedy for this purely statistical, so-called 'base-rate', problem is to characterise a group of offenders of which more than 50% can be expected to cause further harm, so that − other things being equal − assessors may have more than an even chance of being right in their selection of a high-risk sub-group.

The probability of 'false positive' errors of prediction measures the risk imposed on offenders classed as 'dangerous' that they may be deprived unnecessarily of their liberty; the probability of 'false negatives' leaves the public with the risk of serious harm. The one risk cannot be reduced without increasing the other and an efficient classification is, therefore, optimal, minimising the sum of probable errors of both kinds. But justice to offenders requires a high probability of being right in classifying them as *dangerous* and an efficient classification may yet entail an unacceptably high probability of 'false positive' errors of prediction.

Statistical Studies

Various attempts have been made to identify high-risk sub-groups of offenders, usually in conjunction with the construction of 'experience tables' and 'dangerousness' scales, for use in predicting recidivism over short periods during which offenders are on parole or on bail before trial. Several substantial exercises of this kind have been undertaken in the United States, with a view to defining sub-groups of violent offenders who are on average more likely than not to repeat their violent offences; but none have been successful.

Wenk (1972) and his colleagues in the Research Division of the California Department of Corrections made three major attempts to develop means of classifying offenders by *violence-proneness*, with disappointing results. In 1965 they devised a scale incorporating various relevant attributes of offenders, such as age, nature of the instant offence, previous record, use of drugs etc., and were able to identify a small sub-group (3% of the large population of offenders under study) who were three times as likely as the rest of those at risk to commit a violent offence whilst on parole for a period of 15 months. However, the probability was still only 14% for this select group.

A second investigation, in 1968/9, tested the validity of a classification of offenders according to their record of violent behaviour by following their careers in the 12 months subsequent to their release from prison. Of the sub-group deemed to have the highest potential for aggression, the proportion returned to prison for new crimes of actual or potential violence was 3.1 per thousand, as compared with 2.8 per thousand of the group judged to be less potentially aggressive.

Finally, these investigators undertook a more elaborate study of more than 4000 muvenile offenders made wards of the California Youth Authority in 1964/5 and placed on parole. Only 2.4% of them committed violent offences whilst on parole for 15 months. The investigators were able to identify a substantial sub-group who were three times more likely than the rest to commit violent offences whilst on parole; but the rate of violent recidivism for this select group was no higher than 5.2%.

The indices of aggressiveness and scales of violence-proneness used in these investigations were elaborate of their kind and comprehensive. They were based not only on records of violent behaviour but on much other background information about offenders, including the results of psychiatric examination and psychological tests; altogether 100 separate variables were devised. But these predictive devices were put to work on a not very violent group of young offenders who, furthermore, were given only a very short time in which to manifest their 'dangerousness'. As the consulting statistician fairly remarked: 'considering the rarity of the phenomenon, [i.e. violent behaviour whilst on parole for 15 months], it is difficult to imagine that even with the most refined techniques, one could do much better than, say, to double the best rates obtained here'.

In Britain, a comparable investigation (Brody and Tarling 1980) suffered from the same statistical limitation, that serious assaultive crimes are rare. With a longer follow-up period and detailed scrutiny of individual case-histories it proved possible to improve on the rates reported by Wenk et al., but only marginally.

Brody and Tarling (1980) used a representative (one in ten) sample of 811 adult men serving sentences in prisons in south-east England in 1972. They obtained unusually comprehensive access to prison and medical records and were able to identify a sub-group of 77 'dangerous' men (i.e. men they rated from their case-histories, in consultation with prison staff, as likely on release to commit a further serious assaultive crime). By 1979 all but a handful of the whole sample of prisoners had been at liberty for at least five years and the investigators were in a position to examine the validity of their assessments of dangerousness. Of the 77 men classed in some degree as 'dangerous' 18 were still in custody and there were no records for 7 of those who had been released; of the remaining 734, 9 were still in custody and the records of 67 released men were missing. Hence they were left with an effective sample of 710 men who had been at risk of causing further harm, of whom they had classed 52 as 'dangerous'. Inspection of criminal records revealed that only 25% (13) of the 'dangerous' sub-group were convicted of an assaultive crime within 5 years of being released; and if, as seems appropriate, account is taken only of 'dangerous' offences (i.e. serious assaultive offences, consistent with an assessment of 'dangerousness') the figure drops to 17% (9).

Other investigators have been more successful and have managed, using only the variables of age and criminal record, to identify sub-groups of high-risk, violent offenders with probabilities in the range 35 to 55% of doing further serious harm within periods at risk of up to 5 years.

In the United States, Cocozza and Steadman (1974) constructed a summary measure of previous criminal activity which they applied to the 98 offenders who were eventually released into the community from hospitals for the criminally insane following the 1966 decision of the U.S. Supreme Court in the case of *Baxstrom* v. *Herold*. Their fifteen-point Legal Dangerousness Scale took account of juvenile record, number of previous arrests and convictions for violent offences and the severity of the offence which had led to commitment to hospital. Offenders who scored at least five points on this fifteen-point scale and who were not more than 50 years old, constituted a sub-group of 49, of whom 36% went on to commit further violence within two or three years of being released. Koppin (1976) used the same scale on another, similar, group of 111 offenders who had been deemed unfit to stand trial but were eventually released from secure hospitals. This group was somewhat younger on average than the group studied by Cocozza and Steadman and it contained no women: of those who were under 50 and who scored five or more points on the Legal Dangerousness Scale, 48.6% committed violent offences during the same period at risk.

In three different British samples it has been found that one variable alone — having three or more previous convictions for violence — identified groups of offenders of whom more than 1 in 2 were subsequently reconvicted of violence, including robbery. Walker, Hammond and Steer (1970) reported a study of two samples: (a) 264 Scots who incurred their first conviction (being a violence conviction) in Scotland in 1947. For the 11 with a fourth or subsequent conviction for violence, the percentage who incurred a further such conviction was 55%. This was a cohort study: the sample was followed through successive convictions. The follow-up period varied for the later convictions, since the study was cut off at 1958 convictions; so 55% is a minimum percentage and might well have been a bit higher if the follow-up had been standardised at, say, five years after every conviction; (b) 401 'Londoners', convicted of indictable violence in the Metropolitan police district in March or April 1957. For the 21 who incurred a fourth or subsequent such conviction, the percentage who incurred another one in the next 5 years was 52%. Phillpotts and Lancucki (1979) studied a sample of adult men convicted of standard list offences at a court in England and Wales in January 1971. In a sub-sample of 828 men who had been either convicted of an offence with violence or robbery in January 1971 or had at least one such previous conviction, 43 had three or more successive convictions of the kind. Of these, the proportion who were reconvicted of further such offences within six years of sentence was 54%. This group of recidivists was made up of two distinct subgroups: of the 30 men with exactly three convictions for violence or robbery, prior to or in January 1971, 12 were reconvicted of similar offences (i.e. 40% ± 20%) while of the remaining 13 men with four or more such convictions, 11 were reconvicted (i.e. 85% ± 20%). These numbers are small, and the confidence limit wide: plus or minus 20%. But even so, this means that if the exercise were repeated there is a very high probability (0.975) that of men with four or more such convictions *at least* 65% would incur further such convictions; and the percentage might well reach 100%.

Statistical attempts to isolate empirically defined risk-groups are crucially important for the justification of the selection of dangerous offenders. Only if attempts to assess dangerousness are restricted to groups of offenders with a general probability of causing further serious harm of more than 50% are they statistically justifiable; for only so can we ensure that, other things being equal, our judgments are more likely to be right than wrong. Another way of stating the requirement in more familiar terms is to say that, before we are justified in considering whether or not a serious offender is *dangerous*, there must be a *prima facie* case for supposing that he is likely to cause further serious harm; and that *prima facie* case, speaking strictly statistically, rest on his membership of a high risk class of serious offenders, i.e. of a class of which the members are, actuarially speaking, at the very least more likely than not to commit further serious offences.

There is a clear need for a substantial research project designed for the specific purpose of identifying high-risk sub-groups of *serious* offenders. There seems to be no full-scale piece of research which has been based on samples selected with this in view, or has made use of anything like all the information about members of a sample which is likely to be of predictive value. All the well-known statistical investigations have made opportunistic use of information, most of which was not collected with prediction in view. To take personal violence as the most promising example, a sample could not be considered satisfactory unless it were representative of a cohort, appropriately stratified by types of offence, of all adults convicted of personal violence of any kind (or threats or attempted violence) in the course of a year in Magistrates' and Crown Courts. The information to be collected about such offenders ought to include at least the following:

Relationship to the victim and its duration
Circumstances in which the offence was committed
Motive(s) for it (including if possible those offered by victim as well
   as offender)
Evidence that offender had been taking alcohol or drugs
Psychiatric and/or psychological assessments
Evidence of previous violence (whether resulting in convictions or
   not) and its circumstances
Evidence of offender's association with other violent offenders
Previous sentences imposed on the offender, whether for violence or
   other types of offence
The offender's age, sex, country of upbringing, employments

A follow-up of at least five years during which the offender had been at liberty seems essential, and should take note not only of subsequent convictions for violence (and other offences) but also of occasions on which the offender had been allegedly involved in violence, even if these did not lead to a charge or conviction. It should also take note of any reports of supervisors (such as probation officers or social workers), and of any subsequent involvement in the use of drugs or heavy drinking, or situations of the kind in which the sample offence had occurred. Two points must be emphasised however: (i) numbers in high risk sub-groups of serious offenders will always be small and (ii) though it is almost exclusively amongst those with serious records, particularly of violence, that dangerous offenders are to be found, the sub-group will not include all those at high risk of causing serious harm, or even all those with records of violence who are at risk of causing further serious harm.

Brody and Tarling (1980) looked separately at the serious offenders in their sample. Including all the life sentence prisoners, these accounted for 38% of the sample: a group of 312 men stated to include those 'who specialised in lucrative and successful robberies, burglaries or frauds, who had badly wounded or killed their victims or would have carried out threats to do so, and who had sexually assaulted children or adults'. Of these serious offenders 10% (30) were assessed as highly dangerous but only 16 of these judgments could be tested, for 12 of the men concerned were still in custody in 1979 and the records for two others were missing. In the event, only one of the 16 men who could be followed up was reconvicted within five years of a 'dangerous' offence; indeed, only three were reconvicted of any offence at all during this period. It is probable − though not stated − that these 16 men were under some degree of supervision during at least the first year of freedom; and we know that supervision tends to postpone reoffending. Nevertheless the results are striking. Of course, if all 30 of those assessed as dangerous had been released, more 'dangerous' offences would certainly have been committed; but how many more cannot be known. Even if the 12 who were still in custody in 1979 had all been correctly classifed as 'highly dangerous' (i.e. would, if released, have committed a 'dangerous' offence) the proportion of true positive judgments of highly dangerous would not have exceeded 46% (13), for the fact is that 53% (15) were falsified: 13 men stayed altogether clear of the law and two committed property offences not consistent with an assessment of 'dangerous'.

Alternative Methods of Assessment

Statistical studies can obviate the 'base-rate' difficulty but they cannot solve the problem of making just predictive judgments of offenders for sentencing purposes. This must be done by case-study on an individual basis. It will not do to sentence an offender solely on the ground that he belongs to a statistical risk-group, if only because from the fact that, say, 55% of a group are likely to reoffend, it need not follow that each individual member is 55% likely to do so. But this raises the problem of the relative merits of statistical and case-study methods of determining dangerousness.

The superiority of actuarial over clinical methods of assessing dangerousness seemed until recently to be an unshakeable fact. Writing in 1954, Meehl remarked that it was 'hard to show rigorously why the clinician ought to do better than the actuary and even harder to document the claim that he in fact does'. At the end of his extensive and meticulous survey of studies permitting comparison of the results of case-study and actuarial methods, he declared: '. . . it is clear that the dogmatic, complacent assertion sometimes heard from clinicians that "naturally" clinical prediction, being based on "real understanding" is superior, is simply not justified by the facts collected to date'. He pointed to 'the brute fact' that, despite all the defects and ambiguities, 'we have here, depending on one's standards for admission as relevant, from 16 to 20 studies involving a comparison of clinical and actuarial methods, in all but one of which the predictions made actuarially were either approximately equal or superior to those made by a clinician'.

As a clinician himself, Meehl understood the reluctance of his colleagues to accept the implications of his findings but he confessed himself unable to alleviate their horror at the prospect of misclassification by actuarial methods. 'A clinician's departure from the optimal method merely effects an exchange of some cases for others − but doesn't quite break even on the exchange.' The error by clinical ordeal is 'just as blind as one made by the blindest cut-and-dried formula, since the plain fact is that the clinician with wide-open eyes (and supernumerary ear) nevertheless did not see the world rightly. So it is the *number* of errors by the two methods that is all-important.' He concludes: 'Presumably it hurts me as a patient just as much to be misevaluated, regardless of whether the final mistake is made by a PhD or by a clerk.'

Controversy did not, however, die down: for the protagonists of the case-study remained obstinately unconvinced. They clung, in effect, to Meehl's admission that the studies he had reviewed 'do not tell us much about the kind and amount of clinical study which is competing with the actuarial method. On *a priori* grounds we might expect that mediocre or poor clinical methods would be inferior to the actuarial, since the latter is always as good as the sample can make it, but that superior clinical methods might be better than the actuarial.'

In 1966 Sawyer comprehensively reviewed a further selection of 45 new studies, distinguishing explicitly in respect of each, as Meehl had not done, between the way in which information was obtained, selected and measured and the way in which it was put to use or combined to reach a prediction. He concluded: '. . . whatever the data, clinical combination never surpasses mechanical combination; nonetheless, clinical skills may contribute through data collection, by assessing characteristics that would not otherwise enter the prediction. Moreover, it seems likely that inaccurate prediction usually results less from inappropriate combination than from lack of valid predictors to start with. If this is so, then improvement should result from devising better ways for the clinician to report objectively the broad range of possibly relevant behaviour he perceives.' In other words, we do predict better the behaviour we understand and the case-study is, after all, essential to successful prediction.

Progress depended, Sawyer argued, on combining the two methods in such a way that the insights of successful case-studies, turned into new 'predictor variables', could be joined with the advantages of the actuarial method in bringing large amounts of information into economical and effective relationship, to produce an improved actuarial figure.

Authoritative opinion remains divided on the prospects for advance. Commenting in 1972 on the disappointing outcome of the substantial attempts of Wenk and his associates in California to produce a valid classification of young offenders by violence-proneness, Wilkins declared: '. . . research along these lines does not seem worthwhile to press. Perhaps this study should be "the last word" for some time in its attempts to "predict" violence potential for individuals.' On the other hand, Monahan, reviewing the state of the art in 1977, was optimistic and produced a number of suggestions for further work on so-called situational factors (the effects on behaviour of different material and social environments) which would order them into new predictor variables which would enhance the sensitivity of actuarial classifications.

Meanwhile, courts, Parole Boards and others assessing the dangerousness of individual offenders perforce use case-study methods of varying degrees of sophistication. It is worth remarking, in the light of the methodological debate conducted in terms of relative efficiency, that though their verdicts are couched in the language and governed by the logic of probability they are not, as it were, amateur actuaries. It is not simply, as is sometimes said or implied, that case-by-case adjudications do not lend themselves to the use of computerised techniques or actuarial tables. The difference between actuaries and judges, Parole Boards and clinicians, does not lie in the extent to which they are respectively able or inclined to deal with quantified information or to express their findings in arithmetical terms of degree of certainty, but in the requirements of their respective tasks. It is the job of actuaries to construct sound actuarial tables; it is the job of judges and Parole Boards to judge an individual case on its merits. It may well be that in judging the risk represented by a serious offender, sound actuarial information could materially increase the probability of correct determination.

In 1958, Holt described what he called a 'sophisticated clinical' method, which would treat an actuarial prediction as information about an individual to be combined clinically (i.e. judgmentally, not mechanically) with the rest of the available information about him. Prediction tables are not uncommonly provided for use of Parole Boards: candidates for parole are assigned to a risk class according to a score on a prediction table which is meant to be used along with information from sociological, psychiatric and psychological reports and interviews in making the decision whether or not to grant parole. However, the technical problems of making proper use of prediction tables in conjunction with individualised assessments of dangerousness have not been systematically investigated (Glaser 1973) though the practical problems and results of persuading practitioners to make use of such tables were explored by Hoffman et al. (1974).

The Validity of Clinical Assessments of Dangerousness

Great scepticism as to the present and potential validity of clinical assessments of dangerousness prevails in informed circles. Critics of dangerousness predominate in these circles and the tone of their pronouncements is polemical; they rarely give the evidence close critical attention. Cocozza and Steadman (1976) reviewed the position. They noted that much of the evidence cited is indirect and inferential (for example, it is argued that predictive judgments cannot be valid because of the vagueness of the criteria of dangerousness or the statistical difficulty of predicting infrequent events etc.) and that direct evidence, such as would show the extent to which such judgments tend in practice to be valid, is neither plentiful nor of good quality.

For obvious reasons, it is difficult to mount purpose-designed studies of the validity of clinical judgments of dangerousness. Investigators have had to rely on the court rulings which from time to time during the past decade and a half in the US have released allegedly dangerous inmates of prisons and secure hospitals, making it possible to follow their subsequent careers and put the assessments of their dangerousness to the test of experience. But it is difficult to draw sound conclusions from the results of these legal experiments: length of time and conditions in custody and period at risk of reoffending have varied both within and between the sample populations; and when, as is often the case, the assessments themslves are not available for inspection, the criteria that were used can only be inferred and assessment procedures are not precisely known. Moreover, 'dangerous' offenders who are released by the court do not necessarily constitute a representative sample of all those judged *dangerous* by the clinicians; indeed, they may well be marginal cases to whom the court in its wisdom decided to grant the benefit of the doubt. Furthermore, the characteristics from which it would be possible to infer the 'dangerousness' of the wider population of serious offenders from which those assessed as dangerous are drawn (whether or not they are released by the court) are rarely reported in sufficient detail; yet as we have seen, predictive values depend, as much as on anything else, on the prevalence of dangerousness in the population of offenders from which subjects are drawn and the absence of this information makes precise comparisons impossible. These weaknesses and limitations are often overlooked by critics anxious to insist on the proven inaccuracy of clinical assessment.

Steadman and Cocozza (1974) were responsible for the path-breaking *Baxstrom* studies. In 1966, following the decision of the US Supreme Court in the case of *Baxtrom* v. *Herold,* nearly 1000 offenders were removed from the hospitals for the criminally insane in which they had been confined beyond the expiration of their sentences. The opportunity to validate the assessments of their dangerousness which it was presumed had led to their extended detention, was taken by Cocozza and Steadman who followed the careers of a sample of 246 of them for four years after their release from secure hospitals. They found that only 26 of the offenders concerned exhibited sufficiently violent behaviour at the civil hospitals to which they had been transferred to justify their return to hospitals for the criminally insane; and that of the 98 in the sample who were actually released into the community only two committed further serious crimes of violence within an average period of two and a half years outside. These findings were and still are frequently cited as the most striking evidence for the gross inaccuracy of clinical assessments of dangerousness; but Steadman and Cocozza have acknowledged its serious defects.

The clinical verdicts of *dangerous* that were apparently put to the test by the transfer of the *Baxstrom* patients out of hospitals for the criminally insane into civil hospitals or their release into the community are not recorded. No psychiatric reports and recommendations are available for inspection: that these persons had been specifically judged *dangerous* was inferred from the fact of their continued detention in secure hospitals and that 'it was documented in Johnnie Baxstrom's court records that a major factor in the continued detention of patients in [the] Matteawan and Dannemora [state hospitals] was the estimation of their dangerousness' (Steadman and Cocozza 1974: 64). An ingenious comparison was made of the court-released *Baxstrom* patients with a sample of others who had been released with psychiatric approval, as a way of inferring the criteria of suitability for release used by psychiatrists. These turned out to be age and a record of criminal violence. For patients between the ages of 40 and 69 a record of violent crime was the determining factor; for those outside this range, age was what counted. Thus the young were kept in detention and the old were released, regardless of record. The psychiatrists who were presumed to have judged the Baxstrom offenders as *dangerous* were said to have been hopelessly wrong in the light of their relatively peaceable behaviour when transferred to civil hospitals or released from custody: but no account could be taken of other factors, such as administrative discretion or administrative inertia, that may well have played a part; in any case, it would have been surprising if these persons had not behaved peaceably, considering that by the time of their transfer or release they had been institutionalised for an average of 15 years and at the average age of 47 were well past the peak age for violent crime.

The 'natural experiment' provided by the Supreme Court ruling in the case of *Baxtrom* v. *Herold* certainly illuminated 'the careers of the criminally insane' (Steadman and Cocozza 1974); but it was too rough and ready for its outcome to be taken seriously as evidence for or against the validity of clinical determinations of dangerousness. However, Cocozza and Steadman (1976) were able to undertake another substantial study of allegedly dangerous offenders which did not suffer from the same limitations.

The 257 subjects of this investigation had been charged with serious offences but found incompetent to stand trial in New York State in 1971 and 1972. They were young (on average, 31 years old) and had all been examined for a determination of dangerousness by two psychiatrists whose reports to the court were available for inspection. Almost two-thirds (166) of the assessments were put to the test by court-ordered releases. Of the defendants judged *dangerous*, 96 were eventually released from custody. During an unspecified period at risk, 13 (14%) of them were arrested for a violent crime whilst of the 70 judged *safe*, 11 (16%) were so arrested.

The authors claim that the findings of this study, taken with others, constitute 'clear and convincing evidence of the inability of psychiatrists or of anyone else to accurately predict dangerousness'; but this claim is exaggerated. The intensive analysis they offer of the relevant psychiatric reports demonstrates that these were based on routine and slovenly diagnostic procedures. Their study of these procedures, described in detail below, provides better evidence of bad practice than of the state of the art of assessing dangerousness; their findings bear more on the practical then the theoretical problems of ensuring just predictive judgments.

A substantial body of first-hand evidence, which is directly relevant to the present and potential validity of clinical assessments of the dangerousness of serious offenders, comes from the two institutions for the diagnosis and treatment of dangerous offenders in the US, at Bridgewater, Mass., and Patuxent, Maryland, respectively.

The work of Kozol et al. (1972) at Bridgewater well illustrates the theoretical and practical difficulties of assessment and its limited validity even when the task is taken seriously. Cocozza and Steadman (1976) set aside their findings, along with those of their own *Baxstrom* studies, as inconclusive. They refer to the methodological weaknesses of both investigations as though they were comparably damaging in their implications for the value of the findings; but this is hardly the case. The limitations and methodological weaknesses of the Bridgewater study were not unimportant; but it was a true validation study of recorded (not inferred) clinical assessments of dangerousness.

In reporting in 1972 on their ten-year investigation, Kozol and his associates made the bold claim that 'dangerousness in criminal offenders can be reliably diagnosed and effectively treated with a recidivism rate of 6.1%.' As to diagnosis, they pointed to the small proportion the 301 men assessed *safe* and duly released at the end of their sentences who, nevertheless, went on to commit further serious crimes of violence within five years of release, as compared with the much higher proportion of the 49 men who were released by court order, notwithstanding an assessment of *dangerous*, who also did so (34.7%). But they had taken no account of differences in the length of time during which individuals in their sample had been at liberty and, therefore, at risk of reoffending. For example, it was possible for the offenders whom they had diagnosed as *dangerous*, but who were released promptly by the court, to have been at risk of reoffending for as much as four years longer than those who were released with their agreement only after treatment. As Cocozza and Steadman point out, 'such a difference in length of time at risk would certainly account for a large part of the reported differences in recidivism rates'. Unfortunately, it is not possible with the available data to calculate precisely the effect of this method-ological oversight.

The reference to 'effective treatment' concerned 82 offenders who were judged *dangerous*, but released after treatment, of whom only 6.1% reoffended within four years. The claim that 'treatment was successful in modifying the dangerous potential in 94% of the patients we recommended for discharge after treatment for an average period of 43 months' is heavily discounted by Monahan (1973) who defines a notional control group and proposes an adjustment down to 22%.

Critics have emphasised the fact that of the 49 judgments of *dangerous* put to the test by the court-orders for release, only one-third were vindicated; two-thirds of these 49 men committed no further serious crimes of violence during nearly 5 years at liberty. But these 49 cases represent only one-fifth of the total number judged *dangerous* and as a sample of such judgments are probably unrepresentative. It is plausible to suppose that they were borderline cases in which the court decided to give the offender the benefit of the doubt. Had all the judgments of *dangerous* been put to the test by court-ordered releases, it is probable that a higher proportion would have been vindicated.

The evidence for the accuracy of the Bridgewater judgments of *dangerous* is inconclusive, because only an unrepresentative sample of one-fifth of them were actually put to the test. The reasonable inference is that they were more accurate overall than the figures for the court-released group suggest. The results of a later review are relevant. Kozol et al. (1973) have reported that the diagnoses of 29 of the 49 cases released by the court against their recommendation were retrospectively reviewed. The 29 cases were chosen for review because they had been assessed in the early years of the study when experience was limited. With hindsight, 14 were seen to have been misclassified as *dangerous*. Had these men been assessed with the benefit of experience, the num-ber of disputed cases would have been 35 instead of 49; and since 17 went on to commit further violent crimes, the chances of a correct diagnosis of *dangerous*, even at the borderline, would have been 50:50 instead of 2:1 against.

The other first-hand validation study was undertaken at the Patuxent Institution (US State of Maryland 1973). A group of 421 inmates, serious offenders who had been referred for diagnosis and treatment, were considered for release after a stay in the Institution of at least three years. Two-thirds were judged unfit as being *dangerous* but the court released them all, some unconditionally and some conditionally upon their undergoing a so-called 'release experience'. Of those released unconditionally, some 46% committed one or more further offences (not necessarily serious or accompanied by violence) during three years at risk: of those who underwent the 'release experience', 36% did so.

The numbers here are much larger than in the Bridgewater study: 286 positive judgments of *dangerous* were put to the test by the court, as against only 49 in Bridgewater; and the proportion of judgments borne out in the follow-up period (46%) was higher than reported by Kozol et al. (34.7%). Unfortunately, a precise comparison is impossible. Allowances must be made for the following differences, which cut in both directions: (i) all the Patuxent judgments of *dangerous* were put to the test, in contrast to only one-fifth of the Bridgewater judgments and this would make for a higher degree of accuracy; (ii) the period during which the Patuxent offenders were at risk of reoffending was shorter by two years (they were followed up for three instead of five years) which would lower the degree of accuracy; (iii) against this must be set the effect of the fact that in calculating recidivism rates, the Patuxent team took account of all new offences whilst the Bridgewater team allowed only for violent crimes.

To pursue the comparison further, it would be necessary to know more: on the one hand, about the criminal records of the Bridgewater sample; and on the other hand, about the assessment procedures of the Patuxent team. About these, we know only that their subjects were under observation and treatment for as long as three years, whereas Kozol and his colleagues made their recommendations in respect of 77% of their cases at the end of a mandatory diagnostic period of only 60 days. It seems likely that on balance there is little to choose between the ability of the two institutions to produce valid diagnoses of *dangerous* and that their work is representative of the best clinical practice — or, at least, of the best practice of which enough is known in detail and outcome to permit a judgment.

In this country, Brody and Tarling (1980) used lay assessments of *dangerousness.* They themselves, in consultation with prison staff, classed the men in their sample as in varying degree *dangerous,* on the basis of careful inspection of an array of evidence similar in extent and quality to that normally available to courts and Parole Boards. They take the view that their assessments are likely to be least controversial in the cases of life-sentence prisoners, which suggests that they think assessments in general are likely to be more successful when the criteria used by the Court of Appeal (Criminal Division) are applied – principally, a requirement of mental disorder or instability; but this view cannot be put to the test.

Had judges been asked to make the assessments of the fixed-sentence prisoners studied by Brody and Tarling, would they have done better on the basis of the same information? Could they have commanded additional information which would have improved their chances of being right? Would the Parole Board have done better with the same information? Is more or better quality information usually available to them? Brody and Tarling do not give explicit consideration to these questions. They say, merely: 'It can fairly be claimed that the present attempt to distinguish the dangerous from amongst the larger sample of prisoners is the most thorough reported anywhere'; that 'the assessments of psychiatrists and psychologists who have access to much more specialised information have never been shown to be much more accurate than anyone else's'; and that 'as the present classification achieved the highest level of predictive accuracy so far reported, it is improbable that better results could be found with the data available'.

But these statements need to be qualified. Theirs is an important study because it is based on lay assessments of comprehensive case-histories. Their results arguably give a fair, if probably somewhat conservative, indication of the success in assessing dangerousness achieved by Courts and Parole Boards who do not undertake first-hand studies of individual offenders but rely on the scrutiny of written evidence about them. It is true that they correctly identified the perpetrators of 50% of the *dangerous* offences committed by the released prisoners in their sample; but this is the measure of the *protective* value of the classification, not of its *predictive* value: i.e. it measures the proportion of *dangerous* offences which would have been prevented had the men assessed as *dangerous* been kept in custody for at least five years beyond the date of release from their original sentences, not the proportion of true positive judgments of *dangerous* – this was only 17%. On the extreme assumption that the 18 positive judgments which were never put to the test, because the men concerned were kept in custody, would all have been confirmed if they had been released instead, the proportion would have been 46%. The comparable figure on the same extreme assumption for the specialist assessors, Kozol et al., at the Bridgewater Center is 86%; but, of course, the extreme assumption must be much less plausible in this instance since the proportion of positive judgments put to the test was so much lower – only one-fifth in comparison with two-thirds in the British investigation. All the positive judgments made by the Patuxent clinicians were put to the test (the court ordered the release of all the men concerned) and here the proportion vindicated was close to 50%.

Prospects for Improvement

Kozol and his associates and the Patuxent team worked with selected groups of serious offenders suspected of presenting an unacceptable risk of committing further serious offences; and they used intensive case-study methods to assess the risk presented by each individual. On the most favourable reading of their results not more than 50% of their judgments of *dangerous* that were put to the test were borne out. Why were they not more successful?

We cannot estimate the extent to which statistical and clinical factors respectively are responsible. As to the former, we know only that the offenders referred to the Bridgewater Center were a highly selected group of 592 men chosen from among 2000 prison inmates by psychiatrists assigned by the Massachusetts Department of Mental Health; that they had been convicted of serious assaultive crimes; that their offences were untypical (mainly but not exclusively sexual, directed against young victims, compounded by violence, even by extreme violence, including murder); and that their average age was 25–35. The offenders admitted to the Patuxent Institution were apparently a comparable group; Gordon (1977) calculated from their records that they had an average score of 14 on the 15 point Legal Dangerousness Scale constructed by Cocozza and Steadman (1974). As to clinical factors, we know that the assessment procedures were designed to be thorough; though we are told of misclassifications subsequently detected.

On the one side are ranged the critics, among them Cocozza and Steadman, who flatly declare 'inability to predict'; Ennis and Litwack, who compare the procedures unfavourably with 'flipping a coin'; and Monahan, who suggests that clinicians have 'taken their best shot' and that efforts should be directed to refining statistical methods of prediction. On the other is Gordon (1977) who points out that individual probabilities are difficult to determine with more or less homogeneous high-risk categories. He argues that the offenders assessed at Bridgwater and Patuxent do constitute a relatively homogeneous high-risk class within which further classification on the basis of clinical assessments of individuals cannot be more than marginally effective, and that there is little hope of raising the general probability of further serious offending in this group by more refined selection. The predictive values reported by the Bridgewater and Patuxent teams are relatively high, he argues, because they relate to populations of offenders preselected, as it were, for their dangerousness. By the same token, however, they are absolutely low. The predictions refer to the members of subgroups of serious offenders which, though more heterogeneous than if each individual presented a clear and immediate threat of serious harm, or no threat at all, are yet relatively homogeneous in their disposition to inflict serious harm. Chance, Gordon argues, must, therefore, be the prime determinant of the contribution made by particular individuals to the general probability for the class as a whole. Taking into account the infrequency with which offenders convicted of the most serious offences do comparable harm within, say, the next three years in which they are at risk, 'probabilities for individuals . . . may seldom range higher than 0.3 to 0.5 in our society': from which he draws the conclusion that 'if society is ever to protect itself routinely against individuals that it experiences as the most dangerous of all, it is going to have to do so at probability levels between 0.3 and 0.5 or not do it at all'. His case rests equally on empirical and theoretical grounds: validation studies of clinical assessments of *dangerous* have not, in fact, revealed better chances of their being right than those he cites and, moreover, there are good statistical reasons why this should be so. However, the statistical argument is conclusive only if we have reason to believe that the predictive values of clinical assessments so far reported are in fact the maximum obtainable in the present state of the art; only if they are may we fairly invoke the rarity of *dangerousness* even among serious offenders and the homogeneity of the risk classes to which the subjects of the clinical assessments belong, to explain why they are not higher.

Gordon is in danger of overstating the case, though he is right to emphasise the role of chance in individual outcomes. Given the general rarity of the phenomenon of dangerousness, the selected offenders admitted to the Patuxent Institution (and to the Bridgewater Center, too) may, as he argues, constitute high-risk groups; but the *homogeneity* of these groups must be doubted. There seems also to be room for improvement in assessment procedures: for example, the incorporation into the clinical picture of actuarial information about individuals, including new situational variables (Monahan 1977); and, above all, the introduction of checks on the reliability as well as the validity of assessments (i.e. checks on the tendency of independent assessors to agree, as well as on the subsequent behaviour of offenders judged dangerous).

The question, whether clinicians can improve the predictive value of their assessments of dangerousness, surely remains open. Numerous factors may account for the relatively low values so far achieved by clinicians: the characteristics of the offenders under assessment; or of the sample of judgments being validated; routine or slovenly assessment procedures; neglect of situational or other environmental variables affecting behaviour, and the length of time at risk. All of these factors are susceptible to correction or control.

The critics are being nihilistic, rather than merely pessimistic, in urging the unqualified hopelessness of the enterprise of assessing dangerousness and in insisting that, in facing the fact that some serious offenders do present an unacceptable risk of serious harm, we can hope for no expert help of any kind which could materially improve the validity of our predictive judgments. Such nihilism seems unrealistic.

Clinicians at Work

Empirical investigations have been undertaken that question the competence of clinicians, in particular of psychiatrists, not only by attempting to show the limited validity of their assessments of dangerousness but by studying the content of their reports and the reception of these reports by the court (Cocozza and Steadman 1976), and by the direct study of assessment procedures in action (Pfohl 1977).

Cocozza and Steadman (1974) inspected the psychiatric reports and recommendations made to the court in respect of 257 defendants charged with serious offences and found incompetent to stand trial in New York in 1971–72. Each defendant was assessed by two psychiatrists.

Analysis of the recommendations based on these reports showed a strong relationship between the seriousness of the offence and the assessment of dangerousness. The more serious the offence the larger the percentage reported *dangerous*: nearly three-quarters of those charged with crimes of actual violence, such as murder, manslaughter, assault and rape, were reported *dangerous*, but not many more than half of those charged with potentially violent crimes such as robbery or arson, or serious offences against property such as burglary and grand larceny; and of those charged with sundry other crimes such as forgery, gambling or sodomy, fewer than one-third were reported *dangerous*.

The investigators themselves point out that these figures reflected the heavy concentration of findings of *dangerous* in a single hospital, the director of which had instructed his staff, pending clarification of the newly revised Criminal Procedure Law in the courts, to declare *dangerous* any patient charged with violence against the person. In any case, the relationship they disclose is intuitively neither surprising nor unreasonable, bearing in mind that, though making it mandatory for the court to receive the psychiatric reports, the Criminal Procedure Law provided no specification of legal dangerousness: no specification of the nature and gravity of the harmful behaviour to be predicted or of the period for which an assessment of the probability of its occurring was needed.

However, the relationship was present regardless of the defendant's age or race and regardless also of the nature of his mental illness (e.g. psychosis, schizophrenia, paranoia) and it may indicate a tendency to diagnose by rule of thumb. It is noteworthy that the relationship was strongest when the reporting psychiatrists were primarily employed in forensic work; those not regularly engaged in making predictive judgments of this kind were found to be more discriminating in their reports. Further evidence of routine and undiscriminating diagnostic practices was sought by an analysis of the extent to which the probability that a defendant would be found *dangerous* varied in accordance with certain features of his background and of his medical and criminal record: but this yielded nothing.

Scrutiny of the psychiatric reports themselves, however, revealed them to be of strikingly poor quality. The examples quoted *verbatim* are brief to the point of nonchalance and embarrassingly circular in argument, despite the fact that the psychiatrists responsible for them had each affirmed, as required, that 'the following is a detailed statement of the reasons for finding the defendant to be a dangerous, incapacitive [sic] person'.

Cocozza and Steadman examined and classified 390 reasons given for a finding of *dangerous* in 149 of the reports, according to whether they referred to events before the defendant's arrest (criminal record, history of mental illness, nature of current charge) or to subsequent events during the period of his remand under observation (anti-social behaviour, such as threatened or actual assault; indications of mental illness, such as delusions, unpredictability, impulsiveness; and sundry other untoward manifestations). They found that events after arrest were more frequently cited by psychiatrists in support of their diagnoses than events before arrest and further, that the preponderance of reasons concerning events both before and after arrest referred to indications of mental illness and anti-social behaviour.

In discussing the results of their analysis of the reasons given by psychiatrists for their findings of *dangerous*, Cocozza and Steadman remark that the frequency of references to anti-social behaviour before arrest is surprising, in view of the fact that they themselves could find no difference in the criminal records of those judged *dangerous* and *safe* respectively and that references in the reports to the nature of the offences with which the defendants were charged were rare, which is also surprising in view of the strong relationship which in fact exists between the seriousness of the offence and a finding of *dangerousness*. However, underlying this point there seems to be some confusion between reasons for the behaviour of psychiatrists and defendants respectively. The discrepancies could be accounted for by the plausible hypothesis that, according to the degree of violence associated with the offence with which he is charged, a defendant is more or less likely after arrest to present management problems of the kind which were cited by psychiatrists in their reports and categorised by investigators as 'anti-social behaviour'.

However that may be, it is intrinsically objectionable that predictive judgments should rest on so slender a basis as a single, as yet unproven, charge of a violent crime. To have shown that this was the effect of slovenly diagnostic practices is a valuable achievement. But in discussing their findings Cocozza and Steadman reach conclusions that go well beyond them: from a demonstration of slovenly diagnosis they proceed to make charges of professional hubris and bad faith against psychiatrists said to be under pressure 'to play the role [of expert] to meet the expectations of society'. Psychiatrists, they allege, pose as scientists but practice 'magic', in the sense that though claiming special knowledge and granted expert status in law, they make assessments of dangerousness which rely on empirically untested beliefs and represent 'an effort at control of the potentially harmful "other"'. In any case, they have been allowed to exceed their powers: 'they represent an excellent example of professionals who have exceeded their areas of expertise and for whom society's confidence in their ability is empirically unjustified'. But the reporting psychiatrists were neither interviewed nor observed at work; there is evidence to support charges of incompetence or slovenliness but not of professional hubris and bad faith.

The attack on the part played by 'experts' and in particular by psychiatrists in the judicial determination of dangerousness has taken a different turn at the hands of Pfohl (1977), using the opportunity created by an order of a Toledo court in 1974 which required the State to seek the diagnostic services of 'independent mental health professionals' to re-evaluate the status of every patient in the maximum security hospital for the criminally insane at Lima, Ohio. Twelve review teams were formed, each consisting of a psychiatrist, a clinical psychologist and a psychiatric social worker. The teams were required to decide whether a patient was mentally ill or a psychopathic offender, dangerous to self and others, and in need of placement in a maximum security hospital. Patients would continue to be confined to Lima's state hospital only if they were 'immediately dangerous' and needed maximum security or if they were 'psychopathic offenders' requiring further treatment.

Pfohl mounted a field study of the diagnostic proceedings of the review teams. The aim was not to validate the outcome of the proceedings but to reveal the workings in the diagnostic sessions of certain professional attitudes and interests which, bearing in mind the social significance of the assessments of dangerousness forwarded to the court, could be loosely termed 'political'.

In the reported analysis of the dynamics of the working sessions the teams are shown as falling under the leadership of the psychiatrists and consequently succumbing to a professional, scientific ideology, the effect of which was to give a characteristic bias to the diagnoses. 'The review teams did not simply categorize patients (as *dangerous* or *safe*), they provided them with clinical identities that 'explained' (or at least told a story about) why they were dangerous.' Moreover, the teams were led, under pressure from the psychiatrists, 'to depreciate social realities', which is to say, to discount sociological explanations of the past or likely future behaviour of those before them.

A charge of 'false consciousness' is substituted by Pfohl for the charges of professional hubris and bad faith made by Cocozza and Steadman. In searching for a diagnosis under psychiatric leadership, the teams applied a distinctive professional logic to the records and oral evidence of the patients under review and made use of a distinctive abstract professional language, the effect of which, it is argued, was to sustain their sense of identity as experts, whilst they unwittingly furthered 'the interests of the existing mechanisms of social control' by reinforcing 'an assumption within the criminal justice system that systematically prevents the realisation of social justice: the assumption that violent or dangerous behaviour can best be explained at the individual or psychological level'.

The analysis of proceedings in the diagnostic sessions is *ad hoc*: it is informed by no sympathetic reconstruction of the logic of clinical activity, such as is undertaken by Meehl (1954, Chapter 6) and is necessary in order to evaluate it in its own terms. Nevertheless, it is illuminating and on the whole persuasive as having the ring of truth. The hypothesis of *false consciousness* is not inherently implausible; but the account of the origins of *false consciousness* in the suppression of sociogenic in favour of psychogenic explanations of dangerousness is unconvincing. That the suppression took place is clear from the citations of the transcripted proceedings; but it is not evident how it is thought that the search for a diagnosis might have been different had the sociologically trained members of the team been in a stronger position, professionally or personally, to press for consideration of sociogenic factors. (A majority of them were apparently social workers, either women and/or black.) In fact, it is not clear how we are to understand the hypothesis that the assumption that violent, anti-social behaviour can best be explained at the individual or psychological level is inimical to the realisation of social justice.

If it is being said that sociological explanations of behaviour are more powerful than psychological explanations, this is a proposition in need of some clarification. The dangerousness of individuals is being assessed. What is the sociological explanation of *individual* behaviour that is not at the same time a psychological explanation? But if it is being said that the assessments of dangerousness would have been better (that a higher proportion would have been valid) had social factors been given their proper weight by the examining teams, this is almost certainly true, providing that they had known what the relevant social factors were and how to measure and weight them.

As to social justice, two propositions may be latent in the hypothesis. One is, that to explain an individual's past or likely future harmful behaviour as a response to the rewards and punishments of a 'deprived' social background, is sufficient to justify excusing its consequences for others; but it is plainly not sufficient. Another is, that if mental health professionals were cured of *false consciousness* and came to realise the significance of social factors in making people *dangerous*, they would not participate in the administration of justice, since they would see that to do so is to connive at the perpetration of injustice, either by ignoring the distinction between social control and social oppression or, more radically, by failing to see that no such distinction can be sustained. In certain political contexts and circumstances the proposition may be tenable on either of these grounds: but whether it were so would be a matter for rational debate, and what to do if it were would be a matter for the individual conscience.

Experts and the Courts

Cocozza and Steadman made some study of the reception by the court of the psychiatric reports on the defendants in their sample. They report that in a high proportion of cases there was no disagreement between the psychiatric finding and the judicial determination. In 86.7% of the cases the psychiatrists' recommendation about the defendant's dangerousness was accepted by the court. They remark that 'while by law the decision was a judicial one, in reality it was made by the psychiatrists'. But this damaging inference cannot safely be drawn simply from the absence of disagreement: indeed, considerable doubt is cast on it by the 13% of cases in which the courts disagreed.

There was disagreement between the court and psychiatrists in 34 cases. In 28 of these cases the court found the defendant *safe* despite a psychiatric finding to the contrary and in the remaining six cases the court found the defendant *dangerous* despite a psychiatric finding of *safe*. The less serious the alleged offence, the greater the likelihood that the court would disagree with a psychiatric finding of *dangerous*: of the defendants charged with a violent crime against the person and reported *dangerous* by psychiatrists, the court rejected the findings in 13% of the cases. This level of disagreement rose to 17% for those charged with non-violent property offences and to 43% for other felonies. Cocozza and Steadman take these findings to show that the court reinforced the tendency of psychiatrists to use the seriousness of the offence as the sole guide to the defendant's dangerousness. It might be said, alternatively, that the court, as handicapped as the clinicians in arriving at a sound judgment by the vagueness of the statutory requirements for a determination of *dangerous*, was concerned at least to maintain a proper distinction between recidivism and dangerousness where this had been overlooked by the psychiatrists; and to reserve the label *dangerous*, so far as possible, for cases in which the seriousness of the anticipated harm seemed to justify caution and could reasonably be held to outweigh doubts about the certainty and imminence of its actually occurring.

The analysis of concurrence and disagreement between court and psychiatrists presented by Cocozza and Steadman does not unambiguously suggest slovenly adjudication to match the slovenly diagnoses of the psychiatrists. The need for substantive and procedural safeguards against slovenly adjudication as well as slovenly diagnoses of dangerousness is self-evident, and there can be little doubt that these safeguards were missing in the cases they investigated: legal dangerousness was not defined and there were no other provisions to ensure the scrupulous and discriminating assessment of individual cases. There is direct evidence that the consequences of these omissions was disastrous for the quality of the assessments but there is no direct evidence of their effect on the work of the court. The statistical evidence of concurrence between the court and psychiatrists is by itself inconclusive. It is intuitively likely that the mandatory testimony of psychiatrists carried much weight with the court; but the charge of slovenly adjudication is another matter and cannot be proven without full information about the actual reception of this testimony by the court. The investigators did attend the hearing of 55 cases but they have published no account of their observations of the court at work. In referring to the hearings they remark, however, (1978) on the importance of counsel for the defence in securing a legal determination of 'safe' against a psychiatric finding of 'dangerous'. Evidently, then, the court did sometimes pay attention to weaknesses in the expert testimony revealed under cross-examination by counsel for the defence; but there is nothing to show whether or not the court was, in general, mindful or unmindful of the need to test the evidence of experts before it.

Select Bibliography

Items preceded by an asterisk contain further references and bibliographies

The Dangerous Offender: English Law and Practice

Advisory Council on the Treatment of Offenders, 1963, Preventive Detention, *Report etc.*, Chairman, *Bishop of Exeter*, London, HMSO.

Advisory Council on the Penal System, 1968, The regime for long-term prisoners in conditions of maximum security, *Report*, Chairman, Sir L. *Radzinowicz*, London, HMSO.

Advisory Council on the Penal System, 1977, The Length of Prison Sentences, *Interim Report*, Chairman, Baroness *Serota*, London, HMSO.

Advisory Council on the Penal System, 1978, Sentences of Imprisonment: A Review of Maximum Penalties, *Report etc.*, Cmnd 7948. Chairman, Baroness *Serota*, London, HMSO.

Home Office, 1966, *Report* of the inquiry into prison escapes and security, etc., Cmnd 3175. Chairman, Lord *Mountbatten* of Burma, London, HMSO.

Home Office, Department of Health and Social Security, 1973, *Report* on the review of procedures for the discharge and supervision of psychiatric patients subject to special restrictions, Cmnd 5191. Chairman, Sir C. *Aarvold*, London, HMSO.

Home Office, Department of Health and Social Security, 1975, Committee on Mentally Abnormal Offenders, *Report, etc.*, Cmnd 6244. Chairman, Lord *Butler* of Saffron Walden, London, HMSO.

Huber, B. 1977, 'Die Lebenslange Freiheitsstrafe, Rechtsgrundlage und Praxis in England', *Juristenzeitung*, 1, pp. 16–19.

Stockdale, E. 1966, 'The indeterminate sentence in England', *British Journal of Criminology*, vol. 6, no. 1, pp. 65–7.

Thomas, D.A. 1978, *The Penal Equation: derivations of the penalty structure of English Criminal Law*, Occasional Series no. 2, Cambridge, Institute of Criminology.

Thomas, D.A. 1979, *Principles of Sentencing*, Cambridge Studies in Criminology XXVII (2nd edn.), London, Heinemann Educational Books.

Dangerousness and Criminal Justice

*American Friends Service Committee, 1971, Struggle for Justice, a *report* on crime and punishment, Chairman, E.C. *Morgenroth*, New York, Hill and Wang.

Ancel, M. 1965, *Social Defence: a modern approach to criminal problems*, London, Routledge and Kegan Paul.

Bentham, J. 1780, *An Introduction to the Principles of Morals and Legislation*, J. H. Burns and H.L.A. Hart 1970 (eds), University of London, The Athlone Press. (See, in particular, Chapters XII and XVI).

Bottoms, A.E. 1977, 'Reflections on the renaissance of dangerousness', *Howard Journal*, vol. 16, no. 2, pp. 70–96.

*Chappel, D. and Monahan, J. (eds.), 1975, *Violence and Criminal Justice*, Lexington, Lexington Books, D.C. Heath and Co.

Cross, R. 1971, *Punishment, Prison and the Public*, The Hamlyn Lectures, London, Stevens and Sons.

Floud, J. 1975, 'Sociology and the theory of responsibility: "social background" as an excuse for crime', *Psychological Medicine*, vol. 5, no. 3, pp. 227–38.

Ginsberg, P.H. and Klockars, M. 1974, '"Dangerous offenders" and legislative reform', *Williamette Law Journal*, vol. 10, pp. 167–184.

Goldstein, J. and Katz, J. 1960, 'Dangerousness and mental illness', *Yale Law Journal*, vol. 70, no. 2, pp. 225–39.

Greenland, C. 1978, 'The prediction and management of dangerous behaviour: social policy issues', *International Journal of Law and Psychiatry*, vol. 1, pp. 205–22.

*Gross, H. 1979, *A Theory of Criminal Justice*, Oxford, OUP.

Halleck, S.L. 1967, *Psychiatry and the Dilemmas of Crime*, New York, Harper and Row.

Hart, H.L.A. 1968, *Punishment and Responsibility*, London, OUP.

*Klein, J.F. 1976, 'The dangerousness of dangerous offender legislation: forensic folklore revisited', *Canadian Journal of Criminology and Corrections*, vol. 18, no. 1, pp. 109–22.

Levine, D. 1975, The concept of dangerousness: critism and compromise, *Paper* presented at the National Criminology Conference, University of Cambridge, England (unpublished). Institute of Criminology, Cambridge (mimeo).

Levine, D. 1977, 'Crime, mental illness and political dissent' in J.L. Tapp and F. Levine (eds.), *Law, Justice and the Individual in Society: Psychological and Legal Issues*, USA, Holt, Rinehart and Winston, pp. 224–238.

Lewis, C.S. 1948/49, 'The humanitarian theory of punishment', *20th Century*, vol. 3, no. 3, pp. 5–12.

Monahan, J. 1977, 'Social accountability' in B.D. Sales (ed.), *Perspectives in Law and Psychology I, The Criminal Justice System*, New York, Plenum Press, pp. 241–55.

Monahan, J. and Cummings, L. 1975, 'Social policy implications of the inability to predict violence', *Journal of Social Issues*, vol. 31, no. 2, pp. 153–64.

Morris, N. 1974, *The Future of Imprisonment*, Chicago, The University of Chicago Press.

Morris, N. 1977, 'Who should go to prison' in B.D. Sales (ed.), *Perspectives in Law and Psychology I, The Criminal Justice System*, New York, Plenum Press, pp. 151–9.
Radzinowicz, Sir L. and King, J.F.S. 1977, 'Dangerous offenders' in *The Growth of Crime: The International Experience*, London, Hamish Hamilton, pp. 220–4.
Sarbin, T.R. 1967, 'The dangerous individual: an outcome of social identity transformations', *British Journal of Criminology*, vol. 7, no. 3, pp. 285–95.
Schoeman, F.D. 1979, III. 'On incapacitating the dangerous', *American Philosophical Quarterly*, vol. 16, no. 1, pp. 27–35.
Scott, P.D. 1974, 'Solutions to the problem of the dangerous offender', *British Medical Journal*, vol. 4, pp. 640–1.
Scottish Council on Crime, 1975, Crime and the Prevention of Crime: A *Memorandum* by the Scottish Council on Crime, Edinburgh, HMSO.
Shah, S.A. 1974, 'Some interactions of law and mental health in the handling of social deviance', *Catholic University Law Review*, vol. 23, no. 4, pp. 674–719.
Shah, S.A. 1975, 'Dangerousness and civil commitment of the mentally ill: some public policy considerations', *American Journal of Psychiatry*, vol. 132, no. 5, pp. 501–5.
Shah, S.A. 1977, 'Dangerousness: some definitional, conceptual and public policy issues' in B.D. Sales (ed.), *Perspectives in Law and Psychology I, The Criminal Justice System*, New York, Plenum Press, pp. 91–119.
Szasz, T.S. 1963, *Law, Liberty and Psychiatry*, New York, Macmillan.
Van den Haag, E. 1975, *Punishing Criminals: Concerning a Very Old and Painful Question*, New York, Basic Books.
Von Hirsch, A. 1972, 'Prediction of criminal conduct and preventive confinement of convicted persons', *Buffalo Law Review*, vol. 21, no. 3, pp. 717–58.
Von Hirsch, A. (ed.) 1976, *Doing Justice*, Report of the Committee for the Study of Incarceration, New York, Hill and Wang.
Walker, N.D. 1972, *Sentencing in a Rational Society* (2nd edn.), Harmondsworth, Penguin Books.
Walker, N.D. 1976, *Treatment and Justice in Penology and Psychiatry*, The Sandoz Lecture; Edingurgh, The University Press.
Walker, N.D. 1978, 'Dangerous people', *International Journal of Law and Psychiatry*, vol. 1, pp. 37–50 (revised version in Walker 1980).
Walker, N.D. 1980, *Punishment, Danger and Stigma*, Oxford, Basil Blackwell.
White, I., *Wrongs and Rights*. Cambridge, CUP (forthcoming)

Dangerousness in Social Perspective

Ashby, The Rt. Hon. Lord. 1976, 'Protection of the environment: the human dimension', The Jephcott Lecture, *Royal Society of Medicine*, vol. 69, pp. 721–30.

206   DANGEROUSNESS AND CRIMINAL JUSTICE

Baldwin, J. and Bottoms, A.E. 1976, *The Urban Criminal: a study in Sheffield*, London, Tavistock Publications.
Carson, W.G. 1970a, 'White-collar crime and the enforcement of factory legislation', *British Journal of Criminology*, vol. 10, no. 4, pp. 383–98.
Carson, W.G. 1970b, 'Some sociological aspects of strict liability and the enforcement of factory legislation', *Modern Law Review*, vol. 33, no. 4, pp. 396–412.
Carson, W.G. 1975, 'Le délinquant dangereux et les valeurs symboliques de l'orde social', *Revue de science criminelle et de droit pénal compané*, no. 3, pp. 805–13.
Clark, R. 1970, *Crime in Urban Society*, New York, Dunellen.
Cotgrove, S. 1979, 'Risk, value conflict, and political legitimacy', *Paper* presented to the Symposium on the Acceptability of Risk, University of Manchester Institute of Science and Technology, December, Manchester University Press (forthcoming)
*Council of Europe, European Committee on Crime Problems, 1974, Collected Studies in Criminological Research, vol. XI, *Violence in Society;*
Selosse, J., Statistical Aspects of Violent Crime, *report*, pp. 9–60;
Lenke, L., Criminal Policy and Public Opinion towards Crimes of Violence, *report*, pp. 63–123;
McClintock, F.H., Phenomenological and Contextual Analysis of Criminal Violence, *report*, pp. 127–76;
Debuyst, Ch., Etiology of Violence, *report*, pp. 179–256, Council of Europe, Strasbourg, France.
Cressey, D.R. 1969, *Theft of the Nation: The Structure and Operations of Organized Crime in America*, New York, Harper and Row.
Ehrlich, I. 1973, 'Participation in illegitimate activities: a theoretical and empirical investigation', *Journal of Political Economy*, vol. 81, no. 3, pp. 521–65.
Erwin, E. 1978, *Behaviour Therapy: scientific, philosophical and moral foundations*, Cambridge, CUP.
Geis, G. and Meier, R.F. 1977, *White-Collar Crime: Offenses in Business, Politics and the Professions*, revised edn., New York, Free Press.
Geis, G. and Monahan, J. 1976, 'The social ecology of violence' in T. Lickona (ed.), *Morality: Theory, Research and Social Issues*, New York, Holt, Rinehart and Winston, pp. 342–56.
Glover, E. 1960, 'The prevention of pathological crime' in *The Roots of Crime*, London, Imago, pp. 347–51.
Gunn, J. 1973, *Violence in Human Society*, Devon, Newton Abbot, David and Charles.
*Klockars, C.B. 1975, *The Professional Fence*, New York, Free Press.
Le Comité d'études sur la violence, la criminalité et la délinquence, 1977, *Réponses à la violence*, Chairman, Alain *Peyrefitte*, Paris, La Documentation Française.
McClintock, F.H. 1963, *Crimes of Violence*, Cambridge Studies in Criminology, vol. XVII, London, Macmillan and Co.; See also University of Toronto 1975 *Proceedings* of a workshop on Police in Canadian Society.

*McIntosh, M. 1975, *The Orgainisation of Crime*, London, Macmillan.
Madden, D.J. and Lion, J.R. (eds.) 1976, *Rage, Hate, Assualt and Other Forms of Violence*, New York, Spectrum Publications.
Mark, Sir R. 1977, *Policing a Perplexed Society*, London, George Allen and Unwin.
Monahan, J. and Geis, G. 1976, 'Controlling "dangerous" people', *Annals of the American Academy of Political and Social Science*, vol. 423, no. 1, pp. 142–51.
*Packer, H.I. 1968, *The Limits of the Criminal Sanction*, Stanford, Stanford University Press.
Pasternack, S.A. (ed.) 1975, *Violence and Victims*, New York, Spectrum Publications.
Pearce, F. 1976, *Crimes of the Powerful*, London, Pluto Press.
Radzinowicz, Sir L. 1968, 'The dangerous offender', The fourth Frank Newsam Memorial Lecture, *The Police Journal*, vol. 41, no. 9, pp. 411–47.
Rennie, Y.F. 1978, *The Search for Criminal Man* (The Dangerous Offender Project), Lexington, Lexington Books, D.C. Heath and Co.
Rock, P. 1980, 'Public opinion and criminal legislation', *Proceedings of the 13th Criminological Research Conference, 1978*. Council of Europe Directorate of Legal Affairs, Strasbourg, France, pp. 173–213.
Roshier, R.J. 1973, 'The selection of crime news by the press' in S. Cohen and J. Young (eds.), *The Manufacture of News*, London, Constable, pp. 28–39.
Rothschild, Lord 1978, 'Risk', *The Listener*, 30 November, pp. 715–18.
Royal Commission on the Press, 1949, *Report etc.*, Cmnd 7700, Chairman, Sir W.D. *Ross*, London, HMSO.
*Silberman, C. 1978, *Criminal Violence and Criminal Justice*, New York, Random House.
Stone, C.D. 1975, *Where the Law Ends: the social control of corporate behaviour*, New York, Harper and Row.
United Nations Congress on the Prevention of Crime and the Treatment of Offenders, 5th, 1975, *Report* prepared by the Secretariat, United Nations, New York, 1976.
United States of America, National Commission on the Causes and Prevention of Violence, 1969, *Staff Reports*
  *Baker, R.K. and Ball, S.J. (eds), Mass media and violence, vol. 9; Graham, H.D. and Gurr, T.R., Violence in America: Historical and Comparative Perspectives, vols. 1 and 2;
  *Mulvihill, D.H. and Tumin, M.M. (eds.), with Curtis, L.A., Crimes of Violence, vols. 11, 12 and 13;
  US Government Printing Office, Washington DC.
United States National Criminal Justice Information and Statistics Service, 1977, *Criminal Victim Surveys in Cincinnati*, SD–NCS–C–9, July.
United States National Criminal Justice Information and Statistics Service, 1977, *Criminal Victimization in the United States*, SD–NCS–N–7, December.
United States, President's Commission on Law Enforcement and

208 DANGEROUSNESS AND CRIMINAL JUSTICE

Administration of Justice, 1967, *The challenge of crime in a free society*, Report, US Government Printing Office, Washington DC.

United States, President's Commission on Law Enforcement and Administration of Justice, 1967, *Task force report, Crime and its impact – an assessment*, US Government Printing Office, Washington DC.

University of Sydney, Proceedings of the Institute of Criminology 1971, *Report of a seminar on social defence, the contribution of the correctional services*, no. 2, University of Sydney, Faculty of Law.

University of Sydney, Proceedings of the Institute of Criminology, 1979, *Proceedings of a Seminar on White Collar Crime* (2), no. 37, The University of Sydney, Faculty of Law.

University of Toronto, Centre of Criminology, 1975, *Proceedings of a workshop on Violence in Canadian Society, report*, Canada, University of Toronto.
See, in particular, McClintock, F.H., 'Demographic aspects of violence', pp. 13–46.

Wilson, J.Q. 1975, *Thinking about Crime*, New York, Basic Books.

Yoder, S.A. 1978, 'Criminal sanctions for corporate illegality', *Journal of Criminal Law and Criminology*, vol. 69, no. 1, pp. 40–58.

Zehr, H. 1976, *Crime and the Development of Modern Society: Patterns of Criminality in Nineteenth Century Germany and France*, London, Croom Helm Ltd. US New Jersey, Rowman and Littlefield.

Determining Dangerousness

American Bar Foundation, Angel, A.R.A., Green, E.D., Kaufman, H.F. and Van Loon, E.C. 1971, 'Preventive detention: an empirical analysis', reprinted from the *Harvard Civil Rights–Civil Liberties Law Review*, vol. 6, no. 2, pp. 289–396.

Barker, R. 1968, *Ecological Psychology: Concepts and Methods for studying the environment of human behaviour*, Palo Alto, Stanford University Press.

Bern, D. and Allen, A. 1974, 'On predicting some of the people some of the time', *Psychological Review*, vol. 81, no. 6, pp. 506–20.

Carr-Hill, R. 1970, *The Violent Offender – Reality or Illusion? 2 Victims of Our Typologies*, Oxford University Penal Research Unit Occasional Paper no. 1, Oxford, Basil Blackwell; see Walker, Hammond and Steer 1970 and Levine 1976.

Cocozza, J.J. and Steadman, H.J. 1974, 'Some refinements in the measurement and prediction of dangerous behaviour', *American Journal of Psychiatry*, vol. 131, no. 9, pp. 1012–14.

Cocozza, J.J. and Steadman, H.J. 1976, 'The failure of psychiatric predictions of dangerousness: clear and convincing evidence', *Rutgers Law Review*, vol. 29, no. 5, pp. 1084–1101.

Cocozza, J.J. and Steadman, H.J. 1978, 'Prediction in psychiatry: an example of misplaced confidence in experts', *Social Problems*, vol. 25, no. 3, pp. 265–76.

Conrad, J. 1977, "What happened to Stephen Nash? The important questions about dangerousness' in J.P. Conrad and S. Dinitz (eds.),

In Fear of Each Other (The Dangerous Offender Project), Lexington, Lexington Books, D.C. Heath and Co., pp. 1–11.

Dershowitz, A.M. 1970, 'The law of dangerousness: some fictions about predictions', *Journal of Legal Education*, vol. 23, no. 2, pp. 24–47.

Dinitz, S. and Conrad, J.P. 1978, 'Thinking about dangerous offenders', *Criminal Justice Abstracts*, vol. 10, no. 1, pp. 99–130.

Flynn, E.E. 1978, 'A preliminary conceptualisation of a classification for risk and supervision system' in J. Freeman, (ed.), *Prisons Past and Future*, Cambridge Studies in Criminology XLI, London, Heinemann Educational Books, pp. 123–30.

Galen, R.S. and Gambino, S.R. 1975, *Beyond Normality: The Predictive Value and Efficiency of Medical Diagnoses*, New York, John Wiley and Sons.

Gathercole, C.E., Croft, M.J., McDougall, J., Barnes, H.M. and Peck, D.F. 1968, 'A review of 100 discharges from a special hospital', *British Journal of Criminology*, vol. 8, no. 4, pp. 419–24.

*Glaser, D. 1973, *Routinizing evaluation: getting feedback on the effectiveness of crime and delinquency programs*, National Institute of Mental Health, Center for Studies of Crime and Delinquency, Department of Health, Education and Welfare publication no. (HSM) 73–9123, US Government Printing Office, Washington DC.

*Gordon, R.A. 1977, 'A critique of the evaluation of Patuxent Institution, with particular attention to the issues of dangerousness and recidivism', *Bulletin of the Academy of Psychiatry and the Law*, vol. 5, no. 2, pp. 210–55.

Halfon, A., David, M. and Steadman, H.J. 1971, 'The Baxstrom women: a four year follow-up of behaviour patterns', *Psychiatric Quarterly*, vol. 45, no. 4, pp. 518–27.

Halleck, S.L. 1974, 'A troubled view of current trends in forensic psychiatry', *Journal of Psychiatry and the Law*, vol. 2, no. 2, pp. 135–6.

*Hamparian, D.M., Schuster, R., Dinitz, S. and Conrad, J.P. 1978, *The Violent Few* (The Dangerous Offender Project), Lexington, Lexington Books, D.C. Heath and Co.

Kozol, H.L., Boucher, R.J. and Garofalo, R.F. 1972, 'The diagnosis and treatment of dangerousness', *Crime and Delinquency*, vol. 18, no. 4, pp. 371–92. See also Kozol, H.L. 1975, 'The diagnosis of dangerousness' in S.A. Pasternack (ed.), *Violence and Victims*, New York, Spectrum Publications, pp. 3–13.

Kozol, H.L., Boucher, R.J. and Garofalo, R.J. 1973, 'Dangerousness', *Crime and Delinquency*, vol. 19, no. 4, pp. 554–5. Letter in reply to Monahan 1972.

Levine, D. 1976, 'Careers of violence: further comments', *British Journal of Criminology*, vol. 16, no. 2, pp. 161–3; See Walker, Hammond and Steer 1970 and Carr-Hill 1970.

Lucas, W.E. 1977, 'The evaluation of dangerousness: problems for psychiatry', *Seminar paper*, Institute of Criminology, Faculty of Law, University of Sydney, Australia.

McGrath, P.G. 1968, 'Custody and release of dangerous offenders', in A.V.S. de Reuck and R. Porter (eds.), *The Mentally Abnormal Offender*, A Ciba Foundation symposium, London, Churchill, pp. 121–9.

Mannheim, H. and Wilkins, L.T. 1955, *Prediction Methods in Relation to Borstal Training*, Studies in the causes of delinquency and the treatment of offenders 1, London, HMSO.

Meehl, P.E. 1954, *Clinical versus statistical prediction; a theoretical analysis and a review of the evidence*, Minneapolis, University of Minnesota Press.

Meehl, P.E. and Rosen, A. 1955, 'Antecedent probability and the efficiency of psychometric signs, patterns or cutting scores', *Psychological Bulletin*, vol. 52, no. 3, pp. 194—216.

Megargee, E.I. 1976, 'The prediction of dangerous behaviour', *Criminal Justice and Behaviour*, vol. 3, no. 1, pp. 3—21.

*Monahan, J. 1970, 'The prevention of violence' in J. Monahan (ed.), *Community Mental Health and the Criminal Justice System*, London, Pergamon Press Inc., pp. 13—34.

Monahan, J. 1973, 'Dangerous offenders: A critique of Kozol et al.' *Crime and Delinquency*, vol. 19, no. 3, pp. 418—20. Letter in response to Kozol, Boucher and Garofalo 1972.

*Monahan, J. 1977, 'The prediction of violent criminal behaviour: a methodological critique and prospectus', *Paper* commissioned by Panel on Research on Deterrent and Incapacitative Effects, National Academy of Sciences, California, Irvine (unpublished, Institute of Criminology, Cambridge, mimeo). Earlier version of this paper published in *Violence and Criminal Justice*, D. Chappell and J. Monahan (eds.), 1975, Lexington, Lexington Books, D.C. Heath and Co., chapter 2.

Monahan, J. and Cummings, L. 1974, 'Prediction of dangerousness as a function of its perceived consequences', *Journal of Criminal Justice*, vol. 2, no. 3, pp. 239—42.

Moos, R. 1973, 'Conceptualizations of human environments', *American Psychologist*, vol. 28, pp. 652—65.

Moos, R. 1975a, *Evaluating Correctional and Community Settings*, New York, Wiley.

Moos, R. 1975b, *Evaluating Treatment Settings*, New York, Wiley.

Moos, R. and Insel, P. (eds.), 1974, *Issues in Social Ecology*, Palo Alto, National Press.

Morris, N. 1968, 'Psychiatry and the dangerous criminal', *Southern California Law Review*, vol. 41, no. 3, pp. 514, 529—36.

Patuxent: *see* US State of Maryland 1973.

Payne, C., McCabe, S. and Walker, N.D. 1974, 'Predicting offender—patients' reconvictions', *British Journal of Psychiatry*, vol. 125, pp. 60—4.

*Pfohl, S. 1977, 'The psychiatric assessment of dangerousness: practical problems and political implications' in J. P. Conrad and S. Dinitz (eds.), *In Fear of Each Other* (The Dangerous Offender Project), Lexington, Lexington Books, D.C. Heath and Co., pp. 77—101.

Preusse, M.G. and Quinsey, V.L. 1977, 'The dangerousness of patients released from maximum security: a replication', *Journal of Psychiatry and Law*, vol. 5, no. 2, pp. 293—9.

Quinsey, V.L., Warneford, M., Preusse, M. and Link, N. 1975, 'Released Oak Ridge patients: a follow-up study of review board discharges',

British Journal of Criminology, vol. 15, no. 3, pp. 264–70.
Rosen, A. 1954, 'Detection of suicidal patients. an example of some limitations in the prediction of infrequent events', *Journal of Consulting Psychology*, vol. 18, pp. 397–403.
Rubin, B. 1972, 'Prediction of dangerousness in mentally ill criminals', *Archives of General Psychiatry*, vol. 27, pp. 397–407.
*Sawyer, J. 1966, 'Measurement and prediction, clinical and statistical', *Psychological Bulletin*, vol. 66, no. 3, pp. 178–200.
Schwitzgebel, R.K. 1977, 'Professional accountability in the treatment and release of dangerous persons', in B.D. Sales (ed.), *Perspectives in Law and Psychology I, The Criminal Justice System*, New York, Plenum Press, pp. 139–49.
Scott, P.D. 1977, 'Criminal dangerousness and its assessment', *British Journal of Psychiatry*, vol. 131, no. 8, pp. 127–42.
Shah, S.A. 1976, 'Dangerousness: a paradigm for exploring some issues in law and psychology', *The David Levine Invited Address* at the meeting of the American Psychological Association, Washington, DC.
Simon, F.H. 1971, *Prediction Methods in Criminology*, Home Office Research Studies no. 7, London, HMSO.
Soothill, K.L. and Pope, P.J. 1973, 'Arson: a 20-year cohort study', *Medicine, Science and the Law*, vol. 13, no. 2, pp. 127–38.
Soothill, K.L., Jack, A. and Gibbens, T.C.N. 1976, 'Rape: a 22-year cohort study', *Medicine, Science and the Law*, vol. 16, no. 1, pp. 62–9.
Steadman, H.J. 1973, 'Some evidence on the inadequacy of the concept and determination of dangerousness in law and psychiatry', *Journal of Psychiatry and Law*, vol. 1, Winter, pp. 409–26.
*Steadman, H.J. and Cocozza, J.J. 1974, *Careers of the Criminally Insane*, Lexington, Lexington Books, D.C. Heath and Co.
Steadman, H.J. and Cocozza, J.J. 1976, 'Psychiatry, dangerousness and the repetitively violent offender', *Paper* prepared for presentation at the Annual Meeting of the American Society of Criminology, Tuscan, Arizona, no. 6, Institute of Criminology, Cambridge, (mimeo).
Stokols, D. 1977 (ed.), *Psychological Perspectives on Environment and Behaviour: Conceptual and Empirical Trends*, New York, Plenum Press.
Stürup, G.K. 1968, 'Will this man be dangerous?', in A.V.S. de Reuck and R. Porter (eds.), *The Mentally Abnormal Offender*, A Ciba Foundation symposium, London, Churchill, pp. 5–18.
Tennent, G.T. 1976, 'The dangerous offender' in T. Silverstone and B. Barraclough (eds.), *Contemporary Psychiatry*, British Journal of Psychiatry special publication no. 9, Ashford, Headley.
Thornberry, T.P. and Jacoby, J.E. 1979, The Criminally Insane: a community follow up of mentally ill offenders, Chicago, University of Chicago Press.
*Tomasic, R. 1977, 'The dangerous offender – prediction and assessment', *Seminar paper*, Institute of Criminology Faculty of Law, University of Sydney, Australia (unpublished).
Tong, J.E. and Mackay, G.W. 1959, 'A statistical follow-up of mental defectives of dangerous or violent propensities', *British Journal of Delinquency*, vol. 9, no. 4, pp. 276–84.

Underwood, B.D. 1979, 'Law and the crystal ball: predicting behaviour with statistical inference and individualised judgment', *The Yale Law Journal*, vol. 88, no. 7, pp. 1408–48.

US State of Maryland, Department of Public Safety and Correctional Services, 1973, *Maryland's Defective Delinquency Statute, a progress report* (unpublished); see Gordon (1977).

Walker, N.D., Hammond, W. and Steer, D. 1970, *The Violent Offender – Reality or Illusion? I Careers of violence*, Oxford University Penal Research Unit Occasional Paper no. 1, Oxford, Basil Blackwell; see Carr-Hill 1970 and Levine 1976.

Wenk, E.A., Robison, J.O. and Smith, G.W. 1972, 'Can violence be predicted?', *Crime and Delinquency*, vol. 18, no. 4, pp. 393–402.

Protective Sentencing: Law and Procedure

American Law Institute, 1962, *Model Penal Code*, Philadelphia, American Law Institute.

Baldwin, J. and McConville, M. 1979, *Jury Trials*, Oxford, Clarendon Press.

Canada, House of Commons, 18 July 1977, Bill C–51, An Act to Amend the Criminal Code, Part XXI – Dangerous Offenders.

Canadian Committee on Corrections, 1969, Toward Unity: Criminal Justice and Corrections, *Report*, Chairman, Mr. Justice *Ouimet*, The Queen's Printer, Ottawa, Canada, see Chapter 13, *The Dangerous Offender*, pp. 241–71.

Canada, *Canadian Criminal Code* see Martin's Annual Criminal Code, Canada Law Books Ltd.

Denmark, Danish Criminal Code 1973; see Lønberg 1975.

Dershowitz, A.M. 1973, 'Preventive confinement: a suggested framework for constitutional analysis', *Texas Law Review*, vol. 51, no. 7, pp. 1277–1324.

Ennis, B.J. and Litwack, T.R. 1974, 'Psychiatry and the presumption of expertise: flipping coins in the courtroom', *California Law Review*, vol. 62, no. 5, pp. 693–752.

Fokkema, D.C., Chorus, J.M.J., Hondius, E.H. and Lisser, E.Ch. (eds.) 1978, *Introduction to Dutch Law for Foreign Lawyers*. Prepared under the auspices of the Netherlands Comparative Law Association, The Netherlands, Kluwer, Deventer.

Ginsberg, P.H. and Klockars, M. 1974, '"Dangerous offenders" and legislative reform', *Williamette Law Journal*, vol. 10, Spring, pp. 167–84.

Home Office, Lord Chancellor's Office, 1961, *Report* of the interdepartmental committee on the Business of the Criminal Courts, Part B, Cmnd 1289, Chairman, Mr Justice *Streatfeild*, London, HMSO.

Hood, R. (ed.), 1974, *Crime, Criminology and Public Policy*, Essays in Honour of Sir Leon Radzinowicz, London, Heinemann Educational Books. See:
   Christie, N. 'Utility and Social Values in Court Decisions on Punishment', pp. 281–96;
   James, Lord Justice, 'A Judicial Note on the Control of Discretion in the Administration of Criminal Justice', pp. 157–9;

Thomas, D.A., 'The Control of Discretion in the Administration of Criminal Justice', pp. 139—55.
Jackson, R.M. 1977, *The Machinery of Justice in England*, (7th edn.), Cambridge, CUP.
Kress, J.M., Wilkins, T.L. and Gottfredson, D.M. 1976, 'Is the end of judicial sentencing in sight?' *Journal of the American Judicature Society*, vol. 60, no. 5. Reprinted as an annex to appendix C, Report of the Advisory Council on the Penal System, 1978, Sentences of Imprisonment, London, HMSO.
Lønberg, A. 1975, *The Penal System of Denmark*, Ministry of Justice, Denmark.
MacDonald, J.M. 1958, *Psychiatry and the Criminal: a guide to psychiatric examinations for the criminal court*, Springfield, Illinois, Charles Thomas.
Norway, *The Norwegian Penal Code*, 1961. Translated by H. Schjoldoger, Introduction by J. Andenaes, The American Series of Foreign Penal Codes, no. 3, London, Sweet and Maxwell; South Hackensack, N.J., Fred. B. Rothman and Co.
Ormrod, Sir R. 1968, 'Scientific evidence in court', *The Criminal Law Review*, pp. 240—7.
Price, R.R. 1970, 'Psychiatry, criminal law reform and the mythophilic impulse: on Canadian proposals for the control of the dangerous offender', *Ottawa Law Review*, vol. 4, no. 1, pp. 1—61.
Price, R.R. and Gold, A.D. 1976, 'Legal controls for the dangerous offender' in *Studies in Imprisonment*, Ottawa, Canadian Law Reform Commission.
Sleffel, L. 1977, *The Law and the Dangerous Criminal* (The Dangerous Offender Project), Lexington, Lexington Books, D.C. Heath and Co.
Sweden, National Swedish Council for Crime Prevention (Brottsförebyggrande rådet), 1978, *A New Penal System: ideas and proposals*, English summary of Nytt straffsystem, idéer och förslag 1977.
Sweden, *The Penal Code of Sweden* 1965, as amended 1 January 1972. Translated by Thorsten Sellin, The American Series of Foreign Penal Codes, no. 17, London, Sweet and Maxwell; South Hackensack, N.J., Fred B. Rothman and Co.
United States, National Council of Crimes and Delinquency, 1963, *Model Sentencing Act*.
Wechsler, H. 1974, 'The Model Penal Code and the codification of American criminal law', in R. Hood (ed.), *Crime, Criminology and Public Policy*, Essays in Honour of Sir Leon Radzinowicz, London, Heinemann Educational Books.

Control Without Custody

Advisory Council on the Penal System, 1970, Non-custodial and semi-custodial penalties, *Report*, Chairman, Baroness *Wootton* of Abinger, London, HMSO.
Committee on Local Authority and Allied Personal Social Services, 1968, *Report etc.*, Cmnd 3703, Chairman, F. *Seebohm*, London, HMSO.
Davies, M. 1972, *Parole and the Probation Service*, Home Office Re-

214   DANGEROUSNESS AND CRIMINAL JUSTICE

King, J.F.S. with Young, W. (ed.), 1976, *Control without Custody?*, Papers presented to the Cropwood Round-Table Conference, December 1975, Cambridge, Institute of Criminology.
Lawson, C. 1978, *The Probation Officer as Prosecutor; a study of proceedings for breach of requirement in probation.* Occasional Series no. 3, Institute of Criminology, Cambridge.
Morris, P., Beverley, F. and Vennard, J. 1975, *On Licence: a study of parole*, London, Wiley.
Nuttall, C. et al. 1977, *Parole in England and Wales*, Home Office Research Study no. 38, London, HMSO.
Prins, H.A. 1975, 'A danger to themselves and to others, social workers and potentially dangerous clients', *British Journal of Social Work*, vol. 5, no. 3, pp. 297–309.
Studt, E.T. 1972, *Surveillance and service in parole*: a *report* of the Parole Action Study, Los Angeles, Institute of Government and Public Affairs, UCLA.

Quantitative Studies

Boland, B. 1978, 'Incapacitation of the dangerous offender: the arithmetic is not so simple', *Journal of Research in Crime and Delinquency*, vol. 15, no. 1, pp. 126–9; see Van Dine, Dinitz and Conrad 1977 and 1978.
Cohen, 1978, 'The incapacitative effect of imprisonment: a critical review of the literature' in A. Blumstein, J. Cohen and D. Nagin (eds.), *Deterrence and Incapacitation: Estimating the Effects of Criminal Sanctions on Crime Rates*, Washington, DC, National Academy of Sciences.
Freeman, R.A., Dinitz, S. and Conrad, J.P. 1977, 'The bottom is in the hole: a look at the dangerous offender and society's effort to control him', *American Journal of Correction*, vol. 39, no. 1, pp. 25, 30–31.
Greenberg, D.F. 1975, 'The incapacitative effect of imprisonment: some estimates', *Law and Society Review*, vol. 9, Summer, pp. 541–80.
Palmer, J. and Salimbene, J. 1978, 'The incapacitation of the dangerous offender: a second look', *Journal of Research in Crime and Delinquency*, vol. 15, no. 1, pp. 130–4; see Van Dine, Dinitz and Conrad 1977 and 1978.
Pease, K. and Wolfson, J. 1979, 'Incapacitation studies: a review and a commentary', *The Howard Journal*, vol. 18, no. 3, pp. 160–7.
Shinnar, S. and Shinnar, R. 1975, 'The effects of the criminal justice system on the control of crime: a quantitative approach', *Law and Society Review*, vol. 9, Summer, pp. 581–612.
Van Dine, S., Dinitz, S. and Conrad, J.P. 1977, 'The incapacitation of the dangerous offender: a statistical experiment', *Journal of Research in Crime and Delinquency*, vol. 14, no. 1, pp. 22–34. Also published in J.P. Conrad and S. Dinitz (eds.) 1977, *In Fear of Each Other* (The Dangerous Offender Project), Lexington, Lexington Books, D.C. Heath and Co., pp. 103–17.

Van Dine, S., Dinitz, S. and Conrad, J.P. 1978, 'Response to our critics', *Journal of Research in Crime and Delinquency,* vol. 15, no. 1. pp. 135—9; see Boland 1978; Palmer and Salimbene 1978.

*Van Dine, S., Conrad, J. and Dinitz, S. 1979, *Restraining the Wicked* (The Dangerous Offender Project), Lexington, Lexington Books, D.C. Heath and Co.

Review Procedures

Arthur, L.G. and Karsh, K.H. 1976, 'Release hearings: to protect the public!', *Federal Probation,* vol. 40, no. 3, pp. 55—9.

Gottfredson, D.M., Hoffman, P.B., Sigler, M.H. and Wilkins, L.T. 1975, 'Making parole policy explicit', *Crime and Delinquency,* vol. 21, no. 1, pp. 34—44.

Greenland, C. 1970, *Mental Illness and Civil Liberty: a study of Mental Health Review Tribunals in England and Wales,* Occasional papers in Social Administration no. 38, London, G. Bell and Sons.

Hoffman, P.B., Gottfredson, D.M., Wilkins, L.T. and Pasela, G.E. 1974, 'The operational use of an experience table', *Criminology,* vol. 12, no. 2, pp. 214—28.

Mental Health Review Tribunal Rules 1960, SI. 1139, London, HMSO. Reproduced in discussion paper of Committee on Mental Health Review Tribunal Procedures 1978, pp. 7—37 (rules amended by SI 1974, 241 and SI 1976, 447).

Mental Health Review Tribunal Procedures, Committee on 1978, *The Procedures of the Mental Health Review Tribunals,* discussion paper, Chaired by the Lord Chancellor's Office.

Parole Board for England and Wales, *Annual Reports* 1968—

Thomas, D.A. (ed.), 1974, *Parole: Its implications for the criminal justice and penal systems, Papers* presented to the Cropwood Round-Table Conference, 1973, Cambridge, Institute of Criminology.

West, D.J. (ed.) 1972, *The Future of Parole: Commentaries on Systems in Britain and USA,* London, Duckworth.

Wood, J.C. 1976, 'Mental Health Review Tribunals: a reappraisal', *Medicine, Science and the Law,* vol. 16, no. 3, pp. 212—18.

Wood, J.C. 1976, 'Mental Health Review Tribunals and social work', *Social Work Today,* vol. 7, no. 11, pp. 318—20.

Note

We gratefully acknowledge the efficient help with the preparation of this bibliography of Miss Loraine Gelsthorpe, The Institute of Criminology, Cambridge.

References

Advisory Council on the Treatment of Offenders, 1963, Preventive Detention, *Report, etc.*, Chairman, Bishop of Exeter, London, HMSO.

Advisory Council on the Penal System, 1968, The regime for long-term prisoners in conditions of maximum security, *Report*, Chairman, Sir Leon *Radzinowicz*, London, HMSO.

Advisory Council on the Penal System, 1974, Young Adult Offenders, *Report, etc.*, Chairman, Sir Kenneth *Younger*, London, HMSO. See also 'Young Adult Offenders and Younger Report', *letter, Prison Service Journal* (n.s.) no. 18, April, pp. 15−16.

Advisory Council on the Penal System, 1978, Sentences of Imprisonment: A Review of Maximum Penalties, *Report, etc.*, Cmnd 7948. Chairman, Baroness *Serota*, London, HMSO.

American Law Institute, 1962, *Model Penal Code*, Philadelphia, American Law Institute.

Arthur, L.G. and Karsh, K.H. 1976, 'Release Hearings: to protect the Public!', *Federal Probation*, pp. 55−9.

Ashby, The Rt Hon. Lord, 1976, 'Protection of the Environment: The Human Dimension', The Jephcott Lecture, *Royal Society of Medicine*, vol. 69, pp. 721−30.

Baldwin, J. and McConville, M. 1979, *Jury Trials*, Oxford, Clarendon Press.

Bottoms, A.E. 1977, 'Reflections on the renaissance of dangerousness', *Howard Journal*, vol. 16, no. 2, pp. 70−96.

Brody, S.R. 1976, *The Effectiveness of Sentencing: a review of the literature*, Home Office Research Studies no. 35, London, HMSO.

Brody, S.R. and Tarling, R. 1980, *Taking Offenders out of Circulation*, Home Office Research Studies no. 64, London, HMSO.

Canadian Committee on Corrections 1969, Toward Unity: Criminal Justice and Corrections, *Report*, Chairman, Mr Justice *Ouimet*, The Queen's Printer, Ottawa, Canada, see ch. 13, 'The Dangerous Offender'. pp. 241−71.

Carson, W.G. 1975, 'Le délinquant dangereux et les valeurs symboliques de l'ordre social', *Revue de science criminelle et de droit pénal comparé*, no. 3, pp. 805−13.

Cocossa, J.J. and Steadman, H.J. 1974, 'Some refinements in the measurement and prediction of dangerous behaviour', *American Journal of Psychiatry*, vol. 131, no. 9, pp. 1012−1014.

Cocozza, J.J. and Steadman, H J 1976, 'The failure of psychiatric predictions of dangerousness: clear and convincing evidence', *Rutgers Law Review*, vol. 29, no. 5, pp. 1084–1101.

Cocozza, J.J. and Steadman, H.J. 1978, 'Prediction in psychiatry: an example of misplaced confidence in experts', *Social Problems*, vol. 25, no. 3, pp. 265–76.

Cohen, J. 1978, 'The incapacitative effect of imprisonment: a critical review of the literature' in A. Blumstein, J. Cohen and D. Nagin (eds.), *Deterrence and Incapacitation: Estimating the Effects of Criminal Sanctions on Crime Rates*, Washington, DC, National Academy of Sciences.

Committee on Local Authority and Allied Personal Social Services, 1968, *Report, etc.*, Cmnd 3703, Chairman, F. *Seebohm*, London, HMSO.

Davies, M. 1972, *Parole and the Probation Service*, Home Office Research Department, London (mimeo).

Denmark, *Danish Criminal Code 1973*, see Lφnberg, 1975.

Dershowitz, A.M. 1973, 'Preventive confinement: a suggested framework for constitutional analysis', *Texas Law Review*, vol. 51, no. 7, pp. 1277–324.

Dinitz, S. and Conrad, J.P. 1978, 'Thinking about dangerous offenders' *Criminal Justice Abstracts*, vol. 10, no. 1, pp. 99–130.

Ennis, B.J. and Litwack, T.R. 1974, 'Psychiatry and the presumption of expertise: flipping coins in the courtroom', *California Law Review*, vol. 62, no. 5, pp. 693–752.

Erwin, E. 1978, *Behaviour Therapy: scientific, philosophical and moral foundations*, Cambridge, CUP.

European Economic Community Treaty 1964, see *European Community Treaties*, London, ed. by Sweet and Maxwell 1977.

European Convention on Human Rights, 1968, article 5, para. 4. Directorate of Information, Council of Europe, Strasbourg.

Fletcher, G.P. 1978, *Rethinking Criminal Law*, Boston, Mass., Little and Brown.

Geis, G. and Monahan, J. 1976, 'The social ecology of violence' in T. Lickona (ed.), *Morality: Theory, Research and Social Issues*, New York, Holt, Rinehart and Winston, pp. 342–56.

Glaser, D. 1973, *Routinizing evaluation: getting feedback on the effectiveness of crime and delinquency programs*, National Institute of Mental Health, Center for Studies of Crime and Delinquency, Department of Health, Education and Welfare publications no. (HSM) 73–9123, US Government Printing Office, Washington, DC.

Glueck, S. 1960, 'Ten years of unravelling juvenile delinquency', *Journal of Criminal Law, Criminology and Police Science*, vol. 51, no. 3, pp. 253–308.

Gordon, R.A. 1977, 'A critique of the evaluation of Patuxent Institution, with particular attention to the issues of dangerousness and recidivism', *Bulletin of the Academy of Psychiatry and the Law*, vol. 5, no. 2, pp. 210–55.

Hammond, W.H. and Chayen, C. 1963, *Persistent Criminals*, Studies in the Causes of Delinquency and the Treatment of Offenders, no. 5, Home Office Research Unit, London, HMSO.

Hoffman, P.B., Gottfredson, D.M., Wilkins, L.T. and Pasela, G.E. 1974, 'The operational use of an experience table', *Criminology*, vol. 12, no. 2, pp. 214–28.

Holt, R.R. 1958, 'Clinical and statistical prediction: a reformulation and some new data', *Journal of Abnormal and Social Psychology*, vol. 56, pp. 1–12.

Home Office, 1932 *Report* of the Departmental Committee on Persistent Offenders, Cmnd 4090, Chairman, Sir John *Dove-Wilson*, London, HMSO.

Home Office, Lord Chancellor's Office, 1961, *Report* of the Interdepartmental committee on the Business of the Criminal Courts, Cmnd 1289, Chairman, Mr Justice *Streatfeild*, London, HMSO.

Home Office, 1966, *Report* of the inquiry into prison escapes and security, etc., Cmnd 3175, Chairman, Lord *Mountbatten* of Burma, London, HMSO.

Home Office, Department of Health and Social Security 1973, *Report* on the review of procedures for the discharge and supervision of psychiatric patients subject to special restrictions, Cmnd 5191, Chairman, Sir C. *Aarvold*, London, HMSO.

Home Office, Department of Health and Social Security 1975, Committee on Mentally Abnormal Offenders, *Report, etc.*, Cmnd 6244, Chairman, Lord *Butler* of Saffron Walden, London, HMSO.

Home Office, 1977 *Prisons and the Prisoners. The work of the Prison Service in England and Wales*, London, HMSO.

Jackson, R.M. 1977, *The Machinery of Justice in England* (7th edn.), Cambridge, CUP.

Koppin, M.A. 1976, 'A validation study of Steadman's Legal Dangerousness Scale with reference to related data', *Paper*, Colorado State Hospital, Department of Research and Program Analysis (unpublished).

Kozol, H.L., Boucher, R.J. and Garofalo, R.F. 1972, 'The diagnosis and treatment of dangerousness', *Crime and Delinquency*, vol. 18, no. 4, pp. 371–92. See also Kozol, H.L. 1975, 'The diagnosis of dangerousness' in S.A. Pasternack (ed.), *Violence and Victims*, New York, Spectrum Publications Inc., pp. 3–13.

Kozol, H.L., Boucher, R.J. and Garofalo, R.J. 1973, 'Dangerousness', *Crime and Delinquency*, vol. 19, no. 4, pp. 554–5, Letter in reply to Monahan (1973).

Kress, J.M., Wilkins, T.L. and Gottfredson, D.M. 1976, 'Is the end of judicial sentencing in sight?', *Journal of the American Judicature Society*, vol. 60, no. 5.
Reprinted as an annex to Appendix C, *Report* of the Advisory Council on the Penal System, 1978, Sentences of Imprisonment, London, HMSO.

Law Commission Working Party 1968, *The Codification of the Criminal Law*, Working Paper no. 17, London, The Law Commission.

Lawson, C. 1978, *'The Probation Officer as Prosecutor: a study of proceedings for breach of requirement in probation'*. Occasional Series no. 3, Institute of Criminology, Cambridge.

Lipton, D., Martinson, R. and Wilks, J. 1976, *The Effectiveness of Correctional Treatment*, New York, Praeger.

Lønberg, A. 1975, *The Penal System of Denmark*, Ministry of Justice, Denmark.

McClintock, F.H. 1977, *A Study of an English Borstal* (unpublished).

McIntosh, M. 1975, *The Organisation of Crime* London, Macmillan.

Mark, Sir R. 1977, *Policing a Perplexed Society*, London, George Allen and Unwin.

Massachusetts, 1958, Committee on Law Enforcement and Administration of Criminal Justice, *Gen. Laws, Ann.* ch. 12. 3A, S.I.

Meehl, P. E. 154, *Clinical versus Statistical Prediction: a theoretical analysis and a review of the evidence*, Minneapolis, University of Minnesota Press.

Mental Health Review Tribunal Procedures, Committee on, 1978, *The Procedures of the Mental Health Review Tribunals*, discussion paper, Chaired by the Lord Chancellor's Office.

Mental Health Review Tribunal Rules 1960, S.I. 1139, London, HMSO. Reproduced in discussion paper of the Committee on Mental Health Review Tribunal Procedures 1978, pp. 7—37 (Rules amended by SI 1974, 241 and SI 1976, 447).

Monahan, J. 1973, 'Dangerous offenders: a critique of Kozol et al.', *Crime and Delinquency*, vol. 19, no. 3, pp. 418—20. Letter in response to Kozol, Boucher and Garofalo, 1972.

Monahan, J. 1977, 'The prediction of violent criminal behaviour: a methodological critique and prospectus', *Paper* commissioned by Panel on Research on Deterrent and Incapacitative Effects, National Academy of Sciences, California, Irvine (unpublished, Institute of Criminology, Cambridge, mimeo).

Morris, N. 1974, *The Future of Imprisonment*, Chicago, The University of Chicago Press.

Morris, P., Beverley, F. and Vennard, J. 1975, *On Licence: a study of parole*, London, Wiley.

Nuttall, C. et al. 1977, *Parole in England and Wales*, Home Office Research Study no. 38, London, HMSO.

Ormrod, Sir R. 1968, 'Scientific evidence in court', *The Criminal Law Review*, pp. 240—7.

Parker, Lord Chief Justice, Practice Direction 1962, *Criminal Law Review*, 308 (Corrective Training and Preventive Detention).

Parker, Lord Chief Justice, Practice Direction 1967, *Criminal Law Review* 231 (Hospital and Restriction Orders).

Parole Board for England and Wales, Annual Reports 1968—

Patuxent (see U.S. State of Maryland 1973).

Pearce, F. 1976, *Crimes of the Powerful*, London, Pluto Press.

Pease, K. and Wolfson, J. 1979, 'Incapacitation studies: a review and commentary', *The Howard Journal*, vol. 18, no. 3, pp. 160—7.

Pfohl, S. 1977, 'The psychiatric assessment of dangerousness: practical problems and political implications' in J.P. Conrad and S. Dinitz (eds.) 1977, *In Fear of Each Other* (The Dangerous Offender Project), Lexington, Lexington Books, D.C. Heath and Co., pp. 77—101.

Phillpotts, G.J.O. and Lancucki, L.B. 1979, *Previous Convictions, Sentence and Reconviction: A statistical study of a sample of 5000 offenders convicted in January 1971*, Home Office Research Study no. 53, London, HMSO.

Radzinowicz, Sir L. 1968, 'The Dangerous Offender', The fourth Frank Newsam Memorial Lecture, *The Police Journal*, vol. 41, no. 9, pp. 411–47.

Rennie, Y.F. 1978, *The Search For Criminal Man* (The Dangerous Offender Project), Lexington, Lexington Books, D.C. Heath and Co.

Roshier, R.J. 1973, 'The selection of crime news by the press' in S. Cohen and J. Young (eds.), *The Manufacture of News*, London, Constable, pp. 28–39.

Sawyer, J. 1966, 'Measurement and prediction, clinical and statistical', *Psychological Bulletin*, vol. 66, no. 3, pp. 178–200.

Schoeman, F.D. 1979, III. 'On incapacitating the dangerous', *American Philosophical Quarterly*, vol. 16, no. 1, pp. 27–35.

Scott, P.D. 1977, 'Criminal dangerousness and its assessment', *British Journal of Psychiatry*, vol. 131, no. 8, pp. 127–42.

Scottish Council on Crime, 1975, Crime and the Prevention of Crime: a *Memorandum* by the Scottish Council on Crime, Edinburgh, HMSO.

Silberman, C. 1978, *Criminal Violence and Criminal Justice*, New York, Random House.

Sleffel, L. 1977, *The Law and the Dangerous Criminal* (The Dangerous Criminal Offender Project), Lexington, Lexington Books, D.C. Heath and Co.

Soothill, K.L. and Pope, P.J. 1973, 'Arson: a 20-year cohort study', *Medicine, Science and the Law*, vol. 13, no. 2, pp. 127–38.

Soothill, K.L., Jack, A. and Gibbens, T.C.N. 1976, 'Rape: a 22-year cohort study', *Medicine, Science and the Law*, vol. 16, no. 1, pp. 62–9.

Steadman, H.J. and Cocozza, J.J. 1974, *Careers of the Criminally Insane*, Lexington, Lexington Books, D.C. Heath and Co.

Stone, C.D. 1975, *Where the Law Ends: the social control of corporate behaviour*, New York, Harper and Row.

Studt, E.T. 1972, *Surveillance and Service in Parole: a report* of the Parole Action Study, Los Angeles, Institute of Government and Public Affairs, UCLA.

Sweden, *The Penal Code of Sweden* 1965, as amended January 1st 1972. Translated by Thorsten Sellin, The American Series of Foreign Penal Codes, no. 17, London, Sweet and Maxwell. South Hackensack NJ, Fred B. Rothman and Co.

Thomas, D.A. 1979, *Principles of Sentencing*, Cambridge Studies in Criminology XXVII (2nd edn.). London, Heinemann Educational Books.

Thornberry, T.P. and Jacoby, J.E. 1979, The Criminally Insane: a community follow up of mentally ill offenders, Chicago, University of Chicago Press.

Tomasic, R. 1977, 'The dangerous offender – prediction and assessment', *Seminar paper*, Institute of Criminology Faculty of Law, University of Sydney, Australia (unpublished).

United States, National Council of Crime and Delinquency, 1963, *Model Sentencing Act*.

U.S. State of Maryland, Department of Public Safety and Correctional Services, 1973, *Maryland's Defective Delinquency Statute, a progress report* (unpublished). See Gordon (1977).

University of Sydney, Proceedings of the Institute of Criminology, 1979, *Proceedings of a Seminar on White collar crime* (2), no. 37, The University of Sydney, Faculty of Law.

Von Hirsch, A. 1972, 'Prediction of criminal conduct and preventive confinement of convicted persons', *Buffalo Law Review*, vol. 21, no. 3, pp. 717–58.

Von Hirsch, A. (ed.), 1976, *Doing Justice*, Report of the Committee for the study of incarceration, New York, Hill and Wang.

Walker, N.D. 1972, *Sentencing in a Rational Society* (2nd edn), Harmondsworth, Penguin Books.

Walker, N.D. 1978, 'Dangerous people', *International Journal of Law and Psychiatry*, vol. 1, pp. 37–50 (Revised version in Walker, 1980).

Walker, N.D. and McCabe, S. 1973, *Crime and Insanity in England*, vol. 2, Edinburgh, Edinburgh University Press.

Walker, N.D., Hammond, W. and Steer, D. 1970, *The Violent Offender – Reality or Illusion? I Careers of Violence*, Oxford University Penal Research Unit, Occasional Paper no. 1, Oxford, Basil Blackwell. (See Carr-Hill 1970, and Levine 1976). This article first appeared in the Criminal Law Review, August 1967.

Wenk, E.A., Robison, J.O. and Smith, G.W. 1972, 'Can violence be predicted?', *Crime and Delinquency*, vol. 18, no. 4, pp. 393–402.

Widgery, Lord Chief Justice, Practice Direction [1980] 1 *Weekly Law Reports* 270. (Crime: Sentence: Loss of time).

Wilkins, L.T. 1972, Foreword to Wenk and Emrich, *Assaultive Youth*, 1972,

Williams, Glanville 1978, *Textbook of Criminal Law*, London, Stevens and Sons.

Yoder, S.A. 1978, 'Criminal sanctions for corporate illegality', *Journal of Criminal Law and Criminology*, vol. 69, no. 1, pp. 40–58.

Zehr, H. 1976, *Crime and the Development of Modern Society: Patterns of Criminality in Nineteenth-century Germany and France*, London, Croom-Helm Ltd., U.S. New Jersey, Rowman and Littlefield.

222   DANGEROUSNESS AND CRIMINAL JUSTICE

Table of cases

General Index

experts
    and courts 201–202
    versus laymen 32–37
'false consciousness' (clinical) 200
'false negatives' 21, 26, 28
'false positives' 21, 26, 30
firearms 8
Fletcher, G.P. 49n
force
    excused or justified 49n
forvaring: see Danish legislation

Geis, G. 14
Garofalo, R.J. 22
German law 49n
Gladstone, Herbert 79
Glaser, D. 188
Glueck, S. and E. 181
Gordon, R.A. 31, 195, 196

'habitual criminal' statutes (USA)
    33, 103
Hammond, W.H. 80, 184
harms
    'grave' harm 50–51, 106, 110,
    116–118
    irremediable 51–53
    to the person 53–55
    to property 54–55
    psychological 51–53, 106
    'serious harm' 51
Hoffman, P.B. 188
Holt, R.R. 188
Home Office xi, xiii, xv, 78–92,
    94–96, 99, 115, 134, 150,
    153n, 165
Home Secretary 63, 66, 71, 75–
    77, 91, 93, 95, 96, 97n, 125,
    132, 135, 143–146, 149–
    153, 156, 165, 170
Honey, Norman xi
hospital orders xiii
    ineligibility for 120
    release from 94–96
    with restriction orders xv,
    76–78
Howard League for Penal Reform ix

Howden, Brian xi

Immigration Act, 1971 86
impulsive acts 37n
individualisation 109
infants 42
innocence
    detention 45
    presumption of xiii
    and punishment 39–40
institutions visited 179
intentional harm 45–46
internment (Sweden) 103

Jackson, R.M. 36
Jacoby, 29
judiciary (of England and Wales)
    xiii
juries
    as assessors of dangerousness
    34–37

Karsh, K.H. 152
Koppin, M.A. 183
Kozol, H.L. 22, 23, 30, 191–195
Kray and Richardson 83
Kress, J.M. 151

Lancucki, L.B. 184
Law Commission 15
Lawson, C. 142
Legal Dangerousness Scale
    (Cocozza and Steadman's)
    183, 195
Local Review Committees 63, 96,
    146, 151
Lilley Foundation ixn
Lima Hospital, Ohio 199
licences (for conditional release)
    134–135, 136–142
    supervision under 136–142
Lipton, D. 136
Litwack, T.R. 22, 33, 195
Lonberg, A. 107
Londoners, sample of 184
Lord Chancellor 94, 145, 153n
Lord Chief Justice 80, 82, 86, 111,
    116, 129, 130, 144

and see 'Court of Appeal' —
practice directions
Lord Justice of Appeal, review by
122

McCabe, S. 137
McConville, M. 36
McClintock, F.H. 137
McIntosh, M. 11
Mark, Sir Robert 12
magistrates' courts 121
Maryland 191, 193
Massachusetts Department of
Mental Health 195
Massachusetts statute 22
Matteawan Hospital 190
Meehl, P.E. 186, 187, 200
mental abnormality: see 'mental
condition'
mental condition (of offender)
xii, xiii, 42, 71—78
mental disorder: see 'mental condition'
Mental Health Act 1959 xii, 70,
76, 78, 94, 95, 99, 110, 116,
117, 120, 130, 145, 153n,
155, 165, 170
Mental Health Review Tribunals
63, 77, 94—96, 144—149,
152—153, 168, 170
Committee to review their procedures 145—153
mental hospitals
civil commitment to ix
commitment by criminal
courts: see 'hospital orders'
Special Hospitals x
Ministry of Information 9
misdemeanours 75
Monahan, J. 14, 29—31, 188, 192,
195, 196
Morris, Norval 21
Morris, Pauline 138
Mountbatten Report 90, 92, 96n

National Council on Crime and
Delinquency's Model Sen-
tencing Act 105

negligence as source of risk 7
Netherlands' special sentence 107
news media 3—9
non-custodial control 134—142
Nuttall, C. 137

offences
'abnormal' 83
against the State 82, 83
corporate 4, 10—15, 117
details of 91
'grave' 71—72
non-homicidal xii
political 12
professional 12
of terrorists 83
'traditional' 83
Official Secrets Act 91
organised crime 11
Ormrod, Sir Roger 34, 35

Parliament xii, xv, 101, 150
parole xiii, 92—94, 137, 150
in Scotland 165
Parole Board 33, 58, 63, 76, 93,
96, 97n, 107, 108, 112, 117,
134, 150, 151, 153, 165,
168, 170, 188, 193, 194
Patuxent Institution 191, 193—
196
Pease, K. 16
Pearce, F. 13
Pfohl, S. 197, 199
Phillpotts, G.J.O. 184
police records 127—129
Pope, P.J. 61
Powers of Criminal Courts Act
1973 85, 120, 168
prediction xvi, 16, 19n, 24—25,
48, 180—202
by case-study 29—31, 187—189
essential to judicial determination of dangerousness 25
non-statistical 186—196
pessimism about 32
statistical 181—186
and see 'actuarial methods',
'case-study'

protective purposes of xii, xiv
'renewable' (Netherlands') 107
'reviewable' 99, 102, 103
semi-determinate 107
special, need for xv, 38–40,
    100, 101, 108
and see 'proposals of Working
    Party'
sex (and special sentences) 119
sexual offences 50, 175
sexual psychopath statutes
    (USA) 33, 107
Schoeman, F.D. 40, 43
security of custody 90–92
Silberman, C. 18
Sleffel, L. 47, 103, 104, 107
social inquiry reports 129–130
social environment, modification
    of 18–19
social hazards 10–15
social menaces xii, 79, 81
social nuisances xii–xiii, 79, 81
social protest 11, 12
socially powerful, the xv, 9, 17–18
Soothill, K.L. 61
Soviet law 49n
Steadman, H.J. 29, 30, 183, 189,
    190, 192, 195, 197, 198,
    200, 201
Steer, D. 184
Stone, C.D. 17
Streatfeild Committee 126, 130
Studt, E.T. 138
supervision xiii, 136–142
Supreme Court of the United
    States 28, 122, 183, 190
surveillance 138–139
'sus laws' 45
Swedish 'internment' 107
Swedish Penal Code 103
Sydney, University of 13

Tarling, R. 16, 19, 28, 112n, 182,
    183, 185, 193, 194
Thomas, D. 70n, 74

Thornberry, T.P. 29
Thornstedt, H. 107
Tomasic, R. 42
tribunals
    as useful devices 34, 63–66,
    112, 120, 121, 132, 133,
    148–150, 153–156
    objections to 120, 121
    and see 'Review Tribunal',
    'Mental Health Review
    Tribunals'

Uniform Determinate Sentencing
    Act (California) 102
United States Federal Code 103
United States Supreme Court 28,
    122, 183, 190

validating 'dangerousness' 28,
    180–186
violations of rights 52–53
violence, personal 7–8
    and see 'harms'
Von Hirsch, A. 34, 39, 40, 43, 44,
    47

Walker, Nigel xi, 38, 39, 41, 42,
    51, 52, 53, 59, 120, 136, 184
Welsh Office 153n
Wenk, E.A. 183, 188
White, Ian 38
Wilkins, T.L. 151
Williams, Glanville 49n
Wolfson, J. 16
Working Party
    collective responsibility of xi
    procedure x–xvi, 179
    and see 'proposals . . .'
Wormwood Scrubs xi

Yoder, S.A. 13
Young, Graham 15, 96, 97n, 153
Younger Report 141

Zehr, H. 18